UNIV
WOLV

Variety in Written English

Combining insights from a variety of linguistic perspectives including Hallidayan functional linguistics and relevance theory, Tony Bex demonstrates how written texts operate within society to convey meaning. This lively and informative book:

- Looks at a wide variety of written genres: advertisements, letters, poetry and literature.
- Provides an accessible and comprehensive survey of genre theory.
- Proposes a challenging new way of analysing genre which relates communicative function to relevance theory.
- Considers the relevance of linguistic theories of genre to the study of literary texts.
- Includes numerous exercises and annotated bibliographies.

Variety in Written English will be of interest to all students of language and communication. In addition, it will be an invaluable text for those interested in literature, as well as the teaching of English.

Tony Bex is currently senior lecturer at the University of Kent and has previously taught in Papua New Guinea, Saudi Arabia and Algeria.

The INTERFACE Series

> A linguist deaf to the poetic function of language and a literary scholar indifferent to linguistic problems and unconversant with linguistic methods, are equally flagrant anachronisms. – Roman Jakobson

This statement, made over twenty-five years ago, is no less relevant today, and 'flagrant anachronisms' still abound. The aim of the INTERFACE series is to examine topics at the 'interface' of language studies and literary criticism and in so doing to build bridges between these traditionally divided disciplines.

Already published in the series:

THE DISCOURSE OF ADVERTISING
  Guy Cook

TWENTIETH-CENTURY POETRY
  From text to context
  Edited by Peter Verdonk

LANGUAGE, LITERATURE AND CRITICAL PRACTICE
  Ways of analysing text
  David Birch

ENGLISH IN SPEECH AND WRITING
  Investigating language and literature
  Rebecca Hughes

LITERATURE, LANGUAGE AND CHANGE
  Ruth Waterhouse and John Stephens

LITERARY STUDIES IN ACTION
  Alan Durant and Nigel Fabb

LANGUAGE IN POPULAR FICTION
  Walter Nash

LANGUAGE, TEXT AND CONTEXT
  Essays in stylistics
  Edited by Michael J. Toolan

THE LANGUAGE OF JOKES
  Analysing verbal play
  Delia Chiaro

LANGUAGE, IDEOLOGY AND POINT OF VIEW
  Paul Simpson

A LINGUISTIC HISTORY OF ENGLISH POETRY
  Richard Bradford

LITERATURE ABOUT LANGUAGE
  Valerie Shepherd

TEXTUAL INTERVENTION
  Critical and creative strategies for literary studies
  Rob Pope

TWENTIETH-CENTURY FICTION
  From text to context
  Peter Verdonk and Jean Jacques Weber

FEMINIST STYLISTICS
  Sara Mills

The Series Editor

Ronald Carter is Professor of Modern English Language at the University of Nottingham and was National Coordinator of the 'Language in the National Curriculum' Project (LINC) from 1989 to 1992.

Variety in Written English

Texts in society: societies in text

Tony Bex

London and New York

First published 1996
by Routledge
11 New Fetter Lane, London EC4P 4EE

Simultaneously published in the USA and Canada
by Routledge
29 West 35th Street, New York, NY 10001

Typeset in Times by J&L Composition Ltd, Filey, North Yorkshire
Printed and bound in Great Britain by Biddles Ltd, Guildford and King's Lynn

British Library Cataloguing in Publication Data
A catalogue record for this book is available from the British Library

Library of Congress Cataloguing in Publication Data
Bex, Tony 1943–
    Variety of written English: texts in society: societies in text
/ Tony Bex.
        p.   cm. – (Interface)
    Includes bibliographical references and index.
    1. English   language—Written   English. 2. English   language—Social
aspects. 3. English   language—Variation. I. Title. II. Series: Interface
(London, England)
PE1074.7.B49   1996
421–dc20   95–26464
                                                                                CIP

ISBN 0–415–10839–X (hbk)
ISBN 0–415–10840–3 (pbk)

To my mother and the memory of my father who would not agree with what I say; and to Jane who would

Contents

Figures

Preface

This book has been a long time in the making. It originated (albeit unknown to me) in arguments with my parents about how to speak 'properly'. Hence the dedication. It grew during the years I was a teacher of EFL and owes a particular debt to conversations with John Swales when we were both in Khartoum although this might not be at all obvious in the subject matter. It would have remained no more than a future project had I not been disturbed by the ways in which the British Government was trying to straitjacket the English curriculum in the late 1980s. Although not directly concerned with the teaching of English, much of the book has been influenced by a consideration of what we ought to be telling our children about language and, in particular, their own language uses.

However, the book also depended on the intellectual support of a number of friends and colleagues among whom Ron Carter, Keith Green, Mick Short, Paul Simpson, Katie Wales and Rob Veltman deserve particular thanks. Others who contributed, but were not always aware that I regarded them as friends and colleagues, include numerous students on undergraduate and postgraduate courses who didn't have a clue what I was talking about and were prepared to tell me in such a way that I was obliged to clarify my ideas and express them more clearly. Particular thanks go to Marcial Bóo, Alan Dolphin, John Kearns, Misa Kim, Mark Smith, Aphrodite Spanou and Paul Sterne. What is right in this book I happily give to them. The faults are mine alone. I am also grateful to those (anonymous) friends who gave me permission to use their personal communications.

The author and publishers would like to thank the following for permission to use copyright material: M S George Limited for permission to reproduce the Kotex advertisement used as Figure 7.8; Gordon Dickerson for permission to reprint an extract from Tony Harrison's 'v', © Tony Harrison; Faber and Faber Limited for permission to reprint an extract from 'Musée des Beaux Arts', *Collected Poems* by W.H. Auden; Penguin for permission to reprint the recipe for Chermoula from *A New Book of Middle Eastern Food* by Claudia Roden; the Royal Geographical Society for permission to reproduce the article 'Agents of ice', by Gary L. Gaile and Dean M. Hanink, *Area*, 17, 2: 165–7.

While the publishers have made every effort to contact copyright holders of material used in this volume, they would be grateful to hear from any they were unable to contact.

Introduction

When Astrophel ends the first sonnet in his *Astrophel and Stella* sequence with the line, ' "Fool", said my Muse to me, "looke in thy heart and write" ' (Evans, 1977, p. 2), we must assume that the author, Sir Philip Sidney, was being *faux naif*. For most people the act of writing is a difficult and painstaking task. Among other things, it involves having a sense of the intended audience and a means of controlling the language so as to say exactly what is intended. To construct a sonnet requires even more complex skills since it is a highly wrought form that requires considerable control of syntax, vocabulary and sound patterns as well as an understanding on the part of the author of exactly what values sonnets may be said to represent within a particular society at a particular time.

Although it seems likely that few people in late twentieth-century Britain write (or even read) sonnets, the majority of us produce and/or consume a bewildering array of written texts each one of which is different from the others. Some of these differences are very subtle, while others are immediately obvious. This book is about these differences. However, it goes beyond simply describing the various kinds of written texts that exist in English for two reasons. First, there are an inordinate amount of texts that have been produced and these are so widely dispersed through both history and geography that any attempt to describe them would be impossible. But second, and this is more important, such an attempt would reveal little of theoretical interest, being no more than a catalogue. In this book, then, I am attempting partly to show why this variety exists, and why it is that readers and writers characteristically group certain texts together as being of the 'same kind' and, by extension, different from other 'kinds'.

At first sight, this may seem a simple task. Most of us acknowledge that there is a difference between such writings as shopping lists, diaries, letters to friends, job applications, the presentation of CVs, small ads for shop windows or local newspapers, student essays, news reports, graffiti, etc. However, we are often inclined to believe that such differences arise naturally: that it is the situation which calls for a particular type of text.

I shall be arguing that the interrelationship between *texts* and *contexts* is much more complex than this. Of course, it is true that particular situations call for particular types of texts, but this is because in any given situation we want our linguistic contribution to have specific effects. To explain how this is possible, then, we need a theory which links speakers, languages and situations in highly complex ways. Because situations recur (albeit with certain subtle differences) so the ways in which language is used are repeated, and by noticing how specific uses seem to develop for specific functions, we are able to develop a theory of genres.

Genre is a term which has been widely used by literary critics and theorists, but has only recently been adopted by linguists. Its meaning is slippery in that there are a wide number of different uses depending on the theoretical stance of the user. I shall be concentrating on the meaning developed by Swales in his book *Genre Analysis* (1990). However, for various reasons that will become apparent, I shall be suggesting that his view is rather narrow. I shall also be considering some of the arguments developed within the Hallidayan school of Functional Linguistics, although my conclusions will be my own.

The study of non-literary written genres has tended to be associated with the teaching of English to foreign learners, and particularly with English for Specific Purposes and it is for this reason that some of the ideas developed seem to have a rather narrow application. Unfortunately, it has attracted little attention in British schools. The reasons for this are unclear, but it seems most likely because of a strong populist tradition which believes that there is a 'correct' way of writing; that this is what should be taught to our pupils; and that a deeper understanding of how language is variously used for different purposes is unnecessary (and even potentially dangerous). This view has a long tradition and was trenchantly expressed by Swift in his *Proposals* in the eighteenth century, and it finds regular expression today. On the other hand, there are those who insist that what they want to say cannot be constrained by the bounds of so-called 'correct' usage. This view is often attributed to literary authors who attempt to follow Pound's dictum to 'make it new'. But it is also tacitly supported by social groups who develop an 'insider-speak' because they feel that 'ordinary' usage just cannot capture what it is they want to say with appropriate precision. Paradoxically, the development of a particular 'way of saying' frequently becomes normative so that people who wish to join the group have to adapt their styles of writing to suit existing practices. Hence, lawyers learn to write like lawyers, academics like academics and advertisers like advertisers. Linguistic prescriptivism, then, seems to be a natural state of affairs (cf. Cameron, 1995) – although not in quite the ways that Swift had in mind – and the interesting issue becomes *who* is doing the prescribing and for what ends.

This is clearly a naive question, since writing practices develop from a history of previous writing practices and show continuity. The civil servants of today are direct descendants of the chancery clerks of the fifteenth century in more ways than one. However, just as their functions (and the societies in which such functions have meaning) have undergone changes over the last four centuries, so have their styles of writing. So underlying this study of some contemporary genres there will be a tacit recognition that they have developed both as a way of performing certain (linguistic) tasks and in reaction to the ways in which similar tasks have been (linguistically) performed in the past. As Lask memorably says:

> English extends in three dimensions – temporal, spatial and social; and the last two have their own historical background, which is often crucial to our understanding of why things look the way they do at present.
>
> (1987, p. xii)

For these reasons, the book follows an unusual trajectory in that it constantly loops between the society and the individual. It takes as axiomatic the view that language is social, but recognises that language users are making individual contributions to the societies of which they are a part. It begins with a look at some of the complaints made by the Queen's English Society and places them in the context of the 'complaint' tradition. This tradition may be considered to be a populist notion about language use which asserts that there are 'correct' usages of English which should be adhered to at all times and in all circumstances. Although its tenets can be shown to be flawed, the tradition has a powerful hold on the imagination and has influenced the construction of the English syllabus within the National Curriculum.

This version of English is often referred to as 'Standard English', a term which is deeply ambiguous but which is also used by professional linguists. Clear definitions of standard English are difficult to come by, although it is typically associated with uniformity of practice in the construction of written texts. Historically, there would seem to be processes at work which tend to encourage such uniformity, although there are equally powerful forces which have resisted, and do resist, such uniformity and these are investigated briefly at two key points in the development of English. The first of these occurred after the introduction of printing in 1476, and the second in the latter half of the eighteenth century when national 'membership' was a crucial issue (cf. Colley, 1992). Some of the arguments that took place in these two periods are reminiscent of those that have been occurring recently. The tensions within the nation-state *vis-à-vis* Europe, the sense that English is no longer 'our' language and the introduction of the new electronic technologies of communication have all led to introspection on the nature and form of the language. Although it is easy to represent these arguments as those between traditionalists and radicals, this would be misleading since none of the writers who have argued for change believed that all and any mode of writing was acceptable. At the pragmatic level, they were suggesting that language use had to adapt to express the new social realities. However, to the extent that our children have been obliged to learn a very restricted range of written expression, the defenders of the 'standard' are locking them into a very narrow understanding of language.[1]

This brief historical survey is followed by a more detailed discussion of the ways in which written texts operate within society at a general level. Key terms introduced here include *context* and *discourse*. The concept of context is peculiarly difficult to define since it can refer both to the physical settings within which written texts are constructed, the physical setting within which they are read, the cognitive environment of individual producers/consumer, or the wider social relationships that obtain between readers and writers. In this chapter I shall be concentrating on the ways in which writings are socially situated. Swales has developed the notion of discourse communities to try and explain how it is that a certain set of communicative practices develop between people who are engaged in the same (linguistic) task. I shall suggest that Swales's definition of a discourse community is too narrow to show how larger genres than the ones he investigates actually manage to develop. However, I shall suggest that it can be extended to include all those occasions when our social interaction is mediated through the written word. By adapting some ideas developed within sociolinguistics, I believe it can be shown that we have overlapping memberships of a number of different discourse communities, and that we are differently situated in relationship to them. In some, we may be 'experts', in others 'neophytes' and in others, to borrow a term from electronic communication, 'lurkers'. I further argue that it is only in relation to these discourse communities that we manage to construct 'meanings'. This may seem a peculiarly atomistic account of our social lives, but the notion of networks and multiple memberships in fact links us tightly to the larger social grouping which consists of all the discourse communities which make up a society. Although I have argued that meanings are constructed within discourse communities, the meanings of discourse communities require further validation from this larger group, and they only achieve such validation to the extent that they are consonant with the discursive practices of the society.

This chapter is followed by a chapter in which I consider some of the ways in which texts have been characterised. At first sight, there would seem to be little of concern here, but I believe that all too often analysts are caught by the logical contradictions inherent in claiming that text X is performing task Y when it is self-evidently not performing such a task, but is being used as an example or object of analysis. I do not feel that I have escaped from this contradiction entirely successfully myself, but I do suggest that we need to develop new ways of distinguishing between texts, acts of communication and people communicating. I argue that whereas acts of communication (or 'language-in-action') and people communicating (i.e. as individuals who are members of a discourse community) are essentially dynamic and should be analysed as such, textual analysis (or 'language-in-observation') is essentially static and hierarchical in its methodology.

From here I loop back to the individual by considering what kinds of skill are typically required to produce texts that are both _cohesive_ and _coherent_. Again the distinction between language-in-action and language-in-observation is relevant since there are some cohesive devices which are part of the language as system. I look briefly at some aspects of grammatical and lexical cohesion, before going on to explore how writers try to make their contributions coherent both with respect to the situation and with respect to themselves. Because writers cannot in fact _construct_ coherence, since it is a property that is supplied by the reader, they have to signal the intended functions in various ways, and the different ways they choose will necessarily lead to different types of texts.

One way of understanding this phenomenon has been developed within register theory. Register analysis assumes that coherence relations can be achieved by particular combinations of field, tenor and mode. Register theory is based on a functional view of language which assumes that the grammatical systems within language have developed to model and signal particular functions. Thus, although I may be correct in claiming that writers cannot construct coherence, they are able to signal the intended coherence of their texts by making particular selections from the ideational, interpersonal and textual potentials that exist within a given language. By looking at a variety of texts, I shall attempt to demonstrate that although register theory is a useful tool in understanding how a given text 'means' in a specific circumstance, and therefore accounts for what ideas may have been involved in its construction, it cannot easily be generalised into explaining how sets of texts are recognised as performing common social functions.

Staying with the individual, I next look at some of the cognitive skills involved in interpreting texts. I shall take as my model the theory developed by Sperber and Wilson (1986), _relevance theory_, but shall be arguing that it fails to account adequately or clearly for the way readers are able to establish interpretations of texts that take into account the social dimensions of specific wordings. In particular, I shall suggest that recovering given propositional forms and then computing their relevance does not fully explain why different text types exist and why their theory needs to be supplemented by a more social theory of language.

In Chapter 7 I consider the issue of genre in some detail. I start with a brief discussion of parody. Taken at its face value, a parodic text is indistinguishable from a non-parodic text. In terms of register, there is nothing that signifies it is to be treated as non-serious. However, most people recognise parodic texts as attempts to make fun of previous texts *of the same kind*. It would seem then that we need a higher level of analysis which explains how sets of texts are recognised as belonging to the same genre.

I shall illustrate my arguments by a detailed look at the genres of letter-writing and of advertisements. The letters I have included for discussion are quite diverse productions and manifest tremendous variation both in terms of topic and in the ways they situate their intended readers. It seems appropriate, therefore, to make an initial distinction between public and private genres. When we observe public genres, we also notice considerable variation but this seems not to be intrinsic to the letter as letter but has an external motivation. The best way of explaining this is by appealing to the notion of discursive practices. We can observe then how such practices invade and shape genres and lead to the creation of subgenres. Similar kinds of variations are also seen to operate in the genre of advertising. Thus it would seem that genres are distinguished less by text type than by the communicative functions they are performing. We recognise letters as letters and advertisements as advertisements not because all letters and all advertisements are the same, but because they have their own particular functions. To illustrate this more precisely, I consider an advertisement which is in the form of a letter. I then conclude this chapter with a brief discussion of recipes before revisiting some of my earlier arguments.

If the view that I have developed about genre is substantially accurate, then it should also apply to those writings that we consider to be literature. The existence of literary texts seems to present genre theory with a number of problems precisely because there is such a large number of different text types that have been traditionally classified as literary. I shall, by using some of the arguments already developed, attempt to show how literature in itself can be considered to be a genre. Further, I shall sketch a very brief argument to indicate how particular literary texts can be regarded as sub-genres.

In the Conclusion, I shall revisit some of the arguments developed earlier in the book with the purpose of demonstrating how variety in writing is an inevitable consequence of the ways in which different members of the same language group situate themselves differently in relation both to each other and to other groups and that a diversity of genres is the sign of a healthy society.

Each chapter concludes with a list of suggested further reading. These readings have all, in one way or another, influenced my thinking even when they have not been referred to in the body of the text. They are therefore part of my intellectual debt. After the readings I have included a brief section called 'Some questions for consideration'. I have called it this largely because I have little faith in formal textbook exercises. Good teachers will construct their own questions, while students working on their own tend to get frustrated by questions which lack answers in the textbook. Also, when they do have answers, there is a tendency to read the answers before attempting the questions. Therefore my questions really are quite simply for consideration. If you manage to produce answers, you will have helped advance the study. If you avoid the questions, nothing serious is lost.

Chapter 1

Variety and 'Standard English'

PRELIMINARIES

In 1988 Kingman published the *Report of the Committee of Enquiry into the Teaching of the English Language* (the Kingman Report). This was a document commissioned by the British government in response to fears that standards of English were falling. Its object was to propose a basic framework on which more detailed syllabus plans could be constructed so as to produce generations of school leavers who would be equipped with the necessary linguistic skills required for employment. It also had the more humane aim of recommending how teachers might develop and shape their pupils' language so that they could express themselves more articulately in other social contexts. The publication of the Kingman Report is a useful starting point for our discussion of language variety both because of its genesis, and because of the specific recommendations that all pupils should be taught 'Standard English'.

The belief that standards of English are falling is peculiar, although it has a long history. It is peculiar in that it presupposes that there is some universal set of criteria against which the standard can be judged. Usually these criteria are found in the past and they are frequently associated with particular literary writers. It was no accident that Prince Charles, when he wanted to illustrate what he saw as the poverty of modern English speech in the early 1990s, should take Hamlet's famous soliloquy 'To be or not to be' and refashion it so that it became full of contemporary clichés. The reference point would be well known to his audience, and the deviations would both be amusing and make the serious point that we no longer have the facility to construct such penetrating thoughts in language which makes them clear. However, under the surface, a variety of myths and ideologies are at work which serve to confuse the issue quite seriously.

Three of these confusions are particularly illuminating in the ways that they point to underlying myths about English. The first (and perhaps most obvious) is that we no longer speak like Hamlet because we are no longer Elizabethans. Our language has changed in fundamental ways to reflect the changes that have taken place in society over the last 400 years. This might seem trivial, but it is also important because to the extent that we ignore it we imprison ourselves in a myth of historical continuity which asserts that the values obtaining between 1564 and 1616 (i.e. Shakespeare's lifetime) were somehow intrinsically English values which can and ought to be recovered.[1] Further, the implicit appeal is to a time in history when the English were displaying particular vigour in resisting foreign invasions, expanding their influence into the New World, establishing a new vision of Christianity and developing a constitution that would serve as the basis for an expanded parliamentary democracy. Although the detail of the reference may be lost, the nostalgia for Elizabethan England remains powerful.

The second confusion is interesting in that it all too often finds its way into discussions of standards. Loosely speaking, it can be regarded as the elision between what is appropriate in writing and what is appropriate in speech. In this case, it is the apparent assumption that what has been carefully crafted on paper as the soliloquy of a fictional character which is ultimately to be realised as speech by an actor in front of a large (and possibly attentive) audience can, or indeed should, be taken as a model for the normal, conversational interaction of twentieth-century speakers of English.

The third confusion is rather less obvious. In taking Shakespeare as his model, Prince Charles was consciously choosing a writer who is generally acknowledged to be the finest in the English language. However, the specific features of the text as *literary* are ignored. There is the assumption that the model adopted (i.e. Hamlet's soliloquy) is appropriate for use in all circumstances: that it is in some sense a standard against which all other usages should be judged. This assumption goes beyond the simple distinctions between speech and writing mentioned above, since it seems to include *all* kinds of communication in English. But this is in itself confusing on two further counts. First, it is not at all clear to me that the highly imaginative literary language used by Shakespeare *is* necessarily appropriate for, say, leaving a note for the milkman. But even if it were, given that Shakespeare is perceived to be the greatest writer in English, it is unreasonable to expect me to reach his 'standard'.

POPULIST VIEWS OF ENGLISH

I have chosen Prince Charles's speech because it was widely reported and generally praised in the British press. However, it is typical of many pronouncements that occur in the 'complaint tradition' (Milroy and Milroy, 1991, Chapter 2) with regard to the use of English. This tradition can be traced back at least as far as Caxton and seems to be based on the assumption that when two locutions seem to be expressing the 'same' meaning, then one of them must somehow be 'better'. Joseph makes the point neatly when he argues:

> Nevertheless, it seems inevitable that once people do become conscious of variants of behaviour, they evaluate them. It is as though valorization and consciousness are two sides of the same coin. Because of the naturalness of change, no human speech community is without linguistic variation, and my research has turned up no speech community whose members were not consciously sensitive to language quality, whether or not they were literate.
>
> (1987, p. 30)

If this is the case, then it is worth considering on what grounds these judgements are made.

Two recent studies carried out on behalf of the Queen's English Society by B.C. Lamb should be enlightening here since they were mounted precisely because of the perceived drop in standards referred to above. The results are revealing, but possibly not quite in the ways the respondents intended. The first, *A National Survey of UK Undergraduates' Standards of English* (1992)[2] covered 148 different university departments and surveyed one in depth. It found that nearly 20 per cent of students were regarded by their tutors as poor in spelling, 24 per cent as poor in punctuation, 20 per cent as poor in standards of grammar, 18 per cent as possessing a poor vocabulary and 22 per cent as poor in 'written clarity'. The report also includes some of the major solecisms recorded. On occasion, these might lead to serious ambiguities of meaning and therefore have to be regarded seriously. However, if we scrutinise this survey critically, it becomes apparent that some of the comments derive from errors produced in examination conditions. Given that students are required to write at speed, in stressful conditions, often using the relatively unfamiliar mode of handwriting, it is not entirely surprising that their concentration may slip. Even leaving aside such circumstances, it would be interesting to know more precisely what the respondents meant by 'bad grammar'. Spelling is more transparent in that there are dictionaries which have the stamp of authority behind them to give guidance. Grammar is a much more elusive feature of the language system and, as I shall be showing later in the book, what may count as 'bad grammar' in one context may be perfectly acceptable in others. And it is because of this that we have to treat with caution the discovery that so many students are considered to be poor at 'written clarity'. Indeed, it could be said that clarity is achieved by both knowing what one wants to say and knowing the appropriate ways of saying it. Thus, 'clarity' becomes a function of, in this case, entering the academic community in which given modes of expression are acceptable. To the extent that our students lack such clarity, it is at least partially the fault of those lecturers who have failed to offer a clear model for their students.

The second survey, *A National Survey of Communication Skills of Young Entrants to Industry and Commerce* (1994) makes similarly depressing reading. Predictably, the survey came up with equally gloomy results, finding that 32 of the 191 firms contacted reported that their entrants were guilty of bad spelling, 25 of 'bad grammar, syntax or sentence construction', 15 had bad punctuation, 28 'bad writing generally' while 5 resorted to 'bad vocabulary'. Again, this survey is used as a way of berating teachers for failing to give their pupils the necessary linguistic skills for employment, and again there is the underlying assumption that there is a single model of English which will somehow serve the needs of all the different kinds of employment that were surveyed. However, at least this survey was amusing in that it included the errors made by the respondents, thereby seriously undercutting its central thesis that standards were necessarily declining.

The 'complaint tradition' is therefore still thoroughly alive, and still concentrating on similar bugbears: clarity, grammar, spelling. That these three are interlinked is not entirely surprising. Spelling is a particular problem because it is subconsciously linked to pronunciation. English spelling does not have a one-to-one relation to phonology, and some of the simplest English graphemes are likely to be pronounced differently in different parts of the country. To that extent, spelling could be said to be anonymous. When I write <but>, my readers, unless they already know me, cannot be sure how I might say it. Correct spelling, then, serves to iron out differences of region, class and individuality. Indeed, one of Caxton's complaints was precisely that regional differences of English (both dialect and accent in so far as it affected local spellings) made it difficult for him to decide which particular variants were most likely to appeal to his intended audiences when he established his printing press in 1476 (see below, Chapter 2).

However, correct spelling might also be said to demonstrate acquaintanceship with a historically stable view of what the English language is like. Since the publication of Johnson's Dictionary (1755) English spelling has been increasingly regularised, and citation forms help diminish the perception of differences whether these are spatial or temporal. It was not always the case. Most people are familiar with Shakespeare's variant spellings. However, in 1704 Robert Walpole's mother could still write to her son:

I writt to you before which I supposed you reseived before you went into Suffolk and I hoped I should have had your answer for I depended so much upon your promas that I should have money at Xmas that I did not writt for till any necesity made me. Therefore pray doe not faille of takeing care I may have it in a weeke.

(Plumb, 1956, p. 108)

There is no evidence that Mrs Walpole was a particularly uneducated woman, although it is clear that regular spelling was not a matter of very great concern for her. It could be said to have become so in part because the assertion of individuality implicit in idiosyncratic spelling disturbs our view of the unity of the language.[3] It is for this reason, perhaps, that we are far more prepared to accept variant spellings in private letters and postcards than we are in printed material.

Correctness of grammar is also underwritten by various schoolbooks, although it is not always apparent that the 'complainers' fully understand the nature of such rules. Lamb's surveys comment on the concord 'rule' whereby singular nouns are followed by verbs marked for singularity. However, this rule is not part of the grammar of all varieties of English, nor does it apply unequivocally in the 'core' grammar which he is implicitly recommending. Certainly, with some constructions, semantic considerations of plurality seem to come into play (see the discussion in Reid, 1991, p. 197ff). For example, in the following sentence:

A herd of cows **was** crossing the road

the cows are considered to be a single unit, whereas in:

A number of cows **were** crossing the road

the cows are treated as individuals. The number of cows observed may be the same in both instances, and the noun head of the subject may be marked for singularity, nevertheless the pedant who insists that the second sentence is grammatically incorrect is missing an important feature of the ways in which we can manipulate grammar to construct meaning.

More commonly, the 'complainers' focus on areas where the language is clearly undergoing subtle shifts in popular usage. A frequent area of anxiety used to be associated with the contrast between 'who' and 'whom' in such constructions as:

The man **whom** I saw

versus

The man **who** is coming with us.

This has led some linguists to posit the notion that 'whom' is a feature of the written grammar only. However, there is some evidence to suggest that the loss of inflectional case morphemes (a process which has been continuing from at least 1066) might be operating here and that what is now treated as normal in the spoken language will spread into the written language. Further evidence to support this idea can be adduced from the increasing frequency of such constructions (which have also been the target of complaint) as:

Between you and I.

The issue of 'clarity' is rather more problematic. There is little evidence that the 'complainers' genuinely fail to understand the locutions they condemn. Indeed, their ability to correct the mistakes they identify suggests that comprehension has not been seriously impaired at all.[4] It would seem, then, that 'lack of clarity' is to be identified with writing something in a form which transgresses the grammatical rules or uses inappropriate phrases and/or vocabulary. Of course, some writing may be obscure because the ways in which the arguments are linked by discourse connectors has not been made explicit. Where this is the case, then we have grounds for arguing that the writers lack particular linguistic skills. However, this is not a complaint that is often clearly articulated. Other writing may be opaque because the writers lack a clear grasp of what they want to say. In these cases, we can hardly chastise the writers for their failure to write clearly, since it is not obviously their language that is at fault.

Typically, then, the complaint tradition focuses on errors in English at the sentence level in such a way as to suggest that meanings map on to grammatical constructions and *vice versa* in a relatively uncomplicated way. It also tends to ignore the historical processes that are engaged in shaping some of the forms of the language and which are still continuing today, and it is most comfortable when it can appeal to 'authority' without questioning how that authority has been achieved. It is also unable to articulate clearly exactly how longer stretches of text are marred in their construction, preferring to hide behind such phrases as 'clarity of expression'. However, although it is fairly easy to demonstrate how the complainers are confused in a number of ways, it is still necessary to take them seriously and try to understand why this passion for a uniform language develops. Just as Joseph has commented on the universality of such complaints, so Mühlhäusler has found that speakers of Miriam, a Papuan language, also correct each others' speech. However, he makes the interesting point that

> corrections of this type occur in a situational context and are not directed at the grammaticality of decontextualised sentences. Intuitions about that kind of grammaticality are notoriously unreliable or non-existent among speakers of many Pacific languages . . . so deciding on context-less grammaticality is not one of the metalinguistic games they tend to engage in.
>
> (1987, p. 10)

What is interesting is why speakers should engage in this kind of correction and, more importantly, why English speakers are interested in 'contextless grammaticality'.

'STANDARD ENGLISH'

The answers to these questions are highly complex and I can only offer tentative solutions here. However, part of the answer can be found in the deep-seated and widely held myth that there is a coherent and describable linguistic variety of English commonly called Standard English capable of fulfilling all the functions that English speakers wish to fulfil.

A discussion of some of the ideas associated with the term 'Standard English' is pertinent to the theme of this book precisely because such ideas represent the forces which seek to impose uniformity on English writing. Even more important, though, is the view that 'Standard English' is most obviously observable in (certain kinds) of writing. Joseph (1987) has devoted a whole chapter to the importance of writing in creating a 'model' for the language. In particular, he asserts its significance in the development of a meta-linguistic awareness. Writing, he claims, has the effect of giving language 'a much more substantial materiality than it inherently possesses' (p. 38). Further, alphabetic writing contributes to a theory of language by isolating various linguistic symbols. Writing also has important ideological effects in its ability to store and control information.

These claims implicitly assume that speech and writing are significantly different modes of communication. I have already commented (in the Introduction) that writing is artificial whereas speech is 'natural'. However, the differences are more far-reaching than appear on the surface. Some scholars (e.g. Goody, 1977, 1986) have suggested that the introduction of writing into non-literate societies affects the social structure of such societies in incalculable ways. Others argue that it has important cognitive effects. Ong (1982, Chapter 4), for example, has a whole chapter devoted to the proposition that 'writing restructures consciousness'. Although these speculations are outside the scope of this book, there is little doubt that 'visible language' has important effects on people's ideas of language. Because it is static, it offers the possibility of a particular kind of analysis. Words, sentences and paragraphs can be viewed as discrete units and their forms can be scrutinised and rescrutinised. Preferred forms can then be offered as models to writers not simply because of what they *do* (their function) but because of what they *are* (their structure).

However, the existence of writing also leads to the functional elaboration of linguistic communication. Whereas what is said is typically processed in immediate face-to-face situations and then 'dies', written communications traverse space and time. They therefore develop new functions (cf. Halliday, 1985, p. 39ff), gaining authority from their very existence rather than from whoever 'utters' them (consider, for example, the authority of written laws). Although it is possible to exaggerate the differences between speech and writing (Barton, 1994, p. 85ff; McCarthy, 1993; McCarthy and Carter, 1994, pp. 3–9), there is sufficient evidence to indicate that written texts have a normative effect on language use. But what is surprising is that only certain kinds of writing achieve the status of authoritative models and are treated as representative of 'Standard English'.

I shall be arguing later that the myth of 'Standard English' is, and has been used as, part of a discourse that asserts the integrity and conflict-free nature of the nation-state by attempting to suppress variety. By asserting the existence of a variety of English which enables its users to say all that they wish to say, proponents of 'Standard English' are implicitly claiming that it is a variety to which all English speakers can aspire. Further to the extent that it is fully codified and invariable, it would be a variety that could be taught and learned by the whole population.

'STANDARD ENGLISH' AND EDUCATION

Certainly, this is the kind of thinking that is encoded in the Kingman Report (Kingman, 1988, pp. 14–15) and repeated in the two National Curriculum documents, *English for Ages 5 16*, issued by the Department of Education and Science (renamed Department for Education) in 1989 and 1993. Although it would be unreasonable to expect such documents to give a clear and scientific definition of 'Standard English', they are important in that the ways in which they describe it will have an important influence on both teachers of English and their pupils for some time to come. The Kingman Report refers to it in most detail and, in doing so, reveals just what a nebulous entity it is. In paragraph 5 (Kingman, 1988, p. 7), it is distinguished from the 'dialect usages of family' and identified with the dialect of the nation (and, rather grandiosely, the world). This is a subtle distinction that may not be immediately apparent to anybody who believes that the nation is necessarily made up of the families who live in it and who use their own particular dialects. However, such a distinction is conveniently blurred where we are informed that ' "Standard English" is what we have in common' (ibid., para. 31, p. 14). Nevertheless, although we all have it in common, we 'can have only partial access to Standard English: the language exists like a great social bank on which we all draw and to which we all contribute' (ibid.). The document continues:

> It is important to be clear about the nature of Standard English. It developed from one of the Middle English dialects . . . to become the written form used by all writers of English, no matter which dialect area they come from. It is the fact of being the written form which establishes it as the standard.

> (ibid., para. 32, p. 14)

Even allowing for the brevity of this description, it is revealing in the way it mingles fact and metaphor. 'Standard English' is seen first as a national variety that transcends any of the varieties that are spoken by the individuals of the nation. This seems to suggest that it is an artificial variety created to ease communication (and especially written communication) within the nation. However, the subsequent claim that it developed from a particular dialect undercuts this suggestion by indicating that it is a variety that is (or was) used by a specific group of people.

It is then described as something all English speakers hold in common. This is confusing in a slightly different way although it is continuous with the previously unstated claim that it is a national possession. It is true that we may hold things 'in common' without being aware of our ownership. However, implicit in these two claims is the underlying ideological claim that we are not full members of the nation until we have laid claim to this common inheritance. By a sleight of hand, membership of the nation has become intricately bound up with being able to manipulate a variety of the language which is either artificial, or is used by an unidentified group who are asserting that they embody national linguistic values.

The subsequent shift of metaphor that sees the 'Standard' as a bank is also revealing. Whether language can be usefully compared to the kinds of commercial transactions that occur in the financial world is an interesting question, but the comparison inevitably conjures up images of winners and losers, rich people and poor people. Nevertheless, this seems to be a more egalitarian bank than we traditionally encounter since we all contribute to it and we all draw from it. What is not clear is whether we all contribute to it equally. If we do, then the idea that Standard English is a particular variety becomes increasingly untenable since it would seem to include all the varieties that exist among English speakers (including the dialect usages of family). If we do not all contribute equally, then it would appear that some speakers of English (to continue the metaphor) possess more 'symbolic capital' (Bourdieu, 1991, pp. 72–6) than others, while the others remain permanently in debt to these more powerful members of society.

The document continues:

> All of us can have only partial access to Standard English . . . As we grow older, and encounter a wider range of experience, we encounter more of the language, but none of us is ever going to know and use all the words in the Oxford English Dictionary, which is itself being constantly updated, nor are we going to produce or encounter all possible combinations of the structures which are permissible in English.
>
> (ibid., para. 31, p. 14)

Although not overtly stated, the underlying claim here seems to be that Standard English is, in fact, the sum total of the English language. Of course, if this were true, it seems perfectly acceptable that our children should be given an education in the potential meanings underlying all varieties of the language, but if such were the case it seems unnecessary to invoke the notion of a 'standard'. But a more limited definition occurs in the passage I quoted previously. The 'standard' is that used by all writers of English 'no matter which dialect area they come from'. If this were genuinely accepted to be the case then everything I have written so far would necessarily be in 'Standard English', as would the following texts:

1 ADDITIONAL BENEFITS RIGHTS TO EXTEND THIS POLICY AND EFFECT NEW POLICIES BEFORE 19TH MAY 1993 (SEE MORTGAGE ASSURANCE OPTION PROVISIONS).

2 *Then t' Alleluias stick in t'angels' gobs.*
When dole-wallahs fuck off to the void
what'll t'mason carve up for their jobs?
The cunts who lieth ' ere wor unemployed?

3 I enclose herewith the above mentioned policies together with accompanying documentation for your retention as they are not required in connection with your new mortgage.

4 Glad Abo went well. Re your recent PALA newsletter and books to review: I'd be quite interested in Nardoccio's *Reader Response to Literature* (if not already allocated) – I'm teaching a course in that area this year.

5 Symphony No. 0? Surely some mistake! Well, no; originally designated Symphony No. 2 Bruckner turned against this work in a fit of pique following criticism from the conductor due to give it its premiere.

6 GAS BOILER floor stand-
ing, balanced flue, 54,000
BTU, Thorn, good working
order £100. 0843 860929
after 6pm.

It is clear that each of these texts differs from the others in significant ways and at many linguistic levels.[5] Indeed, it might be difficult to decide which one could be taken as representative of the model of 'Standard English' outlined by the Kingman Report and given further flesh by the documents *English for Ages 5–16*. The first seems to be excluded because it lacks a main verb and definite article; the second conforms to the prescribed forms of syntax, but includes vocabulary that is typically taboo and unlikely to be taught in schools; the third is perhaps the most suitable, although the insertion of 'herewith' and the high degree of nominalisation might be frowned upon; the fourth (which was originally handwritten) lacks a subject and verb (i.e. I am) in the first sentence, and mixes formality and informality inconsistently in the ensuing sentences; the fifth also contains incomplete sentence forms as well as moving from the very informal to a highly complex structure in the third sentence; the sixth is punctuated inconsistently and contains no verbs and no articles.

Casual readers of these texts might be surprised that 'Standard English' can contain such an immense variety of forms. Indeed, they may assume that the difference between these texts is so great as to render a description of 'Standard English' impossible. However, such readers may also discern certain features shared by the different texts. Texts 1 and 3 share certain features of lexis (as well as having the common word 'policies'); Texts 1 and 6 share certain features of layout; Texts 3 and 4 share certain modes of address through the use of personal pronouns; and Texts 4 and 5 contain similar features of informality manifested by incomplete sentence forms (among other things). The one text that seems to be unique is Text 2. It might be deduced that where the texts display similarities it is not because they are using a standard (or non-standard) form of the language but because they are engaging in similar communicative purposes. Equally, their differences signal different communicative purposes.

Casual readers may go on to assume that the term 'Standard English' merely refers to the appropriate use of particular forms to achieve given communicative purpose (with particular reference to the written language). If this were the case, then there would be little need to criticise the label beyond pointing out that 'Standard' seems redundant. However, *English for Ages 5–16* (1993) suggests that the term is not being used in quite this way at all. Although there is frequent reference to different styles of writing, the detail concentrates on correctly formed sentences in which the notion of correctness is identified with fully formed sentences consisting of subject/verb agreement, use of tenses, expansion of vocabulary, and correct punctuation. Mention is made of 'the intended audience', but variation is discussed more often in terms of style than of purpose. The document seems to underwrite a view of the language in which a set of grammatical forms is 'given' and variation is a contingent effect of particular communicative circumstances. An unfortunate tension is thereby created in which pupils are enjoined to learn a particular set of forms while being surrounded with written texts which clearly do not use these forms. However, no clear explanation as to why such variation exists, or how it is (grammatically) realised, is offered other than a vague gesturing to notions of 'style'.

LINGUISTIC VIEWS OF STANDARD LANGUAGES

I have already commented that it would be unreasonable to expect a governmental document to establish a full and clear definition of all its terms, although one that is designed to indicate how children are to be taught should be more transparent that the ones discussed above. However, some of this confusion derives, at least in part, from some of the previous attempts made by academic linguists to establish what they mean by a 'standard language'. Sociolinguists recognise that language variation is the norm, but they also recognise that particular varieties seem both to have greater social prestige, and are more likely to undergo a process of codification (see below, p. 40 and Bex, 1994a).

A revealing discussion of the problem occurs in Haugen (1966, reprinted 1972) where he distinguishes between the *structural* and *functional* descriptions of language (p. 102). The structural elements within a language are those formal features such as grammar, phonology and the lexicon which can be isolated and described, or *codified*. Functional descriptions of language are typically undertaken by sociolinguists and concern themselves with the ways in which linguistic choices are made according to such variables as social class, geographical situation or communicative purpose. A standard language is therefore a variety that has minimal variation in form and maximal variation in function (ibid., p. 107).

Haugen then continues by discussing 'the maximal variation or elaboration of function one expects from a fully developed language' (ibid., p. 108), although it is not clear here whether he is discussing 'language' in general, or a standardised form of the language. He recognises that, in principle, any vernacular is capable of taking on the role required of a standard language, but hints that the one chosen is 'by definition the common language of a social group more complex and inclusive' than the vernaculars used by other social groups. Further, he asserts that:

> Writing, which provides for the virtually unlimited storage and distribution of vocabulary, is the technological means enabling a modern standard language to meet the needs of every specialty devised by its users. There are no limits to the elaboration of language except those set by the ingenuity of man.

> (ibid., p. 108)

This seems to me to pose similar problems to the definition offered within the Kingman Report. Although the discussion is considerably more subtle, there is the suggestion that the standard language, once it has developed, becomes fixed in the written forms. If this is the case, it fails to explain the quite considerable variation that we find in different written documents. Haugen attempts to resolve this problem by arguing that 'Elaboration of function may lead to complexity of form, and contrariwise, unity of form may lead to rigidity of function. This area of interaction between form and function is the domain of *style*' (ibid., p. 108, italics in the original). The thrust of this argument seems to be that although different vernaculars may be said to represent different social groupings and interests, once they have been harmonised into a language and some prestigious vernacular takes on the role of an 'official language' partly, at least, by being reduced to writing, such variations in the written forms that may continue to exist or that may develop as a society becomes more complex, are simply to be seen as stylistic variants rather than as variants which represent different, and often opposing, social forces.

Haugen's view is echoed by other linguists working in the area. Trudgill, for example, adopts a similar position where he identifies Standard English as a dialect typically used by 'educated' speakers. He comments on the geographical differences that obtain between Standard American and Standard British spoken forms, but continues by asserting that 'Standard English is accepted as the dialect appropriate for writing throughout the English-speaking world, and pressures for its written use are therefore very strong' (Trudgill, 1983a, p. 197; see also 1983b, p. 138). More recently, in a standard textbook Holmes, while acknowledging the difficulty in defining 'standard', offers the following as a starting point:

> A standard variety is generally one which is written, and which has undergone some degree of regularisation, or codification (for example in a grammar and a dictionary); it is recognised as a prestigious variety or code by a community, and it is used for H[igh] functions alongside a diversity of L[ow] varieties.
>
> (J. Holmes, 1992, p. 83)

Again, the emphasis on the written form is asserted, but with very little reference to the kinds of difference that we have found in my quoted examples.

Stubbs (1986, p. 85), in a chapter given over entirely to a discussion of Standard English, asserts that 'SE is neither merely a dialect of English, nor a style; it is an intersection of dialectal and functional variation, and this makes it particularly difficult to define'. However, he does suggest it is capable of definition and again mentions 'the very fact that it is used in print makes it visible, whereas N[on] S[tandard] varieties are generally restricted to spoken language' (ibid., p. 94). This characterisation of Standard English is helpful to my discussion, in that it indicates that not all varieties of written English necessarily manifest standard forms. By mentioning printed forms only, Stubbs is tacitly admitting that handwritten forms of the language may incorporate other, non-standard forms of the language.

Stubbs's difficulty in defining Standard English may be because there is no such variety. Indeed, the fundamental argument of this book is that different forms of writing have developed, and are developing, precisely because they manifest quite different positions in relation to the social interactions that occur between members of a society. Of course, all written texts from a given language will have certain features in common, and some of these will be features of lexis and grammatical organisation. However, it is misleading to argue that all printed forms manifest the same grammatical and lexical features, and the sheer diversity of written forms is indicative of other more fundamental diversities. That some forms seem to have achieved a particular status in the popular imagination, and have found their way into textbooks, is not in itself proof that a particular functional variety of English exists against which other varieties can be judged. Nevertheless, because the existence of Standard English seems so well attested, even by linguists who admit the difficulty of establishing a coherent definition, it is worth pursuing this discussion a little further so as to establish whether there might be other ways of characterising it precisely because it does play such an important role in educational and political discussion of the language.

Alternative characterisations of standard languages have been offered by, among others, Downes and Hudson. Hudson (1980, p. 34) discusses some of the processes involved in standardisation and asserts that standard languages are 'perhaps the least interesting kind of language for anyone interested in the nature of human language . . . For instance, one might almost describe standard languages as pathological in their lack of diversity.' This comment is opaque, unless we consider it in the light of Haugen's view that the ideal standard language has minimal variation of form. However, if we acknowledge a close interrelationship existing between form and function, we shall discover that Hudson is making a very important claim. If, as we shall see, a standard language has a relatively limited number of functions within any given society, then we can assume that it also has a relatively limited number of forms. Indeed, I shall be arguing that partly because of its relatively limited range of function and form, Standard English would be more appropriately labelled 'core' English. However, as Hudson points out:

> The irony, of course, is that academic linguistics is likely to arise only in a society with a standard language . . . and the *first* language to which linguists pay attention is their own – a standard one.
>
> (ibid., p. 34; see also Bex, 1994a)

Downes (1984, pp. 32–8) constructs a slightly different argument. While suggesting that Standard English does exist and, like the other linguists we have considered, reaches its apotheosis in the written language, he is altogether more wary of identifying it with a set of forms. He asserts that a 'standard language is a social institution and part of the abstract, unifying identity of a large and internally differentiated society' (ibid., p. 34). Later, he refers to it as an 'institutionalised form of language' (ibid., p. 38) that arises from a complex of social attitudes towards nationhood. As such, it becomes increasingly difficult to talk about Standard English since English is no longer the possession of a single nation-state. However, to suggest that there might be 'Standard Englishes' (e.g. Standard American English, Standard Australian English, Standard Singaporean English, etc.), is also problematic since it would suggest that there were competing varieties of English, each one of which claimed to be superior to the others. Of course, a way round this problem would be to argue that the Standard English of, say, the USA was not in itself better than the Standard English of Britain since each variety was performing a similar function in relation to their respective societies. But by focusing on a functional definition we would need to be precise both about the functions of Standard English and the ways in which particular forms realised these functions. With an internationally fragmented English, defenders of particular forms could no longer argue for their intrinsic superiority (cf. above, the recommendations in the National Curriculum). 'Correctness' would become relative rather than absolute, and it would be correctness according to task or function rather than according to form. Standard English, in so far as it exists, would then become one variety among many which was used for particular purposes.

THE PROCESS OF STANDARDISATION

Whether this will ever come about is an open question, but it seems unlikely precisely because, in the words of Downes (1984, p. 34) standardisation is 'a social behaviour towards language'. But as a form of social behaviour, attitudes towards language are subject to other social pressures. Just as there are forces which are driving varieties of English apart, and we can see this most obviously in the development of geographical varieties around the world, so there are contrary forces, most of which can be observed in the continuities which underlie the existence of generic forms, which are holding it together. These forces have been in play, although on a smaller scale, throughout the history of English, and it is now appropriate to turn our attention to a brief discussion of the process of standardisation as it has applied to English, and more particularly to written English.

However, I should make clear what I am referring to when I talk about language. I am assuming that language is an independent sign system which is ordered according to a set of intrinsic rules. The status of these rules is somewhat mysterious. Chomsky (1959, 1965, 1980, 1986, 1988), the most influential theorist in current linguistic theory, has consistently suggested that they are biologically innate and independent of other perceptual and reasoning mind/brain processes. Certainly, the fact that all children exposed to language eventually develop a linguistic competence can be regarded as evidence that there are certain universal principles common to all languages, and this has led Chomsky to hypothesise the existence of a Universal Grammar. Such a grammar is represented in the mind as a set of principles which determine what counts as language. These principles are very general and are supplemented by a number of parameters which account for the variety of languages which exist in the world. Thus, for example, while there may be a general rule which states that all languages are structure-dependent such that syntactic constructions typically contain a head and a modifying element, this rule does not specify whether the modifying element should precede or follow the head. However, children analyse the lexical input they receive from the particular language they are exposed to, and decide how the principles of Universal Grammar are being realised in specific instances.

Chomsky has suggested that language is, therefore, best seen as a developmental process that occurs independently of any instruction that may be given:

> Language learning is not really something the child does: it is something that happens to the child placed in an appropriate environment, much as the child's body grows and matures in a predetermined way when provided with appropriate nutrition and environmental stimulation.
>
> (1988, p. 134)

A serious problem with this formulation is that it empties language of its interactive component. The child is seen as a disembodied mind/brain analysing data in terms of its structure rather than its social meaning. While recognising that linguistic rules are both complex and subject to their own logic, we need also to acknowledge that language has developed to perform a range of communicative functions, and that these functions also have an effect on the ways language is perceived and produced (Bex, 1993c, p. 259). Thus although the Chomskyan paradigm may be a source of fascinating intellectual enquiry into the structure of the brain and its phylogeny, ultimately it tells us very little about the ways in which language is developed ontogenetically within particular social groups.

Language, in fact, cannot usefully be abstracted from its social functions. Although we may be born with some innate awareness as to what constitutes language, our experience of it is determined by the ways in which we use it and suffer it as an instrument of social identity and control. It precedes the individual's existence, surrounding us when we are born. Typically, children's first experience of language is in a family group which may manifest a variety of idiosyncratic and potentially ungrammatical forms. Children, however, are more than passive observers of such forms, since their own speech self-evidently has important consequences both for them and for the other speakers surrounding them. Their linguistic interventions can be seen as an attempt to symbolise a range of functions which are both expressive, exploratory and regulatory (cf. Halliday, 1975, p. 37). Of necessity, they will draw on and select from the symbolic forms that surround them, and that seem to perform similar functions for other members of the social group with which they are identified. The construction of a language ontogenetically, then, should be seen as part of the ways in which children establish their social identity within a social grouping that existed before them. Although they may be able to influence the shape of the language which is used to mediate social interaction within the family, this will only be in very small ways precisely because the 'ways of saying' are already established. As Halliday has argued:

> Every instance [of language use] whether repetitive or unique is a configuration of meanings of different kinds, available to the child both for storage as coded text and as evidence for construing the system that lies behind. There is no mystique in a child's ability to construct a language on the evidence of what he [sic] hears.
>
> (1988, p. 42)

This process is repeated and expanded as children leave the tightly knit family group and move into the more linguistically varied world of school. In particular, they are introduced to another type of linguistic interaction using written symbols (Augst, 1992; Barton, 1994; Kress, 1994; Perera, 1984).

This entry into the greater variation of language use continues as we grow up, establish friendships, enter higher education, start work, etc. In each case, we elaborate on our basic linguistic repertoire. In school, we construct written texts designed to express, to explain, to report. Equally, we read texts that instruct, amuse and control. And we have to recognise how these various functions are signalled through the linguistic organisation of the texts themselves. No written text is ever 'innocent' in that it always performs some function within a particular context. In higher education we may be presented with texts that go beyond the pedagogical function of textbooks, becoming rather explorations of ideas within a particular intellectual discipline. At work, we have to manipulate texts, either as managers or employees, which carry authority; we may be required to read or write instructions for manipulating machinery, for carrying out various commercial transactions, for persuading people to buy particular goods and services. Further, at home (and elsewhere) we may write and receive messages of affection; read newspapers and magazines, novels and poetry; construct and read advertisements; write letters of enquiry and complaint. Each one of these activities is differentiated from the others both in terms of social activity, and in the ways that social activity is symbolised through linguistic choice, and it is for this reason that it is misleading to suggest that there is a single variety, Standard English, which is capable of performing such a diverse set of acts.

If variation is the condition of language, it becomes relevant to discuss how it is that a given society develops particular varieties and in particular how it develops the concept of 'a' language which it calls its own. Most readers of this book are likely to feel that there is some entity that can usefully be described as the 'English' language, just as many of us are likely to be aware that there was a time when such a language did not exist and that there may come a time in the future when 'English' ceases to exist.

Further, they are likely to feel that the kinds of variations I have described above are varieties of a particular language rather than variations in the abstract. Kress has argued that texts are always

> the encoding of a past history, and of the realignment of the elements of that past history in response to the demands of a present social complex. History is an inevitable element of text: history of differing kinds and dimensions – the micro-history of an interaction now, itself formed out of the history of prior social/linguistic experience, which in its turn records the macro-history of a language and a culture.
>
> (1989a, p. 449)

Textual variety is therefore both a function of the particular situation and a function of the historical events which have led to that situation. By analogy, we can argue that 'English' exists as a language both because of a congeries of circumstance which encourage all English speakers to feel that they are writing and/or speaking the 'same' language, and the set of historical changes which have led to, and sustained, this belief.

The history of English is obviously far too extensive to be discussed in any detail here, although in order to understand existing textual variety it is necessary to look at some of its salient moments. If we follow Chomsky (1986, p. 15), where he refers to the idea attributed to Weinreich that 'language is a dialect with an army and navy', then we would have to admit that most historians of the language have been on the side of the armies (Crowley, 1990). This is perhaps understandable since historians have to conceptualise and delimit their object of study and it may be for this reason that the history of the English language has tended to be the history of the dominant dialects and, all too frequently, the history of that variety used by the historian (Bex, 1994a; Hudson, 1980, p. 34). One of the things that we can observe in all histories of the language is a continuous dispute as to the 'correctness' of various usages. These disputes typically focus on different areas at different times, but they support Downes's view (quoted above) that attitudes towards language are a form of social behaviour. Thus, rather than searching for a contemporary linguistic variety which corresponds to Standard English, it is more valuable to investigate the processes which have been, and continue to be, associated with the standardisation cycle.

Joseph (1987), who has written the most comprehensive account of the standardisation process, has identified nine features which he claims are possessed by standard languages (see also Crowley, 1989; Haugen, 1966; Kachru, 1985; Leith, 1983). The first of these is that a standard language should 'be underlain by a system of non-standard x dialects' (Joseph, 1987, p. 6). The special feature of a standard language is that it is positively valued in such a way as to be synecdochic of the language as a whole. This value is achieved through codification preeminently by the regular use of a writing system. However, part of its value derives from the authority of its codifiers. In Bourdieu's terms (1991, pp. 72–6), its users possess 'symbolic capital'. Although it is capable of change, usually to achieve functional diversity, such change is always driven by people with 'linguistic authority'. Chronologically, the standardisation process can be seen as a cycle (Figure 1.1):

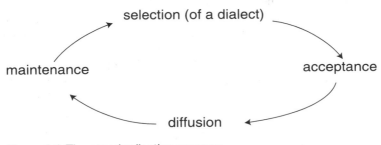

Figure 1.1 The standardisation process

Maintenance depends on the elaboration of its functions, the prestige of its users, the codification, typically, of its written forms and its prescription by means of education, etc. (Leith, 1983, p. 27). Because language is always evolving to meet new needs and express new purposes it is more appropriate to see these processes as a continuing cycle rather than as something which can ever be completed. Within any language there will always be new ways of expression which are in competition with the old forms and for this reason the only fully standardised language will always be a dead language as seen at a particular moment in its development.

In the following chapter I shall be investigating particular moments in the history of English to demonstrate how these processes were evolving since a discussion of contemporary varieties requires some understanding of the historical varieties from which they have evolved.

FURTHER READING

The Kingman Report (1988) is a useful document in that it represents the findings of a Government commission comprising both experts and lay people. Its brief was, among other things, 'To recommend a model of the English language, whether spoken or written, which would: i] serve as the basis of how teachers are trained to understand how the English language works; ii] inform professional discussion of all aspects of English teaching.' Its findings were not acceptable to the government of the day (and not for the reasons given in this section), and it became the subject of dispute. An enlightening chronology of this dispute is given in *Cox on Cox* (1991).

Milroy and Milroy (1991) *Authority in Language* (Chapter 2) are particularly good on the 'complaint tradition'. A more recent work, which covers similar ground but which takes into account the contemporary arguments concerning Political Correctness, is Cameron's *Verbal Hygiene* (1995). This appeared too recently for me to consider its arguments in any detail, but it is to be recommended both for its wit and its humanity.

My discussion of standardisation is necessarily cursory. A good chapter on the difficulties of achieving a satisfactory definition of Standard English can be found in Stubbs's *Educational Linguistics* (1986). Although he does not adopt quite the same position as I have done in this section, he does review the problems in an interesting way. Also, he has a useful bibliography which will supplement my own references. Joseph's *Eloquence and Power* (1987) is a scholarly treatment of the standardisation processes that occur in national languages. Although he does consider English, he concentrates on the standardisation of French. A more Anglocentric perspective is offered by Milroy and Milroy (see above).

Studies of child language abound. The most satisfying general account which attempts to report and review the various current theories fairly is Aitchison's *The Articulate Mammal* (various editions). However, it is worth investigating the ideas in their original form. Chomsky's *Knowledge of Language* (1986) is an accessible introduction to his thoughts on language acquisition and other linguistic matters. From a radically different perspective, Halliday's *Learning How to Mean* (1975) is still highly relevant.

The development and meaning of 'literacy' in individuals has been well discussed by Barton in *Literacy* (1994). The place of literacy in a more general history of humanity remains a matter of considerable scholarly disagreement, but Ong's *Orality and Literacy* (1982) can be recommended both for its scholarship and its breadth of reference. For those who are interested in the place of literacy in the current debate on the National Curriculum, Carter's *Keywords in Language and Literacy* (1995) is particularly valuable. Not only is it an indispensable glossary to 'some central concepts in the teaching and practice of literacy in English' (p. ix), it will also illuminate the ways in which I have used some of the terms.

SOME QUESTIONS FOR CONSIDERATION

A On the day of writing this I have looked at a variety of different texts including the following:

> i We need him. Five years after his invasion of Kuwait, we love him –
> in the sense that we feel affection for familiar ogres, like Dracula or
> James Cagney. Saddam Hussein even looks like the man who tied ladies
> to railway lines in silent movies.[6]

ii For services from LGW to MAD key MD Enter Selection . . . MM
Main Menu HE Help E? Expand Details RF Re-select Flights MD Move
Down RL Fares List
Please enter selection[7]

iii A particular text is thus the encoding of a past history, and of the
realignment of the element of that past history in response to the
demands of a present social complex. History is an inevitable element
of text: history of differing kinds and dimensions – the micro-history of
an interaction now, itself formed out of the history of prior social/
historical experience, which in its turn records the macro-history of a
language and a culture.[8]

iv   To Jane and Tony
                      with seasons
                       Greetings
              love from Jacky, Brian and Rachel[9]

v Notice is hereby given that a Petition was on 13th July 1995 presented
to Her Majesty's High Court of Justice for the confirmation of the
reduction of the capital of the above-named Company from
£8,500,000 to £969,228[10]

vi   INGREDIENTS
                    CHINA TEA, OIL OF BERGAMOT
                      STORE IN A DRY PLACE
                    FOR BEST BEFORE END DATE
                       SEE TOP OF PACK
                      PRODUCT OF CHINA
                    PACKED IN THE UK FOR
                       WAITROSE LIMITED
                    BRACKNELL BERKSHIRE
                      FOODSHOPS OF THE
                  JOHN LEWIS PARTNERSHIP[11]

Are any of these incomprehensible? Can you imagine the circumstances in
which you would find such texts? Are they all in Standard English? If so,
what are the features which define it? If not, what distinguishes those texts
that are in Standard English and those that are not? What is the relationship
between comprehensibility and Standard English?

B From time to time advertisements appear in the press offering courses to
improve your English. They frequently offer illustrations of so-called
solecisms. Also, the correspondence columns of papers often carry examples of the complaint tradition – the *Radio Times* is a particularly good
source because the broadcasting media are both very public and supposed
to set 'standards'. Make a collection of 'errors' and try to assess their kind

(e.g. grammatical, logical, obfuscation, etc.). To what extent do you feel these errors actually interfere with successful communication?

C i A typical children's game involves the production of messages by the use of letters, e.g.

> YYUR
> YYUB
> ICUR
> YY4ME

What might this tell us about the perception of literacy by young children?

ii A 25-year-old man, discussing a trip to South America, is reported as saying: 'On my first trip there, I travelled all around Brazil, Chile, Bolivia and Peru, staying in guest houses and B&Bs for about £1–£4 a night. To get to Caracas, to my flight home, I took a river boat through the heart of the Amazon jungle.'

What accent did he use? Do you think he used exactly these words? In this order? Without any pauses? How did he pronounce '£1–£4'?

iii If somebody could not understand A ii above, how would you 'spcak' it?

What do these examples tell us about the similarities and differences between speech and writing? Does it make sense to suggest either that we should 'speak as we write' or 'write as we speak'?

Chapter 2

A (very brief) history of English

INTRODUCTION

In this chapter I shall be discussing salient moments in the history of English with reference to the standardisation cycle. The two periods which are of particular interest are the years which followed the introduction of printing by Caxton in 1476 and the development of a fully codified educational model of English grammar which was significantly advanced by various writers in the late eighteenth century. However, since changes in language tend to be slow moving (particularly in written language) I shall need to situate these moments within the broad sweep of history. I shall, though, be concentrating on discussions of variety as they occurred at the time and try to locate these discussions within the social contexts which motivated them.

English, which was brought to Britain in the fifth century by the Anglo-Saxon invaders, originally developed from the dialect of a group of languages spoken by various West Germanic tribes. Although structurally related to other contemporary Germanic languages – the *International Encyclopedia of Linguistics* (1992) lists eighteen such languages – it developed sufficient *abstand* (i.e. distinctive structural features, Joseph, 1987, p. 2) to be recognisably different from these other related dialects. As the language of a dominant and militarily powerful group within the British Isles, it was also instrumental in largely overwhelming Celtic and Latin, the other languages that were spoken by the indigenous inhabitants (Burnley, 1992; Leith, 1983). A significant feature of Anglo-Saxon was that it was used for writing. This had the effect of producing 'visible' language which could act as a model both for future writings in the language and also for those speakers who were able to read.

One dialect, the West Saxon, was developed quite considerably as an instrument for learning under Alfred in ninth century Winchester and a number of manuscripts survive that were written in this dialect during the following two centuries. However, West Saxon suffered a severe setback with the advent of the Normans. Norman French replaced Anglo-Saxon[1] for all the functions associated with governance, while Latin was typically used for functions associated with religion and learning. In particular, the practice of writing in English was no longer sustained by any centralised authority (Burnley, 1992, pp. 65–6). The situation in England in the centuries immediately following the Norman Conquest has been well-described by Clanchy:

> English, French and Latin performed distinct social and intellectual functions in twelfth- and thirteenth-century England. No one language could serve all the diverse purposes required because their struggle for dominance was still undecided. English appeared to have given way to Latin as the standard written language of government in the century after the Norman Conquest . . . A century later, in Edward I's reign, it looked as if French might replace Latin as the commonest written language in England. Yet throughout the whole period from 1066 to 1307 English had remained the commonest spoken language, and this is probably the reason why it emerged in the fourteenth century, transformed and fortified, to take its place as the principal language of literature and ultimately of record.
>
> (1993, p. 200)

Of course, English would not have emerged in quite the way Clanchy mentions, nor would it have remained the commonest spoken language, had there not been powerful social forces at work driving such developments. Various explanations have been offered, including the loss of Normandy in 1203, with the consequence that 'those who elected to remain in England devoted themselves to English affairs and English interests untrammelled by continental complications' (Poole, 1955, p. 433). However, this in itself would be unlikely to be decisive without significant pressure from English speakers to reassert their rights in English. Sometimes this power would seem to have been exercised unwittingly. For example, the letters patent sent out by Henry III in 1258 were produced in Latin, French and English, at least partly because Henry was appealing over the heads of the sheriffs that he was criticising to a wider audience (Clanchy, 1993, p. 221) many of whom would have been monolingual. At other times, the writing of texts in English was a necessary function of good governance. The king's subjects were unlikely to obey what they could not understand. Although the Statute of Pleading (1362) relates to spoken language, it makes the interesting observation that 'French is much unknown' in the kingdom. Nevertheless, as Briggs points out, the use of spoken English in the courts was not introduced for entirely philanthropic reasons, rather 'it was doubtless to try, through improved communication, to maintain law and order' (Briggs, 1994, p. 93). The loss of French is also attested to by the production of the Wycliffite Bible in the later part of the fourteenth century. This was prompted by a desire to reach speakers of

English with a comprehensible version of the gospels, but it was clear that it had political as well as religious repercussions (Goodman, 1992, pp. 242–3; Ormrod, 1990, p. 37). What should be stressed here, though, is that all these manuscript documents manifest two distinct kinds of variation: dialectal and functional. Burrow and Turville-Petre comment that the 'main source of diversity in written Middle English is regional and local variation' (1994, p. 5). Although this may well be what strikes the modern eye, there was also considerable generic variation. After all, a prayer or a gospel are as different from a governmental statute as is Chaucer's *A Treatise on the Astrolabe* from *Troilus and Criseyde*.

This brief foray into the history of the language before Caxton is instructive in that it shows how various languages were in conflict during the period, and how a particular dialect (the West Saxon) was entering into the standardisation cycle before it was interrupted by the Norman Conquest. However, Caxton must be seen as the key figure in the standardisation cycle because his introduction of the printing press in London in 1476 was crucial in establishing which dialect was to be selected as synecdochic of the English language, and the mass production of printed materials made possible by printing was to have a profound effect on the ways in which language was discussed in the ensuing centuries.

CAXTON AND THE PRINTING PRESS

Printing was significant in the development of written texts for a number of different reasons. In the first place it allowed for the diffusion of a considerable quantity of texts that were identical in form. This is in marked contrast to the copying of manuscripts which were subject both to the idiosyncrasies and errors of individual copyists, and to the adoption of regional variations to suit the dialects of the immediate audience. Second, by choosing particular forms, the printers were instrumental in disseminating them as models for other writers (and printers). And third, there is some evidence to suggest that the existence of printed texts encouraged the growth of literacy (Barton, 1994, p. 124).

Although it is misleading to personalise historical developments, in this case it is instructive to look at Caxton's own practices as a way of understanding some of these developments in detail. It is generally accepted that Caxton was primarily interested in making a living from his press rather than legislating on matters of 'correct' English (Blake, 1969). Nevertheless, for his translations, he was obliged first to identify a potential audience and then select forms that would be recognised and understood by that audience. His much-quoted preface from *Eneydos* makes this clear. Having bewailed the variety of dialects which make the translator's task so difficult: 'Loo what sholde a man in thyse dayes now wryte. egges or eyren

/ certaynly it is harde to playse euery man / by cause of dyuersite &
chaunge of langage' (Bolton, 1966, p. 3), he continues:

> And for as moche as this present booke is not for a rude vplondyssh man
> to laboure therin / ne rede it / but onely for a clerke & a noble gentylmen
> that feleth and vnderstondeth in faytes of armes in loue & in noble
> chyualrye / Therfor in a meane bytwene bothe I haue reduced &
> translated this sayd booke in to our englysshe not ouer rude ne curyous
> but in suche termes as shall be vnderstanden by goddys grace accor-
> dynge to my copye.
>
> (ibid.)

These words are revealing in the range of concerns they address. Of
course, in the very act of selection, Caxton was performing the function of
a 'gatekeeper'. Those 'termes' that he admitted would be available as
models; those that he denied would remain invisible. In this way, he was
behaving very much like contemporary editors who correct the English of
their contributors and establish 'house styles'. However, whereas now the
functions of editing are typically divided between commissioning editors,
whose job is to determine that the text conforms to the appropriate genre,
and copy editors, who correct errors of grammar and spelling, Caxton
combined these two functions. We can see this in the Preface where he
seems to be making a threefold distinction between dialect forms, social
status and text type.

The first would be determined largely geographically in that it would
depend on where he was most likely to be able to sell his books. The second
was intimately bound up with the educational attainments of his potential
readers. So, the 'rude vplondyssh man' presumably refers to people who are
uneducated, which at the time was synonymous with being ignorant of the
classical writers. This observation seems borne out by a later passage, where
Caxton advises readers who cannot understand his English to 'goo rede and
lerne vyrgyll / or the pystles of ouyde / and ther he shall see and vnderstonde
lyghtly all' (Bolton, 1966, p. 3). Such advice would be pointless for anybody
who had not already got some control of Latin.

The third is hinted at through the distinction he makes between 'clerke'
and 'gentylmen'. If we can assume that 'clerke' is roughly synonymous
with the modern 'cleric', it is revealing that Caxton should mention that
'honest and grete clerkes . . . [have] desired me to wryte the moste curyous
termes that I coude fynde' (ibid.). That he refused is evidence that he may
have considered that such terms were only appropriate for certain kinds of
religious writing. Mueller (1984, pp. 56–7), for example, discusses the
appearance of 'high' and 'moderate' prose styles in the fifteenth century
and notes that they are distinguished according to intention. He claims that
the high style is 'aureate' and aimed at emotional intensification for readers
with a religious vocation whereas the 'moderate' style was chiefly used for

instruction. It would seem, then, that Caxton was rejecting use of the aureate style in this passage. Thus, Caxton was not only instrumental in furthering the process of selection of a dialect, he was also influenced by generic considerations as to the selection of particular registerial elements.

Caxton's choice of dialect was largely drawn from the East Midland variety (the same as that used by Chaucer). Given that Bennett (1952, p. 225) has estimated that Caxton initially worked to a print run not exceeding 4–500 copies, this had particular advantage since it was the dialect that was understood in the London area (Blake, 1992, p. 13). He could therefore assume that patronage would be forthcoming from those associated with the court. However, his choice of forms was not solely dependent on a regional dialect. He also selected from the practices of the most experienced writers, the scriveners of the Chancery, whose writing would necessarily be familiar to court functionaries. Such selections would also tend to increase his potential sales. Although there is some disagreement as to the extent of Caxton's borrowings from Chancery English (Blake, 1969; Cable, 1984), Fisher has stated the case most positively:

> Caxton's place in the development of a standard written English must be regarded as that of a transmitter rather than as an innovator. He should be thanked for supporting the foundations of a written standard by employing, 86 per cent of the time, the favourite forms of Chancery Standard, but he is also responsible for perpetuating the variations and archaisms of Chancery Standard to which much of the irregularity and irrationality of Modern English must be attributed.
>
> (1984, p. 168)

Caxton, then, may legitimately be regarded as a key figure in the process which led to a particular variety of English being regarded as synecdochic of the language as a whole. His choices of dialect have heavily influenced the ways in which we tell our histories. Thus, Dryden, in his 'Preface' to *Fables Ancient and Modern* (1700), refers to Chaucer as the father of English poetry. Had Caxton selected the West Midland dialect, this accolade would probably have gone to Langland.

ELABORATION

I have suggested that printing may have encouraged literacy. Keith Thomas, argues that:

> there was a large reading public in the later Middle Ages; and its relationship to the written word was not very different from what it became in the age of print. There was much continuity between the content of medieval manuscripts and of printed books. Until 1640 religious works still account for nearly half the press's output . . .
>
> (1986, p. 169)

However, this conceals important economic differences between manuscript culture and print culture. Bennett (1952) points out that Tyndale's *New Testament* had an edition of 3,000 in octavo in 1525. No doubt some of these copies would have been sold to people who already had manuscript copies of the Wycliffite Bible, but Hill has estimated that Tyndale's version 'cost 3/- - not a small sum. But Lollard Testaments had cost from seven to eighteen times as much' (1993, p. 11). Thus the sheer accessibility of printed materials was likely to have encouraged the reading habit even if it was largely confined to religious works (ibid., pp. 7–21).

If there was a new market for printed materials developing, it would be seeking a variety of different types of texts. The half of the press's output that was not devoted to religious works would be of texts of diverse types, and the concern of the next century was to identify a national variety of written English which would be flexible enough to accommodate the various genres that were developing. Again, we can see the tensions between centralising and diversifying forces at work as written English became more elaborated.

Puttenham, writing in 1589, recommends that writing (and particularly poetry) should be both modernised and centralised. He rejects the old English of Gower, Lydgate and Chaucer on the grounds that their language is no longer common, and he also discommends the use of dialects spoken north of the Trent even when used by noblemen, although he acknowledges that 'theirs is the purer English Saxon at this day'. The reason he offers is that it is 'not so courtly nor so curant as our Southerne English is, no more is the far Westerne mans speach'. His choice for poets is that they should take as their model: 'the vsuall speach of the Court, and that of London and the shires lying about London within lx myles, and not much aboue' (Blake, 1981, p. 58).

Thus, although he found the written English of the East Midlands increasingly remote, he endorsed Caxton's recommendation made a hundred years earlier. His reasons were no doubt founded on a belief that writing should be constrained by a national variety that was centred on the most influential social forces within the country.

The desire to have a centralised 'national' language was associated with the growth of nationalism that was an inevitable concomitant of the Reformation. We have seen how Caxton distinguished between religious and secular audiences in the late fifteenth century, but we have also noted that 'being literate' was largely perceived as having some competence in the classical languages, and particularly Latin. The desire to bring the Bible to the commonalty had led to its translation into the vernacular and, by association with the 'word of God', such translations gave the new vernacular new standing. However, Latin remained the language of religion and, because learning was necessarily associated with the church, the language of the scholarly professions. The break with Rome in 1534 was a powerful force in undermining this relationship. The creation of a national church and the growth of nationalism in general inexorably pushed English into areas where it would previously not have been used. As it invaded religious functions, so it took over some areas of scholarship, particularly those associated with the new learning in science. Interestingly, at the same time science was slowly becoming secularised, so the use of a language which typically realised religious functions became increasingly inappropriate. To trace the detail of the invasion of English into discourses which were traditionally associated with Latin is an aspect of macro-history (Kress, 1989a) that is beyond the scope of this book. However, it is interesting to observe that Latin was retained as a necessary matriculation subject for entries into the universities of Oxford and Cambridge until the 1960s. Presumably the possession (however rudimentary) of a classical language was seen as the mark of an educated person, although it also served to discriminate between those schooled in institutions which offered tuition in the classics and all other educational institutions.

Recognition that the various languages were in competition, coupled with a sense of national pride, is evident in Mulcaster's oft-quoted words from *The Elementarie* (1582): 'I love Rome, but London better; I favor Italie, but England more; I honor the Latin, but I worship the English' (Crystal, 1988, p. 195). His faith in the stature of English is touching, but it took some time before the language was able to fulfil all the functions associated with a national language, and much of this time was taken up with disputes about the best ways of strengthening the language so that it became more 'eloquent'. These arguments illustrate the kinds of centripetal and centrifugal forces that I have referred to above. The centralising effects implicit in the selection of a dialect associated with a particular geographical and social group of speakers were subject to the fissiparous tendencies involved in functional elaboration.

Initially such arguments were focused on the lexicon. Elyot, for example, writing in the mid-sixteenth century, undertook self-consciously to expand the vocabulary by borrowing a number of Greek and Latin words and 'Englishing' them:

> I intend to augment our Englyshe tongue wherby men shulde as wel expresse more abundantly the thynge that they conceyued in theyr hartis (wherfore language was ordeyned) hauing wordes apte for the pourpose: as also interprete out of greke, latyn/or any other tonge into Englysshe. as sufficiently/as out of any of the said tongues into another
>
> (Jones, 1953, p. 79)

This was certainly one way of solving the problem since it allowed into the language a range of new terms whose etymology would be recognised by the learned. However, it necessitated the production of wordlists to gloss these 'hard words' for the ordinary reader, which led in time to the production of dictionaries. It also encouraged neologisms of an occasionally grotesque kind. The 'cod' letter by Thomas Wilson (1553) ridicules these:

> Ponderyng expendyng, and reuoluting with myself your ingent affabilitee, and ingenious capacitee, for mundane affaires: I cannot but celebrate and extolle your magnificall dexteritee, aboue all other. For how could you haue adepted suche illustrate prerogatiue, and dominicall superioritee, if the fecinditee of your ingenie had not been so fertile, and wounderfull pregnaunt . . . [etc.]
>
> (Barber, 1976, p. 82)

What we can observe here, in what came to be known as the 'Inkhorn' controversy, is an important struggle between those who favoured a self-consciously 'literary' language (i.e. a language constructed from written, largely classically based models) and those who felt that writing should adapt itself more to spoken forms. So, for example, Mueller points out that the desire for 'aureation' was fostered by a belief that:

> orality in written language should be cultivated in a direction counter to that of actual speech, that prose should resonate with curious polysyllables and flocks of suspended constructions; the other assumption was the more removes from the spoken language there were, the better the prose was likely to be.
>
> (1984, p. 158)

Whatever the virtues of such a style, it was clearly unlikely to be immediately comprehensible to the common people, and was therefore unsuitable for works of instruction (whether religious or otherwise).

Although the effects of the Inkhorn controversy on the development of written English are unclear (Adamson, 1989, p. 208), what is clear is that the debate about vocabulary significantly enlarged the lexicon. However, it also had unexpected side effects, as Adamson convincingly shows. The introduction of an elevated variety designed to express elevated thoughts was instrumental in creating a diglossic situation which has left its traces in modern written texts.

Perhaps the most obvious example of a diglossic text from this period is the King James Bible (1611). Because it contains so many diverse books it can also accommodate a range of written styles. There are traces of the 'aureate', or H[igh] style in such books as the *Revelations*, and the relatively simple, or L[ow] style as in the Sermon on the Mount. In the *Psalms*, it even combines H and L. Hebraic poetic patterns of parallelism are often rendered so that one half of the verse is in H and the other in L, as can be seen in the following example from Psalm 24:

The earth is the Lord's, and all that therein is: the compass of
the world, and they that dwell therein.
For he hath founded it upon the seas: and prepared it upon the
floods.
Who shall ascend into the hill of the Lord: or who shall rise up
in his holy place?
Even he that hath clean hands, and a pure heart: and hath not
lift up his mind unto vanity, nor sworn to deceive his
neighbour.
He shall receive the blessing from the Lord: and righteousness
from the God of his salvation.

A cursory count reveals that 16 per cent of the lexical items in the first half
of each verse are of Latin origin whereas 40 per cent of the items are in the
second half. Perhaps more revealing are such couplings as: *is/dwell;
founded/prepared; ascend/rise up; clean hands/hath not lift up his mind
unto vanity; pure heart/ nor sworn to deceive his neighbour; blessing/
righteousness.* Of course, at the didactic level each pair is saying something slightly different, but it is interesting that these differences are realised
by subtle shifts of style.

Hill (1993) has recently argued for the transcendent importance of the
Bible in seventeenth-century English thought. I would go further and say
that its effects on the development of written English are incalculable. Not
only was it possessed by a significant proportion of households in the
country and read regularly, it was also an official publication of the state
'appointed to be read in churches'. Because attendance at church was
compulsory at this time, it could be claimed that a greater proportion of
the population of England was exposed to this model of English writing on
a regular basis than has occurred with any other text, written or spoken.
Although many millions may watch US films or TV soaps, they are not
constrained by law to do so. Nevertheless, as a model it was slightly
ambiguous in that the H and L styles were either offered as alternatives
or subtly intermixed. The pragmatic advantages of such alternation were
obvious: the gospel would be understood by all its hearers while its dignity
would be retained. But the ways in which the various styles might be
manipulated by writers of other texts was less clear.

However, while we can accept Adamson's argument as to the development of a diglossic society (at least in written forms of the language), and
while it may be broadly acceptable to suggest that in the seventeenth
century the H style was typically associated with conservative social
tendencies while the L style was typically associated with Puritanism
and the revolutionaries, we should not overlook the existence of significant textual variety according to function even among writers who, from
this historical distance, may look similar. A comparison between the prose

writings of Donne, Bacon and Burton in the early part of the century, or Browne, Bunyan and Milton in the second half of the century reveals immense variety in syntactic organisation, lexical choice and rhetorical structure depending on subject matter and intended audience. Further, we can observe changes developing within specific genres throughout the century which reflect shifts of belief. Bach's study of Puritan wills (1992) demonstrates that one genre which might be assumed to be stable because it was subject to certain legal requirements in fact altered quite significantly to incorporate the ideological concerns of Puritan evangelic-alism. Thus we have to recognise two slightly different kinds of variation: that between text types as Latin increasingly gave way to English for various functions, and that within text types as different social discourses developed and changed historically.

Contemporary commentators tended to discuss functional elaboration in terms of lexical and rhetorical choice, largely because codification was still in its infancy. There was a significant increase in the production of word-lists, and the first recognisably modern English dictionary appeared in 1604, but the study of syntax was relatively underdeveloped, being based on models more applicable to the analysis of Latin. Bullokar's *Pamphlet for Grammar* (1586) was an early attempt to describe the grammar of English, and his introductory comments on the title page are interesting in that they hint at two slightly different programmes:

> This being sufficient for the speedy learning how to parse English speech for the perfecter writing thereof and using of the best phrases therein and the easier entrance into the secrets of grammar for other languages and the speedier understanding of other languages ruled or not ruled by grammar.

On the one hand, we can see the beginning of a prescriptivist (and pedagogical) tradition that was to be considerably developed in the coming centuries; on the other, there is the suggestion that the study of grammar is valuable precisely because it can serve as an aid to translation not only of the classical languages, but also of the other languages that were being increasingly encountered as English (and European) ships explored more of the world. Fifty years later, Ben Jonson's *Grammar* ([1640] in Herford and Simpson, 1947) was to echo Bullokar, but with an increased sense of self-confidence. Now the study of English grammar is seen metaphorically in commercial terms: 'THE profit of *Grammar* is great to Strangers, who are to live in communion, and commerce with us; and, it is honourable to ourselves' (1947, p. 465). However, the prescriptive concerns are also augmented:

> We free our Language from the opinion of Rudeness, and Barbarisme, wherewith it is mistaken to be diseas'd; we show the Copie of it, and

Matchableness, with other tongues; we ripen the wits of our own Children, and Youth sooner by it, and advance their knowledge.

(ibid.)

Nevertheless, it was not until the eighteenth century that the drive towards codification and (ultimately) prescription really gained momentum.

CODIFICATION AND PRESCRIPTION

The urge to codify English was the result of a complex of social forces. Linda Colley has commented:

Great Britain in 1707 was much less a trinity of three self-contained and self-conscious nations than a patchwork in which uncertain areas of Welshness, Scottishness and Englishness were cut across by strong regional attachments, and scored over again by loyalties to village, town, family and landscape. In other words, like virtually every other part of Europe in this period, Great Britain was infinitely diverse in terms of the customs and cultures of its inhabitants.

(1992, p. 17)

The integrity of the new nation, following the Act of Union, remained precarious and appeared to be seriously threatened by the Jacobite rebellions of 1715 and 1745. Indeed, a virulent form of anti-Scottishness feeling persisted at least until the late eighteenth century, leading Wilkes 'to remind his readers of the linguistic divisions between the two countries (ibid., p. 116). The attempts to define the English tongue were therefore an integral part of the discourse of nationalism. This discourse lay behind Swift's recommendation that a commission should be established for 'correcting, improving and ascertaining the English language' (Crowley, 1991, pp. 30–41). Swift contrasts English with Italian, Spanish and French, asserting that these other languages are more 'refined' because Latin was '[n]ever so vulgar in *Britain* as it is known to have been in *Gaul* and *Spain*' (ibid., p. 31). The contrasting epithets 'refined' and 'vulgar' are revealing. Although they have shifted their meanings since the eighteenth century, the connotative references to social manners which have become more prominent in the twentieth century were clearly present.

Swift's model of the language was to be derived from the practices of the 'learned and polite' (ibid.). It is not entirely clear who was to be counted among the 'learned', but his earlier intervention in the controversy between the Ancients and the Moderns which led to *The Battle of the Books* (1697) suggests that he would not have included the theorists of the new sciences. If we consider Thomas Sprat's (1667) description of the new 'scientific style':

a close, naked, natural way of speaking; positive expressions; clear senses; a native easiness; bringing all things as near the Mathematical

plainness, as they can: and preferring the language of Artizans, Country-
men, and Merchants, before that of Wits, or Scholars.

(Barber, 1993, p. 215)

We can see that Swift's proposal was not simply rooted in a discourse of
nationalism, but was also representative of a particular social class. And
this impression is confirmed if we consider the kinds of writings that he
parodies (for more on parody, see Chapter 7), and the kinds of people he
satirizes in such pamphlets as *A Modest Proposal* (1729), or his great
classic *Gulliver's Travels* (1726).

Swift, as a Tory writer, was certainly taking up cudgels against certain
Whiggish tendencies which had emerged as part of the revolution settle-
ment, and which were to have their apotheosis under Robert Walpole.
However, it is misleading to see these exclusively in political terms since
England was undergoing a major social revolution during the eighteenth
century which manifested itself in a variety of ways. Holmes (1993, p. 66)
documents the importance of the 'commercial revolution' which took place
in the late seventeenth and early eighteenth centuries, and he particularly
notes that 'the Commercial Revolution brought an access of wealth to the
merchant class the importance of which can hardly be over-estimated'
(ibid., p. 67). The development of trade and commerce encouraged the
growth of a new vocabulary with an '"unintelligible jargon"' (ibid., p.
273). Although largely restricted to London and the stock market, no doubt
aspects of 'trade-speak' percolated through the country, particularly among
the increasing numbers who were enjoying the fruits of the new prosperity.
While the population of England and Wales is estimated to have
increased by only 18.6 per cent between 1681 and 1761, those engaged
in trading over a similar period increased by 228 per cent (ibid., pp. 403,
411; Holmes and Szechi, 1993, p. 345). Correspondingly, there was a
significant growth in the urban population which suggests that there
might have been a slow homogenisation of urban dialects and an
increase in written communication connected with trade.

What is clear is that a number of writers set out to appeal to this new
audience, either by amusing them (as in the case of Samuel Richardson and
the new novelists), or by instructing them (Porter, 1982, pp. 252–3).
Publication of such journals as *The Tatler* (1709–11) and *The Spectator*
(from 1711) were clearly designed to indicate correct forms of behaviour to
the new merchant class so as to draw them into the orbit of 'polite' society.
Corresponding to these writers who wished to inculcate social manners
were a number of authors who wished to advise them on linguistic
behaviour. For example, Sheridan was particularly keen to introduce
elocution classes into schools to remove '"Odious distinctions" among
social classes' (Bailey, 1991, p. 185). One way of achieving this general
improvement was to construct a grammar conceived according to the best

authors and demonstrate how users of the language might emulate, or fall short, of this standard.

As a project this was bedevilled by two problems. The first was that the study of grammar had tended to be the study of Latin grammar with the consequence that English grammar was viewed through Latin spectacles. Michael (1987, p. 319) comments that:

> The grammars of modern European languages, and of Latin, ancient Greek and Hebrew, were variations of a general grammar common to most languages, and even of a universal grammar common to all. Such a view obscured the distinctiveness of first-language teaching, inhibited attempts to develop a grammar and a mode of teaching appropriate to English-speaking pupils, and tended to keep English subordinate to the elaborate and prestigious grammars of the classical languages.

Whatever effect it may have had on the teaching of English, it could only have had negative effects on the learning of both English and 'English-ness' since pupils were bound to feel that they were excluded in important ways from those who were assumed to speak and write in this latinate way. The second problem was more complex. Not only were the selected 'best' authors usually literary, these authors' grammatical solecisms were also displayed. Thus, the kinds of writing that pupils would typically expect to engage in when they left school were considerably underrepresented (Sundby *et al.*, 1991, pp. 35–7), but also they were shown that composition in English was so difficult that even the best authors could get it wrong. To put it briefly: the process of codification was conducted according to a false model while the prescriptions were for an inappropriate style of writing.

Of course, these faults were not manifested equally in all the grammars that were produced in this period. Priestly's *Rudiments* (1761) was far less infused with Latin models than most other grammars, and he was also prepared to admit variation of text type (Leonard, 1929, p. 241). Even Lowth, whose *Short Introduction* (1762) was heavily plagiarised by Murray and became the template for nineteenth-century pedagogical grammars, recognised that Latin grammar was an inappropriate model for English. However, he clearly saw his task as reforming and refining the manners of the nation since his purpose was 'to teach us to express ourselves with propriety' (ibid., p. 11).

There were, though, other traditions at work in the eighteenth century and these became prominent in the years following the loss of the American colonies and the beginning of the French revolution. Colley (1992, p. 192) has pointed out that this period saw a crisis of confidence in the 'power elite', in that their legitimacy was under increasing challenge. Among the most vocal of these were Horne Tooke and William Cobbett. Tooke's *Diversions of Purley* (1798/1805) is primarily interesting from a philosophical point of view. His initial concern was the way in which language could be used to legitimate power. The dominant eighteenth-century philosophy derived from Locke in whose writings language was seen as the outward manifestation of ideas. Vulgar language is thus indicative of vulgar thought. While it is necessarily possible to argue about ideas, successful argument depends on the use of correct language:

> The proper signification and use of Terms is best to be learned from those who, in their writings and Discourses, appear to have the clearest Notions, and apply'd to them their Terms with the exactest choice and fitness. This way of using a Man's Words, according to the Propriety of the Language, though it have not always the good Fortune to be understood: Yet most commonly leaves the blame of it on him, who is so unskilful in the Language he speaks, as not to understand it, when made use of, as it ought to be.
>
> (Crowley, 1991, p. 23)

This is a view which is likely to appeal to both the 'power elite' and the prescriptivist grammarians since they can annex the argument and assert that their use of language most successfully corresponds to the 'clearest Notions'. Further, they can recommend their uses as models for other speakers, while rejecting other uses as obscurantist or simply representing confused ideas. Tooke, while acknowledging the force of Locke's position reverses the direction of the relationship between words and ideas. Through a complex series of etymological arguments he claims that instead of ideas leading to words, it is words that create ideas. Aarsleff (1983, p. 54) claims that Tooke's philosophy 'contains the germs of a very romantic and nearly mystical notion of language . . . If thought resides in language, then one may also think that language has a soul and a genius.' But one might equally suggest that Tooke's view is deeply realist and rooted in a perception that how we say is how we mean. In its social dimension it recognises that where a particular social group uses characteristic ways of speaking, it is because that group is expressing different meanings rather than saying the same things in different ways. Tooke, therefore, gives clear philosophical support to the values of language variety (Smith, 1984, Chapter IV) in ways that run counter to the majority of eighteenth-century grammarians.

Cobbett is philosophically less radical, although equally determined to resist the prescriptive grammars produced post-Lowth. Writing to his son in 1819, he says:

> Grammar perfectly understood, enables us, not only to express our meaning fully and clearly, but so to express it as to enable us to defy the ingenuity of man to give to our words any other meaning than that which we ourselves intend them to express.
>
> (1819, pp. 7–8)

However, he follows the practices of other grammarians of the period by selecting passages, frequently from those authors who have written treatises on rhetoric, to demonstrate how bad grammar can distort meaning. Unlike them, though, his purpose is empowering, and his sly digs at the more famous writers is an ironic comment on the ways in which writers are able to manipulate language to serve their own purposes. His intention was surely defensive in that he was proposing a way of writing that could not be twisted to mean other than he intended. Cobbett was, therefore, writing within the same radical tradition as Horne Tooke, and he was no doubt reacting in part to the fact that Parliament had consistently rejected petitions for the extension of male suffrage between 1793 and 1818 because of their language (Smith, 1984, p. 30). Although Parliament may choose to reject such petitions, and although it may do so on the spurious grounds that they were formulated in inappropriate ways, it was important to Cobbett that the meanings of such petitions should be absolutely clear and incapable of misinterpretation.

However, the voices of radicalism did not prevail. Although the kinds of debate as to the importance of establishing a single variety of English which could usefully be taught as representative of the language as a whole continued into the nineteenth century, it is convenient to end our review here since many of the discussions tended to focus on similar issues. A model of the language was produced in the eighteenth century which by and large continues to dominate popular views of the language today. Where these are challenged, then the existing social order is also challenged since contesting views of language represent contesting views of the social order. The standardisation cycle, as we have seen, has largely been driven by the twin forces of nationalism and who best represents the nation. Given that Britain appears to be undergoing another crisis of identity, it is not surprising that the question of Standard English should have reappeared, nor is it surprising that notions of 'correctness' in language should be intimately linked with 'correctness' in social behaviour.

As an illustration of this link we can consider the intervention of Norman Tebbitt, at that time a government minister, who observed on the radio in 1985 that

> we've allowed so many standards to slip . . . teachers weren't bothering to teach kids to spell and to punctuate properly . . . if you allow standards to slip to the stage where good English is no better than bad English, where people turn up filthy . . . at school . . . all those things cause people to have no standards at all, and once you lose standards then there's no imperative to stay out of crime.
>
> (Carter, 1993)

It is not at all clear whom Tebbitt is blaming in this outburst, although it is apparent that for him good English (which is rather meagrely defined as correct spelling and punctuation) is equated with virtuous social behaviour, while bad English is, rather surprisingly, seen in the same terms as bad hygiene and criminal behaviour. Clearly, in some deep recesses of Tebbitt's mind, good English, however ultimately defined, leads to social cohesion, and in failing to teach it, teachers are destroying the fabric of the nation. Similarly, John Rae, an educationist, who opined in the *Observer* that 'As nice points of grammar were mockingly dismissed as pedantic and irrelevant, so was punctiliousness in such matters as honesty, responsibility, property, gratitude, apology and so on' (Carter, 1993). Nice points of grammar (and there is an interesting ambiguity in the choice of 'nice') lead, it appears, to social qualities of deference. They have the same social effects as respect for property, gratitude (but for what?) and apologetic behaviour.

SOME EDUCATIONAL CONSEQUENCES

The preceding discussion, then, has tried to demonstrate that although some people wish to assert the existence of a 'superior' form of English that can be regarded as a standard, they can only do so by ignoring, or repudiating, the existence and functions of all other varieties. Those periods when debates about the language become particularly virulent involve defenders of the 'standards' in reifying English so as to make it a symbol either of the nation as a whole or one dominant group within the nation. Particular usages are treated either as synecdochic of the language that is to be emulated, or as exemplary behaviour to be avoided. Frequently, the forms that are treated with contempt are selected from the spoken language and are compared unfavourably with written forms. In this case, the written language is seen as the repository of what is fixed and therefore normative. Nevertheless, the samples of written language which are held in high esteem tend to be those which belong to the genre of literature.

Nevertheless, the preceding discussion has demonstrated, however briefly, that written forms also manifest tremendous diversity. The search for a Standard English which is capable of performing all the written functions required in our society is therefore doomed to failure, although the process of standardisation is likely to continue unabated. As James Milroy tellingly argues:

> Standardisation is not primarily about *varieties* of language, but about processes. Therefore it must be treated as a process with an underlying socio-political motivation, which attempts to promote uniformity and suppress variability for reasons that are considered functional.
>
> (1992, p. 130)

However, this provides us with a clue as to why there should be such a stress on the teaching of Standard English in schools. One function of education is to socialise children into the practices of the society beyond the walls of the school. It is convenient (at least for governments), to indicate that this society is homogeneous and that the homogeneity is realised through particular shared linguistic practices. The children will be perfectly well aware that such is not the case, but a little social engineering on the part of the teachers may help it to become the case.

Nevertheless, it is undoubtedly true that there *are* some shared social practices within the community of English speakers, even if these may be fewer than governments would wish to admit, and that these are realised through shared linguistic practices. It is perfectly appropriate, therefore, to teach these practices (and their linguistic realisations) in school so that each child can become a fully functioning member of this larger society. However, if we consider the communicative acts of reading and writing, we are faced with a considerable imbalance. While the quantity of written text likely to be processed by people in their lifetime in a literate society is probably vast, the quantity of writing they will be required to do will be considerably less. Few people are likely to write an essay once they have left their educational establishment; although most people are likely to have to fill up some kind of questionnaire whether it be related to tax, medicine or transport. Few people will have to write formal reports, although rather more may be invited to read them. Many are likely to have to write letters of application for jobs, and some may choose to write personal letters. All people will be exposed to various kinds of advertising, instructional material, and a majority may choose to read some form of newsprint and recreational writing, although few will be engaged in actually writing them.

Writing in the public sphere is, therefore, likely to be a minority occupation for the majority of school leavers in terms of their total linguistic activity and it is most likely to be directed towards official purposes. Writing skills should be taught which will further these purposes, but it is misleading to suggest that the acquisition of such skills is equivalent to learning Standard English. Rather we are dealing with a 'core' English which is appropriate for certain highly limited transactions. Typically, these are service encounters in which there is an asymmetry between the writer and the audience and in which certain standards of politeness are expected. This 'core' English is well documented in pedagogical grammars, and is often used as the basis for teaching non-native speakers of English (Bex, 1993c, 1994b).

I recognise that this is a meagre grammar, but a 'core' grammar is sufficient for most people's production of written texts. However, quite clearly we would want to go beyond this 'core' within our educational system since it is self-evident that the majority of texts we are exposed to are constructed according to quite different principles. If we want our children to write more extensively for other purposes (whether privately to expand their imaginative expression, or publicly), and to understand fully the texts they are likely to read, then we need to help them understand how texts are constructed so as to represent particular social institutions and forces. In other words, we need to recognise the variety of written texts and try to account for such variety. Whereas Cobbett argued in favour of teaching grammar so as to encourage his son to speak 'fully and clearly . . . [so that nobody can] give to our words any other meaning than that which we ourselves intend them to express', I am arguing that we also need a clear science of written text so that we can prevent our children from being misled by the words of others. The following chapters, therefore, will investigate how it may be possible to develop such a science. As will become apparent, they take as axiomatic the view that texts are individually various in that they represent one person's intervention within a particular range of social discourses, but that such variety is subject to coherent explanation and classification according to the genres which express these social discourses.

FURTHER READING

One of the prices paid for the expansion of information has been increased specialisation. Any good history of the language should pay attention to *all* the varieties of language that have existed, the social circumstances in which such varieties were used and a detailed description of the variants. Inevitably, this is beyond the scope of any individual, and most histories relate the story of the dominant variety with only cursory mention of other varieties. Crowley (1989, Chapter 1) has a fascinating chapter on the historiography of English, and he has also produced an interesting paper (1990) on the development of linguistics as a science which shows why linguists sometimes tend to objectify language and treat it independently of its users.

Leith's *A Social History of English* (1983) is a good attempt to describe the development of the language within its social context although it is too brief to cover the area in much detail. Bailey's (1991) *Images of English* is a most enjoyable book that touches on many of the concerns of this chapter and can be highly recommended.

A useful introductory history is Barber's (1993) *The English Language: A Historical Introduction.* More technical is Strang's *A History of English* (various editions) which unusually is written in reverse. The advantage of this is that it starts from what the reader already knows about contemporary English and shows how we have arrived where we are. Cambridge University Press is currently engaged in producing a multi-volume history, although the volumes that have appeared so far are variable in their coverage.

It is, of course, useful to supplement such reading with examples of texts from the different periods. Burnley's (1992) *The History of the English Language: A Sourcebook* links a number of texts with an illuminating commentary as does Wakelin's *Archeology of English* (1988). It is also essential to read what historians have to say. Although they rarely mention language (with the notable exception of Clanchy (1993) and Smith (1984)), they can offer a fuller context for the understanding of why language use might have been changing in a particular historical period.

SOME QUESTIONS FOR CONSIDERATION

1 The following two texts were both published in the early seventeenth century. The first is an extract from Francis Bacon's *Advancement of Learning*, a philosophical work that was published in 1605, the second from Robert Burton's *Anatomy of Melancholy* (1621) which is half meditation and half medical textbook.

a The knowledge of man is as the waters, some descending from above, and some springing from beneath; the one informed by the light of nature, the other inspired by divine revelation. The light of nature consisteth in the notions of the mind and the reports of the senses: for as for knowledge which man receiveth by teaching, it is cumulative and not original; as in a water that besides his own spring-head is fed with other springs and streams. So then, according to these two differing illuminations or originals, knowledge is first of all divided into *divinity* and *philosophy*.

(Bacon, 1605, p. 85)

b *Melancholy*, the subject of our present discourse, is either in disposition or habit. In disposition, is that transitory *Melancholy* which comes and goes upon every small occasion of sorrow, need, sickness, trouble, fear, grief, passion, or perturbation of the mind, any manner of care, discontent, or thought, which causeth anguish, dulness, heaviness, and vexation of spirit, any ways opposite to pleasure, mirth, joy, delight, causing frowardness in us, or a dislike. In which equivocal and improper sense, we call him melancholy, that is dull, sad, sour, lumpish, ill-disposed, solitary, any way moved, or displeased.

(Burton, 1621, p. 164)

How do these texts differ in respect of their vocabulary? (e.g. is one more Latinate than the other? How do they differ in their syntactic constructions? Are the clauses related to each other in similar logical ways? How do the texts differ in respect of the ways in which they construct their arguments? To what extent are these differences the result of the different functions of the two texts?

2 The following three texts were all produced in the mid-seventeenth century and are all religious meditations. The earliest is by Milton and was probably written about 1650. The second, by Thomas Browne was

written in about 1656, while the third, by Bunyan, was published in 1666. In what ways do the texts differ in their construction? Given that they all have similar themes and are addressed to similar readerships, what reason might there be for such differences? Can you find evidence to suggest that the writers have different views of Christianity?

a Under the gospel we possess, as it were, a two-fold Scripture; one external, which is the written word, and the other internal, which is the Holy Spirit, written in the hearts of believers, according to the promise of God, and with the intent that it should by no means be neglected; as was shown above, chap.xxvii. on the gospel. Hence, although the external ground which we possess for our belief at the present day in the written word is highly important, and, in most instances, at least, prior in point of reception, that which is internal, and the peculiar possession of each believer, is far superior to all, namely, the Spirit itself.

The Christian Doctrine
(cd. Patterson, 1933, p. 1041)

b *Pyramids, Arches, Obelisks,* were but the irregularities of vain-glory, and wilde enormities of ancient magnanimity. But the most magnanimous resolution rests in the Christian Religion, which trampleth upon pride, and sits on the neck of ambition, humbly pursuing that infallible perpetuity, unto which all others must diminish their diameters, and be poorly seen in Angles of contingency.

Pious spirits who passed their dayes in raptures of futurity, made little more of this world than the world that was before it, while they lay obscure in the Chaos of pre-ordination, and night of their fore-beings. And if any have been so happy as truly to understand Christian annihilation, extasie, exolution, liquefaction, transformation, the kisse of the Spouse, gustation of God, and ingression into the divine shadow, they have already had an handsome anticipation of heaven; the glory of the world is surely over, and the earth in ashes unto them.

Hydrotaphia
(ed. Keynes, 1968, p. 154)

c In which condition I have continued with much content thorow Grace, but have met with many turnings and goings upon my heart both from the Lord, Satan, and my own corruptions; by all which, (glory be to Jesus Christ) I have also received, among many things, much conviction, instruction, and understanding, of which at large I shall not here discourse; onely give you, in a hint or two, a word that may stir up the Godly to bless God, and to pray for me; and also to take encouragement, should the case be their own, *Not to fear what men can do unto them.*

Grace Abounding to the Chief of Sinners
(ed. Sharrock, 1966, p. 98)

3 The following texts are all taken from the eighteenth century. They
appear in order of publication. By paying attention to the differences
you can observe, where would you typically expect to find them? What
textual evidence can you produce to support your assumptions?[2]

a Any able young Man, strong in the Back, and endow'd with a good
Carnal Weapon, with all the Appurtenances thereunto belonging in good
Repair, may have Half A Crown per Night, a Pair of clean Sheets, and
other Necessaries, to perform Nocturnal Services on one Sarah Y-tes,
whose Husband having for these 9 Months past lost the Use of his
Peace-Maker, the unhappy Woman is thereby driven to the last
Extremity.

b Last Saturday a ragged beggar came to a Public House in Puckle-
Church in Gloucestershire, to ask Charity of some countreymen who
were drinking there, who told him in a joking manner, they used to hang
all Beggars and would hang him; he told them he was not fit to die; but
they taking hold of him, he begged they would do him no harm; however
they got a Rope, put it about his Neck, and drew him up to a Bacon
Rack, and bid him cry Bacon; to which they hung him so long, that he
seem'd without Life, his tongue extending from his Mouth, so let him
fall again, and perceiving they had carried their Folly too far, and being
frightened with the Apprehension of what might ensue, carried the
Beggar to a neighbouring field, and laid him under a Hay-Rick for dead.

c My notion is, that your Nephew, being an only Son, & rather of a
delicate constitution, ought not to be exposed to the hardships of the
College. I know, that the expence in that way is much lessen'd; but your
Brother has but one Son, & can afford to breed him an Oppidant. I know
that a Colleger is sooner form'd to scuffle in the world, that is, by
drubbing & tyranny is made more hardy or more cunning, but these in
my eyes are no such desirable acquisitions . . .

d This his to asquaint you that We poor of Rosendale Rochdale Oldham
Saddleworth Ashton have all mutaly and firmly agreed by Word and
Covinent and Oath to Fight and Stand by Each Other as long as Life doth
last for We may as well be all hanged as starved to Death and to see
ower Children weep for Bread and none to give Them nor no liklyness
of ever minding wile You all take Part with Brommal and Markits drops
at all the principle Markits elceware . . .

Chapter 3

Texts in societies: societies in texts

INTRODUCTION

In the previous two chapters I have tried to show both how popular conceptions of English assume that there is a 'best' English which should be promulgated (or prescribed) in schools, and how many writers professionally concerned with the language have, wittingly or unwittingly, given comfort to these popular notions. In particular, I have discussed some parts of the 'standardisation cycle' with a view to showing how different concerns have been paramount in different historical periods during the development of the language. These concerns have usually been driven by forces from outside the language. For example, Caxton's 'editorial' work was undertaken primarily to make money. In the process, he was instrumental in selecting a particular regional and functional variety of the language as the model for future written English. In the seventeenth century, writers wished to expand what could legitimately be written in English, thereby contributing to functional elaboration, but also adding to the vocabulary and the development of different ways of writing. In the eighteenth century, the need to forge a United Kingdom which included the new merchant classes encouraged a form of prescriptivism which in turn depended on a way of describing the language. Inevitably, the variety selected for description tended to be that used by the 'best' writers from within the most 'polite' stratum of society.

While these might be thought of as centralising tendencies, we have also observed significant divergent processes at work which encourage textual variety. Functional elaboration carries with it the risk of specific and idiosyncratic usages developing which subsequently become the 'jargons' of particular social groups. These 'jargon' users emerge because they wish to proclaim their membership of a particular group, while asserting their distinctiveness from other groups who do not use such jargon. However, such uses also carry social risks since the more idiosyncratic they become the less likely their users will be understood by non-members of the group. Unless such groups intend to form secret societies, their particular uses of language will always be in tension with the users of 'ordinary' language (i.e. the language used by non-members of the group), so membership of the group has to be weighed against the advantages offered by society at large.

Similar tensions manifest themselves when a particular social group attempts to prescribe its uses as equivalent to the 'national' language. As we have seen in the eighteenth century, where those who are doing the prescribing are sufficiently powerful then their views will apparently prevail. However, they will be met by pockets of resistance which may, on the one hand, attempt to re-define the ways in which language and society are related, or, on the other, assert alternative views of nationhood which are associated with different memberships (cf. Wordsworth's attempts to resurrect 'the language really spoken by men', [de Selincourt, 1936, p. 736]). In this chapter I intend to explore more fully the nature of these tensions and their effects on written texts. Inevitably, this involves considering the notion of *context*.

A PRELIMINARY VIEW OF CONTEXT

Enkvist has explored the concept in various interesting ways, but has tended to view it as something brought by the reader to the written text. He has argued (1990, p. 170; cf. also 1994, p. 49) that 'the successful discourse-producer must enable his communication partner to build a scenario around the discourse'. He has further expanded on this by suggesting that text producers construct a 'text world' which is in some important respects reinterpreted by readers according to the latter's knowledge of communicative behaviour in general and the extent to which they can reconstruct a 'world' in which such a text may be true (1991, p. 10).

But written texts are not simply mental entities. They have a materiality and physical presence both of which contribute to their potential meaning and which I shall be referring to in due course (cf. also Bernhardt, 1985). However, at this point, while acknowledging the potential importance of cognitive and physical contexts, I wish to concentrate more precisely on social contexts. Language is produced by people, and the relationships that cohere between the users of language and the circumstances in which such use occurs influence interpretation in significant ways. All linguistic signs carry with them traces of the ways in which they have been used before. The production and interpretation of texts are, therefore, integral ways in which we reproduce (and change) our social relationships and our knowledge of the world in general. For individuals, the production of a text is an insertion into a nexus of practices which precedes it, but an insertion that is mediated by the particular constraints and potentials that exist within the language as it has been used before (Kress, 1993).

Thus texts are never self-contained, but are always part of an ongoing linguistic interaction. Although this is obvious when we consider conversational texts, it is less clearly observable with written texts. Because they appear inert, written texts' dynamisms are often overlooked. Although a personal letter, or the signing of a cheque are clear examples of texts that are preceded by, and may initiate subsequent, (linguistic) transactions, textbooks, novels or dictionaries are often viewed as 'free-standing'. But written work is never produced in a vacuum. Even the most private diary assumes a reader (the self) and is constructed according to conventions which have been derived from previous written texts (whether these are diaries or some other model). Even the most revolutionary work is only revolutionary when viewed against existing texts and can, therefore, be said to enter into dialogue with such anterior texts. Thus, although written text may be considered to be a 'product' (Fairclough, 1989, p. 24), it is the product of a process.

If we characterise this process as a form of dialogue, then it is a dialogue involving a number of participants. On the one hand, it is a dialogue with all previous written texts; on the other, it is a specific dialogue with its intended audience. In the construction of a text world, writers, to a greater or lesser extent and deliberately or otherwise, refer to such anterior texts as will situate their texts in an ongoing dialogue and in the process reorder the text-world that has been constructed through these anterior texts. Readers, on the other hand, also need to appreciate where the new text stands in relation to previous texts in order to interpret texts successfully. Halliday (1978, p. 109) has captured this insight where he states that '[t]he situation is the environment in which the text comes to life'. One essential element of this environment is the dialogue of which the new text is a part. Thus, in the activation of text we are no longer treating the linguistic signs solely as manifestations of an underlying linguistic system – *langue,* to use Saussure's terminology – but as utterances which gain their meaning within, and through, particular contexts.

Bakhtin (1986, p. 83) has argued that any communication 'has a particular purpose, that is, it is a real link in the chain of speech communion in a particular sphere of human activity or everyday life', and part of the 'meaning' of any utterance is the purposes that it signals, and which are recovered by the audience. However, written texts are unlike spoken texts in that these purposes are always signalled exclusively from within the text itself. Whereas it is possible for a guard, for example, to block a doorway physically while denying someone entrance, a sign which orders:

KEEP OUT

depends entirely on the linguistic signs that it manifests to convey its meaning. To interpret it successfully, readers need to be aware that it has the force of an injunction, that it refers to a specific space and that the text creator has the authority to enforce the injunction. These three kinds of knowledge are inextricably linked such that a change in any one particular will lead to a change of interpretation. For example, readers completely unfamiliar with English may fail to interpret the sign success- fully; i.e. its 'perlocutionary effects' may be other than intended (Austin, 1976, pp. 101–3; Levinson, 1983, p. 237), and find themselves engaging in antisocial behaviour by being in breach of the law.[1] Other readers may recognise the force of the injunction but, by virtue of their privileged position, know that it does not apply to them (e.g. MPs entering the Palace of Westminster); while yet others may decide that it has no authoritative force at all (e.g. parents or elder siblings who encounter the sign on young children's bedroom doors). Thus the meaning of KEEP OUT is not stable, but varies according to given situations.[2]

However, it is equally clear that linguistic signs are not completely indeterminate. Although they may convey different messages to different people in different circumstances, the possible range of these messages is constrained by a number of factors. For example, if we consider the following text (Figure 3.1):

FOR YOUR INFORMATION

TELEPHONE NUMBERS

Lost or stolen cards (telephone *immediately* – 24 hour, 7 day service)	0383 621166
CardCall (automatic account information – 24 hour, 7 day service)	0383 621122
General enquiries	0383 621155

Figure 3.1 Lost or stolen cards notice

we might notice a number of ambiguities. Indeed, on the linguistic evi- dence alone, it would be possible to produce the following absurd inter- pretation: 'Lost or stolen cards should telephone immediately and for twenty-four hours a day for seven days', and certain dramatists (e.g. N.F. Simpson) have constructed plays around this kind of ambiguity. Exactly how readers avoid such fantastic interpretations will be explored more fully later. However, at this juncture we can suggest that they are ruled out *both* by specific semantic knowledge (e.g. 'card' is polysemous and inanimate,[3] and inanimate objects do not engage in telephone calls), and the ways in which previous texts have been constructed to convey similar information. This latter is particularly important when faced with ellipted elements. So in the current example, readers have to decide whether the text is intended as an injunction or a piece of advice, and whether it is directed to all readers or only some subset. Further, they have to choose between interpreting 'Lost or stolen cards' as referring to all such cards, or (again) to a particular subset of cards. These ambiguities cannot be resolved with reference to the linguistic system alone but by the likely pragmatic effects of choosing one interpretation over another, and by their awareness of how other, similar, texts operate. Thus, readers who have already encountered the following text (Figure 3.2):

TELEPHONE NUMBERS

Lost or stolen cards (24 hour service)   (0702) 364364[4]

Figure 3.2 Lost or stolen cards notice

will have additional clues to work from, since they would almost certainly have encountered the different texts in similar circumstances. Nevertheless, at first sight it might still seem that the two texts are giving conflicting advice as to which telephone numbers should be rung. This confusion, though, is more apparent than real since the meanings of the texts are established in use, and readers are likely to be aware that 'cards' has a different referent in the two texts. Thus, although we have seen that given wordings have the potential for a wide variety of different interpretations, we have suggested that only highly particular interpretations achieve meaning. Further, we have indicated that this meaning depends on readers having experienced similar kinds of texts in similar circumstances. We therefore have the beginnings of an understanding as to why text types which are similar in form also perform similar social functions.

The similarity of wording in these two texts suggests that lexico-grammatical choices are associated with particular meanings at a quite fundamental level. The ellipses that we have noticed in the texts above (and they are more extreme in the second example than the first) are ellipses that can be filled in precisely because the options are constrained by the potential uses of the texts. But an ellipse can only be filled successfully if readers know what has been omitted. On their part, readers can only know what is absent if they are familiar with the elements that might *typically* be present. In other words, writers make particular lexico-grammatical choices because of the situations in which the texts will occur, and conversely particular lexico-grammatical choices are recognised by readers as (partially) defining features of the situations in which they might be supposed to occur. This seems to suggest that texts are both dynamic in that they create (through lexico-grammatical choices) the conditions for their interpretation, and static in that they refer to the conditions under which they are to be interpreted. Thibault expresses this duality clearly, when he states:

Realization embodies the formal copatterned lexico-grammatical selections in textual productions in the sense that these textual productions are both the *realization* of something as the finished product and the process that enacts or *realizes* this product.

(1991, p. 13)

If this enactment is an essential part of the meaning of texts, it remains to be seen how such meaning is achieved by readers. I have suggested, in relation to Figures 3.1 and 3.2, that there is nothing which gives a clear indication as to which cards can be reported missing. Even if we assume that readers are sufficiently familiar with the text type evidenced by these examples, the balance of probability may suggest that *all* lost credit cards can be reported on the given numbers. This indeterminacy can only be resolved in action. If I try to report my lost Access card to the Bank of Scotland and they show no interest, then I have established a more restricted meaning than my original interpretation suggested. Thus, although there is a congruent relationship between the lexico-grammatical realisations of texts and the social event that they enact, that social event is not fully contained within the text but has to be confirmed in action. And as I have suggested above, it is the confirmation in action which guarantees the text's meaning.

DISCOURSE

This indicates that 'meaning' lies partly beyond language, and indeed this is the case. Meanings are established and verified by reference to social *discourse*. The term discourse has been used variously in linguistics (Pennycook, 1994; Widdowson, 1995). Here, it refers beyond individual texts, or even groups of texts, to the kinds of social behaviours which recognise and confer meaning on such texts. I have commented that I can best verify the intended meanings of my example texts by phoning the appropriate institutions. I could also complain about the apparent ambiguity of the wording. However, it would be open to the institution to reject my complaint on the grounds that banks are not expected to concern themselves with the general welfare of their customers. In this case, they would be appealing to a higher level of discourse which asserts the limits of certain kinds of commercial transaction. Although this higher level of discourse is not directly encoded in the text, it is part of the society in which the text occurs and is therefore part of the meaning of the text. It is in this way that meaning can be said to lie partly beyond language.

We can see this much more obviously in spoken interactions. When a given interpretation is at odds with the speaker's intended meaning, the first recourse of the speaker may well be to a metalanguage which glosses what has been said. If that fails, then the challenge is often rejected by an appeal to some kind of authority which is assumed to guarantee the intended meaning. However, the same processes are also at work in the production of written texts. For example, the whole of this chapter, in its attempt to define and clarify what it is I am talking about, depends on my attempts to re-interpret previous writings (and discussions) on similar topics. It therefore presupposes a number of things, including the authoritative nature of the people I quote, the recognition that I am discussing a topic of appropriate importance and that the method of argumentation is being conducted in the same way as other arguments on the same, or similar topics. In short, it appeals to a social discourse which guarantees that what I am writing will not be treated as the outpourings of a maniac. Of course, it cannot guarantee that my particular interpretations and re-interpretations will be acceptable, but to the extent that I can persuade you to agree with my own claims, then my interpretations will have entered the realm of meaning. To the extent that I fail, then there will be an area of dispute. But this dispute will be carried out within the parameters of a particular social discourse which is recognised as meaningful. In fact, of course, I can never entirely succeed, but then neither can anybody else, since my own intended meanings will be subject to the same kinds of interpretations and re-interpretations as those which I am applying to others. For this reason, meanings are often the site of struggle.

Nevertheless, it will be apparent that there are occasions where meanings seem relatively stable. These can be explained by referring to the centralising tendencies I mentioned above. There are moments in history when a given discourse achieves broad consensus across a given society. On such occasions the meanings associated with this discourse tend to remain unchallenged. There are, also, other moments when a particular social group exerts so much power that it is considered too dangerous to challenge its meanings. At the macro-level, we might consider the use of the term 'victory' by British English speakers throughout most of the second world war as an example of the first type. Initially, it tended to mean 'victory over'. However, as the war drew to an end, the meaning underwent a subtle shift towards 'victory for' and became a site for dispute. Whereas there had been social consensus as to what Britons were fighting against, there was less agreement as to what they were fighting for and this was reflected in the broad support for Churchill as a leader 'against' but his rejection as a peacetime prime minister. As an example of the second type we can mention the meanings of the word 'democracy' within a totalitarian state. To the extent that its leaders can annex the term to refer to its own practices and silence those who challenge its annexation, then they can control the meaning of the term.

At the micro-level, we can consider the normative practices of teachers who instruct learners that a given term has a particular meaning within a particular academic discipline and that to conform to the practices of that discipline essay writers must use the term with that meaning only. Again, the instruction is open to challenge, but at great personal risk to the student.

Of course, these are only partial examples since discourses are never constructed around single items of vocabulary, as we shall see, but invade areas of syntax and rhetorical organisation as well. However, they do serve to demonstrate that social discourses, and the meanings associated with them, are inherently unstable. This is because they are always constructed between people who are differently situated in relation to the social groups in which such discourses operate. Disagreement may occur when individuals try to reject those meanings which are not confirmed by their own experiences and offer other meanings which are more comfortable for them. Of course, there is a risk here since people need to identify with particular social groups for both emotional and economic well-being and the demands of solidarity exert powerful pressures to accept and contribute to (rather than challenge) the meanings associated with that group. However, few individuals belong to one group alone – monks and nuns may be exceptions here – since their different needs are met by different sets of people. So typically, individuals establish networks of social relationships whereby membership of one does not preclude membership of another and where the meanings established with one may not be entirely congruent with the meanings employed in another (cf. L. Milroy, 1987, Chapter 6). This situation has been described by Bakhtin (1981, p. 263) as fundamental to all human societies and manifests itself as 'heteroglossia'. Social groups develop characteristic forms of discourse by which they challenge and confirm the meanings of that group, and membership of the group requires aspirants to learn and use such modes of discourse. However, such groups impinge on other groups and may be absorbed into larger social units. Discourse forms, then, are never entirely 'pure' being subject to leakage and change as new members join the social group, or other forms become dominant.

DISCURSIVE PRACTICES

These particular discourse forms achieve status to the extent that they conform to the *discursive practices* of the larger social unit. Such practices are those which regulate the conduct of society as a whole and they inform the constructions of particular discourses in subtle but important ways. In particular, the discursive practices of a given society determine what counts as 'sense' and, perhaps more importantly, 'common sense' within that society. The phrase 'discursive practice' is particularly associated with Foucault who, interestingly, offers a definition in peculiarly negative terms:

> It must not be confused with the expressive operation by which an individual formulates an idea, a desire, an image; nor with the rational

activity that may operate in a system of inference; nor with the 'competence' of a speaking subject when he constructs grammatical sentences; it is a body of anonymous, historical rules, always determined in the time and space that have defined a given period, and for a given social, economic, geographical area, the conditions of operation of the enunciative function.

(1972, p. 117)

If we adapt this definition so that the 'enunciative function' is considered to be equivalent to the text as utterance, then it would seem Foucault is suggesting that texts, which may be constructed according to text producers' competence in a given language, only achieve meaning within the parameters established by a given society. Thus, for example, certain writings may be treated as evidence of schizophrenia simply because they do not make 'sense', although they may consist of grammatically well-formed sentences (Mey, 1993, pp. 238–40). Although Foucault's reference to 'competence' evidently indicates his allegiance to the Chomskyan paradigm within linguistics, his comments are even more suggestive with other linguistic theories of how grammars are constructed and represented in the mind/brain. In fact, if we adopt a 'conventionalist' position (i.e. that grammars are constructed through interaction and agreement [cf. Halliday, 1988]), then his arguments are even more powerful since the discursive practices of a given society will also account for what counts as a grammatical sentence.

A further intrinsic claim in Foucault's definition is that discursive practices may be the possession of particular social groups *within* a larger society and that contradictory practices may co-occur within this larger society. To a large extent such contradictions can be absorbed until one practice clashes with another in an overt way. In this case the dominant practice tends to insist (usually successfully) on the superiority of its own meanings. An interesting example of this occurred recently in the United States. Astrology claims to predict the future lives of individuals and nations with reference to the properties and conjunctions of planets and stars, and astrologers regularly produce texts (i.e. horoscopes) that are treated as meaningful by (some of) their consumers. Astronomy also makes claims as to the properties of these same celestial objects. In some areas, then, astronomy and astrology are competing discursive practices. However, whereas astrology can only refer to itself for its authority, astronomy can appeal to the higher-level discursive practice of science. Thus, when it was discovered that Nancy Reagan was in the habit of consulting astrologers before her husband took any major political decisions, there was a furore. Of course, there are various ways of analysing this incident, but what we can observe is the confluence of three different discursive practices which are normally kept separate: politics, science and magic. Within political discourse events and decisions can either be explained (i.e. given meaning) as the result of the chance meeting of certain planets (i.e. astrology) or as the result of rational, scientific political processes (cf. the area of study known as 'political science'). In this instance, most Americans preferred to reject the authority of magic in favour of the authority of science. So we can assume that one of the dominant discourses within US society is that of science. However, 'science' is an imprecise term which includes a number of disparate areas of operation including astronomy. Therefore, we can consider 'science' to be a powerful nexus (or discursive practice) which informs a range of secondary discursive practices. Although these other practices construct and report their findings in quite distinctive ways, there would seem to be a general consensus that it is possible to distinguish between science and non-science. Discursive practices which are regarded as non-scientific but which make claims to producing accurate reports of phenomena which are investigated 'scientifically' are either dismissed as 'meaningless' or are assigned other kinds of meanings, e.g. mystical and/or religious.

Thus, discursive practices can co-exist and even be in competition with each other, which is why Foucault's mention of history is significant. The discursive practices of a given society always contain traces of the history of that society (which is presumably why astrology can co-exist with astronomy) and therefore contain traces of the struggles which have allowed one kind of discursive practice to dominate over another. But history is a continuing process and new discursive practices are developing which will challenge the existing order. One that has emerged within Britain recently might be characterised as the discursive practice of marketisation (cf. Fairclough, 1995, Chapter 6 for a fuller discussion). Currently, all political parties seem to agree that economic policy is the function of politics. Economic policy, in this case, has been formulated as 'getting value for money' in all areas of social life, and it is assumed that such value is best achieved through the marketing of all goods and services. One result has been that the discourse of the market place has invaded other discourses (e.g. medicine, social services, public transport, education). A typical linguistic manifestation of this invasion is the use of the term 'customer'. Whereas users of different services were once referred to in ways that signalled particular kinds of relationships (e.g. 'patients', 'claimants', 'passengers', 'students', etc.) such descriptions are increasingly being replaced by the blanket term 'customer' which had previously been reserved solely for buyers within a commercial transaction.[5] Of course, the different parties dispute with each other which particular policy is most likely to succeed, but it has become virtually 'meaningless' to demand value without payment or payment without return.[6]

Following Foucault to his logical conclusion, it would seem that we are imprisoned within sets of discursive practices which determine what we can say (cf. also Mey, 1993, p. 263). Indeed, Foucault seems to adopt this position in his essay 'What is an author?' (Rabinow, 1986, pp. 101–20). Here, he explores the 'author function' as a development of particular historical moments. In particular, he suggests that the attribution of author-ship is both an act of appropriation and a means of social control. It is an act of appropriation to the extent that it assigns property rights to a discourse that is communally constructed; and a means of social control in that it enables society to identify and punish particular individuals who engage in subversive discourses. Foucault's argument is logically coherent, but tends to ignore the role that individuals have in contributing to and altering particular discourses. Taken to its extreme, we end up with the claim that 'the author is dead' (Barthes, in Lodge, 1988). But this is clearly to follow logic beyond the bounds of human experience. Although individual texts draw on the discourses from which they are constructed, by their very existence they subtly alter that discourse. Of course, individuals' contributions may have very paltry effects on dominant discursive prac-tices, but they may be able to shift local practices in significant directions and thereby contribute to more global changes. The ways in which these more local discourses are constructed will be the topic of the next section.

DISCOURSE COMMUNITIES

The view that we do not speak language but rather 'language speaks us' has been interestingly explored by Lecercle (1990). He demonstrates that the boundaries of language are always being extended, but they are being extended in use. Utterances are produced which are unique not merely in the Chomskyan sense, but because they go beyond the parameters of grammatical selection. They can, therefore, be said to be creating new potential meanings. It is true that these meanings still need to be verified by society, but they do indicate the potential role of individuals in escaping from the historically determined discursive practices they have inherited.

One way of exploring this is to describe the notional linguistic biography of people as they expand their linguistic contacts. Children are born into language. Their initial experiences of language, however, are twofold. On the one hand it can be perceived as an expressive medium through which they can make their needs known (albeit imperfectly); on the other, it is a medium which (partly) defines and gives shape to them and the world around them both by regulation and description (Halliday, 1975). However, at this stage, babies' own language is literally 'meaningless'. Rather it is interpreted by carers and given meanings which are then relayed back to them (Vygotsky, 1986). Occasionally their own uses will be adopted by the family as an amusing instance of 'babytalk' and persist as part of the family discourse in that it serves to identify the family as a particular kind of social unit which is, in this respect, separable from other social groupings.

My brother, for example, had difficulty in articulating (according to the family norms) the preposition in the phrase 'cup of tea'. After much correction, he exasperatedly produced the phrase '*of* cuppa tea' which has now passed into family usage. This phrase, though, only has 'meaning' within the family, and even my repeating it here cannot convey the sense of family solidarity its utterance captures.

As they broaden their social contacts, initially by going to school, so they are presented with new social forms of language. For many children, school will be their first introduction to the written word. They will learn that written texts can be used for a variety of functions. They can be regulatory in the form of instructions, informative in certain kinds of text books, or creative in the form of free writing. They will further discover that different kinds of writing seem to represent different constructions of reality. A poem clearly does not construct the world in the same way as a physics textbook. In this way, children are at the centre of a nexus of different ways both of representation and of power relationships. To the extent that they choose to interact with such texts, they establish a network of overlapping memberships. Although they cannot hope to influence the discursive practices of the school to any great extent, through the production of their own (written) texts they may be able to influence (in a very small) way the school's (and fellow pupils's) evaluation of what is acceptable since such texts are often displayed in classrooms and therefore act as alternative models.

Such memberships expand as children leave school to become unemployed, employed or students, and the forms of linguistic interaction required to show memberships of such groups vary and have to be learned. Students, for example, may encounter a vast number of different kinds of written texts during the course of a single day. The reading of textbooks and the writing of essays are part of what it means to be a member of the academic community, but textbooks and essays have to be constructed in certain ways to be recognisable for what they are. In the act of reading, students are expected to defer to some kind of (supposed) authority; in writing essays, however, they are supposed to display knowledge (which is a kind of authority) although this knowledge will be assessed and commented on by people with more authority. Interestingly, this authority, and the power relations which derive from it, is not intrinsic to the people who wield it but depends (in part) on the manipulation of language within a recognised social group. The recognition, however, comes from outside the group itself but endorses the activities that occur within it.

At other times of the day, students may be required to fill in forms to register course choices. Here, the wordings are highly constrained and an inappropriate choice may have unhappy consequences. In this case, although the specific wordings may belong to the institution, the construction of forms and the practice of form-filling pervades other areas of social life and there are likely to be easily recognisable similarities between different kinds of forms. We can see, then, how the authoritative practices of a relatively homogeneous community are affected by, and imitate, the practices of the larger social group of which it is a part. Further, students may write cheques. Again, the activity of completing a cheque is highly constrained, but here there is an interesting trade-off between the authority of individuals to dispose of their money and the authority of banks to dictate the linguistic forms which they recognise as successful. Finally, students may write letters to their friends. Here it would be regarded as generally inappropriate to adopt an essay-style. And this is partly because the degree of intimacy between reader and writer is radically different, and partly because the construction and sharing of knowledge within the two activities is perceived as different.

But if membership of different social groups (and the power relations within such groups) is realised through language[7] we need some way of describing such groups which takes linguistic practices fully into account. Swales has attempted to do this by introducing the concept of *discourse communities* (1988; 1990). His choice of the term refers indirectly to earlier sociolinguistic attempts to define the 'speech community', but he wished to distinguish between *sociolinguistic* and *sociorhetorical* memberships (1990, pp. 24–7). In the former, he claimed, 'the communicative needs of the *group*, such as socialization or group solidarity, tend to predominate . . . The primary determinants of linguistic behaviour are social', while in the latter, 'the primary determinants of linguistic behaviour are functional'(ibid., p. 24). He further identifies six defining characteristics of a discourse community, which are that it:

1 has a broadly agreed set of common public goals;
2 has mechanisms of intercommunication among its members;
3 uses its participatory mechanisms primarily to provide information and feedback;
4 utilizes and hence possesses one or more genres in the communicative furtherance of its aims;
5 in addition to owning genres, has acquired some specific lexis;
6 has a threshold level of members with a suitable degree of relevant content and discoursal expertise.

Swales takes as a prototypical example of a 'discourse community', the Hong Kong Study Circle which gathers and disseminates to its members information about the stamps of Hong Kong. He demonstrates how membership of this group conforms to all the six criteria mentioned above, and concludes that 'distance between members geographically, ethnically and socially presumably means that they do not form a speech community' (ibid., p. 29).

One is inclined to agree that the Hong Kong Study Circle may have particular features which identify it as a group whose members engage in particular linguistic behaviours in the furtherance of their aims. However, it is difficult to decide exactly where to draw boundaries between this kind of tightly knit group whose interactive aims are limited and larger communities whose aims are more diffuse but which conform to the same criteria. A university clearly manifests all six features, and yet it is not clear whether Swales would consider it to be a 'discourse community' in the sense he means. Further, the set of universities that exist in Britain also share the criteria listed in that they communicate between each other either formally through the CVCP or informally through 'invisible colleges': that is, groups of people from different institutions who share the same interests and transfer information about these interests between each other. Such communities may also, to a greater or lesser extent, contain members who socialise with each other (i.e. interact with each other in a way that is not immediately concerned with the furtherance of the institution's aims), and I presume that when members of the Hong Kong Study Circle meet by chance, they discuss other matters than stamps.

If we continue with the university as an example, we could make the point that universities are one part of the educational system and therefore share common ground with other parts. Although the links between the members of this system are considerably weaker than those evinced by the kinds of smaller groupings that Swales has in mind, as a social institution, educational practices, and the discourses which realise such practices, will give rise to a set of shared linguistic behaviours which will be held in common by all people engaged in education. There will, however, be subtle differences in the ways in which the behaviours develop within particular memberships. The boundaries, then, between discourse communities are not at all clear nor, in spite of Swales's sixth criterion, is the optimum size. Certainly, on the face of it, it would seem entirely appropriate to refer to people engaged in similar forms of employment as members of the same 'discourse community', and yet Swales's characterisation seems to deny them such membership.

Swales (1990, p. 25) refers to this as the 'Café Owner Problem'. He comments on how it may be possible for individuals to be engaged in a similar set of practices, but who never interact with each other, concluding 'even if this sharing of discursive practice occurs, it does not resolve the logical problem of assigning membership of a community to individuals who neither admit nor recognize that such a community exists'. However, I believe the difficulties are more apparent than real. If we re-consider how individuals are situated in relation to society as a whole we will find that some memberships are imposed rather than freely chosen. Thus, membership of a community may not always be apparent until faced with an outside threat. Given that there are laws which regulate terms of employment within cafés, then there must be a community which is affected by such laws.

Having said this, it is still important to acknowledge that people have different degrees of membership. And it seems likely that the degree of identification with particular groups will depend partly on the frequency with which individuals interact with each other in the pursuit of common aims, and partly on the perceived strength of external threats. At a personal level, I feel weak allegiance to the body of people who are engaged in educational pursuits. But this sense of allegiance becomes stronger as it becomes more localised first to my own university and finally to the department within which I work. And my linguistic practices (within the educational system) reflect this in significant ways. To the extent that this is a textbook, it employs various linguistic selections appropriate to the construction of textbooks which it shares with all other textbooks. However, in that it is a textbook designed for relatively advanced students, its selections are constrained in particular ways. Further, in that it is a textbook within the general field of linguistics, so the constraints are tighter. Barton has captured this fuzzy nature of discourse communities neatly, where he writes:

A discourse community is a group of people who have texts and practices in common, whether it is a group of academics, or the readers of teenage magazines. In fact, discourse community can refer to several overlapping groups of people: it can refer to the people a text is aimed at; it can be the people who read a text; or it can refer to the people who participate in a set of discourse practices both by reading and by writing. People's preferences in how they wish to define it are dictated partly by their purposes.

(1994, p. 57)

Swales has recently withdrawn slightly from his original conception of the discourse community arguing that 'the "true" discourse community may be rarer and more esoteric than I once thought' (1993, p. 695). However, this is largely because his earlier characterisation tended to ignore the overlapping memberships that make up discourse communities and the historical circumstances in which they arise. If by 'true', Swales means 'pure' discourse community untouched by other, external communicative practices, then such a community cannot exist. Even the Hong Kong Study Circle depends for its existence on a network of activities and circumstances that stretches far beyond the activities of the stamp collector, including the need to communicate in writing across large geographical spaces and to pay for such communication. Traces of this (historical) development will necessarily be inscribed within the language of the stamp collectors, but they will incorporate and change such inscriptions and therefore develop a particular discursive activity with its own additions and peculiarities of expression. Although its 'meanings' will be unique, they will also be derivative.

One way of developing Swales's characterisation of the discourse community would be to consider Lesley Milroy's (1987) view of the relationship between social networks and language maintenance. She argues that communities consist of memberships that are 'close-knit' or 'loose-knit'. Close-knit communities are characterised by a high-density personal network structure, and most linguistic interactions take place within the community and are distributed equally among members of that community. Loose-knit communities, on the other hand, have a low-density personal network structure and linguistic interactions are distributed variously according to function. Members of the loose-knit group also have frequent interactions with people outside the community. Milroy goes on to argue that close-knit communities are 'an important mechanism of language maintenance' (ibid., p. 182). Although Milroy's work is centrally in the field of sociolinguistics, her observations are also pertinent to the discussion of discourse communities. There will be some such communities which develop for highly specialised purposes (and Swales's Hong Kong Study Circle would be a case in point). To join such communities may well require specific forms of induction (e.g. passing exams) for which appropriate (or 'correct') language is essential. Further, the meanings generated within such discourse communities will tend to the local and specific and be relatively distinct from those that obtain outside. Other discourse communities will be more open and will therefore admit a greater variety of linguistic behaviours. The former will tend to preserve their linguistic behaviours in order to preserve the specific meanings that are captured within them (cf. the church), while the latter will be subject to frequent change to accommodate changing and casual membership (cf. teenage magazines). Correspondingly, their 'meanings' will also change rapidly. Neither of these types, though, will be completely free of the meanings (or discourses) which hold in the larger community precisely because their members will also be members of this larger community.[8] Of necessity, these different discourse communities will produce different kinds of texts both because they are directed to different kinds of people and because they are conveying a different (social) interpretation of their writers' experience. However, because the texts will have been constructed differently, they will contain clues (in ways to be discussed later) as to the ways they are intended to be interpreted.

What I am proposing then is a complex interrelationship between social discourses, discourse communities, text production and text reception. The model I have in mind is entirely dynamic. Individuals either produce, or produce interpretations of, texts according to the norms of the discourse community and the functions which the text is intended to serve within that discourse community. These are then either verified by the group as meaningful, or challenged and refined. Such groups may develop highly characteristic modes of expression that remain internal to the group. However, these modes of expression are always situated historically, in that they develop from earlier 'ways of saying', and socially, in that they interact with and take on (some) of the meanings of the larger social groups of which they are part. Some discourse communities may also attempt to get their meanings accepted by this larger society. If they succeed, their interpretations achieve wider social meaning. The residue of these attempts can be found in dictionaries which list the range of meanings which attach to a given word within different groups or at different historical moments, while also offering that meaning which is most broadly accepted. At times, these attempts to impose meanings may develop into sites of struggle – cf. the range of interpretations attaching to the word 'democracy'. However, acceptance is also sometimes the result of cooperation. The important point is that 'meanings' are never simply immanent, but are always developed by people interacting in particular communicative situations. Further, because people interact to achieve different goals in different situations, the meanings that might develop within one discourse community will be different from those that may develop within other discourse communities. Such communities will therefore develop characteristic methods of linguistic behaviour which will vary, and this variety will lead to different text types.

CONCLUSION

In this chapter, I have attempted to deal with a very difficult and contentious area of context. My central argument has been that meaning does not lie in the language but is created between people. Although texts occur in physical contexts and are interpreted according to cognitive contexts, these are only partial indicators of what a text might mean. Far more important is the social context. Written texts are interventions into a communicative interaction which necessarily preceded them and which will continue after they have been discarded. They therefore contribute to, and are shaped by, the broad ways in which society speaks to itself (i.e. its discursive practices) and validates some communications as meaningful and others as meaningless. However, they tend also to be specific interventions with specific purposes, and to that extent are directed towards specific groups of people. As specific interventions they have their own particular shape, but they also have to conform to the norms of the group to which they are directed, otherwise they will be rejected. In the act of conforming, writers incorporate and reproduce the linguistic behaviours of that group in such a way as to signal their membership. If they are accepted (i.e. treated as meaningful) they become members of that discourse community. Most people are members of a variety of discourse communities, therefore there will be some leakage between communities as the practices of one may be introduced and accepted by another. Also, people are differently situated in relationship to their membership of given discourse communities. Within some they may be apprentices, within others consumers, and within others both consumers and producers. Discourse communities are therefore typically resistant to precise definition either in terms of their membership or in terms of their practices since they are in a constant state of flux. Nevertheless, in order to understand and be understood, writers and readers need to know how it is that a given discourse community creates and verifies (linguistic) meaning at any particular moment.

FURTHER READING

It is extremely difficult to produce a list of recommended reading to support this chapter because any discussion of the social context of written texts inevitably touches on a number of different academic disciplines, each one of which approaches the topic using its own techniques of analysis. A useful introductory textbook is Mey's (1993) *Pragmatics: An Introduction*. He demonstrates convincingly how linguistic meaning always depends on the pragmatic circumstances in which language is produced. This can be usefully supplemented by Lecercle's (1990) *The Violence of Language*. This is a fascinating discussion of how language is more than we can describe. In particular, he looks at the so-called 'nonsense' produced by writers such as Lear and demonstrates how it hovers on the edge of meaning. This leads him to argue that, although we are constrained in various ways as to what we can say, these constraints are less rigid than many linguists would have us believe.

I have indicated that the term 'discourse' has been used in very different ways by different theorists – indeed, its use might well be described as a site of struggle – and an excellent introduction to the confusions which surround the term is offered by Pennycook in his (1994) paper 'Incommensurable discourses?' For a fuller understanding of how I am using it, readers are referred both to this paper and to Foucault. Within linguistics the term has tended to be used to describe the ways in which linguistic interactions achieve success largely by reference to the internal properties of language use. This area of study, known as *discourse analysis*, uses a variety of techniques to investigate its subject matter and these are well documented by Coulthard's *An Introduction to Discourse Analysis* (1977) and Brown and Yule's *Discourse Analysis* (1983). This sense of the term is the one used by McCarthy and Carter (1994) in their excellent *Language as Discourse* which touches on a number of issues relevant to this chapter. With this sense discourse is seen as being influenced by ideologies in the ways discussed by Simpson in *Language, Ideology and Point of View* (1993).

Lee's *Competing Discourses: Perspective and Ideology in Language* (1992) is ambiguous as to his use of 'ideology' and 'discourse', and occasionally it seems that he is using them as synonyms. Nevertheless, his book is well worth reading. He has been strongly influenced by people working in the area of critical discourse analysis (CDA). Fairclough's *Critical Discourse Analysis* (1995) is a useful collection of papers which explains the CDA project, but is not an easy read. Another branch of CDA is represented in Kress (1989b) *Linguistic Processes in Sociocultural Practice* which should be regarded as essential reading.

As the title of Kress's book indicates, some understanding of related work in sociolinguistics would be helpful. Apart from Lesley Milroy (1987) which I refer to in the chapter, a good introduction is Holmes's *An Introduction to Sociolinguistics* (1992). For a thorough discussion of the 'speech community', Hudson's *Sociolinguistics* (1980) is very useful. Swales introduced the term 'discourse community', and his discussion in *Genre Analysis* (1990) still remains the best introduction.

SOME QUESTIONS FOR CONSIDERATION

1 British Railways used to have a sign in their train toilets that read:

Gentlemen lift the seat

   a How many different interpretations can you construct from this sentence?
   b Under what circumstances would your different interpretations be validated?
   c To what extent do you feel that the 'correct' interpretation is guaranteed by the physical circumstances in which the sign appeared?

2 To what extent does it make sense to consider your college or university as a discourse community? In attempting to answer this question, you might like to consider the following further questions:

   a In what ways is your own institution like/unlike other colleges and universities? To the extent that it is like them, would it make more sense to refer to higher education as a discourse community?
   b Are there any written texts either produced or read by you which are unique to the institution?
   c Which, if any of these, are completely new to you? And are any of them developments of texts that you may previously have encountered or produced at school?
   d How many written texts have you encountered which are clearly typical of the institution but which show traces of the discursive practices which occur outside your college or university?

3 I cannot predict where you may be reading this text (cf. question 1 above), but are there any circumstances where you would *not* be reading it?

   a To what extent does this text depend on its physical context in order to make sense?

   b In the act of reading, how are you drawn into a discourse community?

   c How would you characterise this discourse community, and what is your place in it?

Chapter 4

Some definitional problems

INTRODUCTION

In Chapter 1 I discussed populist notions of language and argued that they ignore language variation. I further claimed that such views militated against a full understanding of how language is situated socially. In Chapter 2 I showed how (some) of these views had developed histori-cally, and what the driving forces were that persuaded different writers to argue for 'correct' forms of the language. In the previous chapter I sketched out a theory of the relationships that exist between language users and social networks. So far though, I have been deliberately vague as to what is meant by language variety. The purpose of this chapter then is to refine the discussion by defining certain key terms. In particular, I shall be concentrating on what I mean by 'text', since it has been variously defined and its meanings are not always clear. But if we want to make the claim that variation resides in texts, it is essential to know what we are talking about.

Language use can vary according to a number of parameters. In the spoken language people employ different *accents*. These are typical ways of pronunciation and relate exclusively to the sound patterns of the lan-guage. They can only be accurately rendered in writing by means of phonetic script. Although some writers attempt to represent different pronunciations by deviant spellings, such representations are doomed to failure because writers cannot predict how readers will normally pronounce the written word. Thus if I, as a southerner, attempt to indicate a northern pronunciation by writing <boot> in place of <but>, northern readers may well assume that I am referring to an item of footwear. In fact, of course, the context will indicate the intended meaning of the word, but the technical point that alphabetic writing does not accurately represent fea-tures of accent remains true and therefore this form of variation need not be included in our discussion.

A feature of variation that is often associated with accent is *dialect*. This refers to given combinations of grammatical and lexical features that occur systematically in speakers from different geographical regions, or (less frequently) particular social classes. Dialectal variation may appear in literary texts (Blake, 1981) and local news reports. Even in the latter, however, there is a tendency to adapt reports of speech according to the norms of writing.[1] As I have indicated in Chapter 2, these norms derived from the English used by the chancery clerks of the fifteenth century and included a predominance of dialect forms from the East Midlands variety. Although they have undergone significant modification over the ensuing centuries, written forms still tend to appeal to South East English dialects.

A more noticeable feature of variety in written texts is that manifested by the different functions that they may perform. Halliday refers to this kind of variation as a variation in *register*. Although I shall be discussing registerial variation in greater detail later, it is worth pointing out that the distinction between dialectal variation and register variation is not at all clear cut. Halliday (Halliday, 1978, p. 225; Halliday and Hasan, 1985, p. 43) suggests that dialect refers to variety according to the user, while register is variety according to use. He also argues that dialects are 'saying the same thing differently' while registers are 'saying different things'. Thus, although dialects can be distinguished through different choices within phonetics, phonology, vocabulary and grammar, they select from the same semantic range. Registers, on the other hand, are chosen precisely because they manifest different semantic choices. In consequence, they are realised by different selections from the grammatical and lexical options within the language (Halliday, 1985, p. 43). Halliday recognises that there is considerable overlap between dialect and register since 'ways of seeing' are also 'ways of meaning' (Hasan, 1984b). In the context of written language, where phonetics and phonology play minimal roles, the distinction is even more blurred. What is meant is intrinsically signalled by what is said and, as we shall see, no two documents, however similar, mean the same thing.

We have already seen that English underwent considerable functional elaboration in the seventeenth century and, given the arguments developed in Chapter 3, this development resulted in new text types to represent the new meanings being expressed. Because of the essentially conservative (or preservative) nature of written forms, this was a slow development. Nevertheless, the expression of new meanings required the introduction of new grammatical forms, new lexis and new ways of linking sentences. Since these are systematic choices in the construction of given texts, text types might be considered to exhibit dialectal variation at least according to the definition of dialect offered above. In spite of this, it is convenient to distinguish between written and spoken text along a number of parameters, and therefore variation between written texts will be discussed in terms of register, although some registerial features might well exhibit distinctions which can also be described in terms of dialect.

Although this might seem confusing, it is intrinsic to the nature of language, since choices are dependent on a variety of factors which are all operating simultaneously. Individuals construct written and spoken texts from a complex of personal choices (or *idiolects*) which have been developed through a network of interactions with a variety of people in a variety of situations. These idiolects are always subject to the constraints of intelligibility, and are therefore modified and developed in reaction to the particular purposes of the interaction. While it might be perfectly appropriate to write a letter to one's lover using a number of expressions that were developed during private moments of intimacy (some of which might exhibit particular dialectal features associated with class or region), it would be inappropriate to use the same phrases in a letter addressed to one's bank manager requesting an overdraft.

Precise characterisations of these distinctions are therefore extremely difficult. Indeed, other writers (e.g. Lyons, 1981, p. 292) have suggested that this type of variety is best seen as a distinction between formal and informal usage. This argument seems to rest on the assumption that writing is best seen as a single variety but, as I shall be demonstrating, since this kind of variation also manifests itself through different lexical and grammatical choices, it becomes increasingly difficult to maintain a clear difference in kind between those texts which vary because of their relative formality and those texts which vary because they have been produced for different purposes. Rather, it might be safer to argue that variation according to formality is one kind of variation according to function, and is better analysed within a general theory of variation (i.e. that of register). This point will be discussed in greater detail in a later chapter where we look more closely at the ways variety derives from the different situations of writers in relation to their intended audiences.

TEXT

So far, I have discussed variation in written texts using *text* in a relatively informal way. Most readers will probably have had an intuitive notion of what I am talking about, but it is now necessary to define much more clearly how I intend to use the term. Although the following discussion may be reminiscent of sledgehammers cracking (crushing?) nuts, there is a serious issue here. If we look at the ways the term is employed in everyday use we come across a number of apparent inconsistencies. Anglican vicars, for example, typically start their sermons by announcing 'My text for today is taken from . . .'. The implication here is that one part (or verse) of the Bible can be treated as a free-standing text for particular purposes. Equally, we may find people hotly disputing the meaning of a word or a phrase separated from its *co-text*. On other occasions, though, the term is taken to refer to some kind of completed communicative event as when we refer to the Bible (which is a collection of disparate books) as a text, or even to Shakespeare's text, by which we mean the whole body of his works. In each of these occasions, text seems to refer to 'what is being talked about' rather than 'what is being meant'. And this can be a very useful distinction since there are times when writers quite deliberately transfer texts (in this sense), either in the form of direct quotation or more indirectly (as in parodies) and destabilise the meanings these texts may have had in their original utterance. Indeed, in these cases, the text may be said to have three 'meanings': the first is that which it had in the original utterance; the second is what it achieves in the new text; and the third is the set of meanings it has independently of either text, but which allows it to mediate between the two longer texts in which it occurs.[2] Although I shall be adopting this sense of the term, it is not one that has appealed to recent linguists who wish to construct a more functional definition.

One of the most thorough discussions of the term is that offered by de Beaugrande and Dressler (1981). Prior to defining text they offer seven 'standards of textuality', and these will serve as a very useful framework for the fuller discussion which will follow in subsequent chapters. These standards can be represented schematically as follows (Figure 4.1):

1 COHESION   4 ACCEPTABILITY
2 COHERENCE   5 INFORMATIVITY
3 INTENTIONALITY   6 SITUATIONALITY

7 INTERTEXTUALITY

Figure 4.1 Standards of textuality, after de Beaugrande and Dressler (1981)

The first three may be considered as largely writer-oriented in that the features are signalled directly by the choices selected by writers in the construction of texts. So the cohesiveness of a text depends on such grammatical markers as 'and', 'but', 'therefore', 'nevertheless', 'first', 'next', etc. Texts are cohesive to the extent that the grammatical relationships between their constituent sentences are recoverable. 'Coherence' refers to the ways in which writers create text worlds which can be related to our experience of the phenomenal world. One way of describing this would be to consider how far the concepts signalled by the linguistic signs are congruent with each other. This depends less on the selection of overt cohesive markers and more on the ways in which situations are described and sequenced. De Beaugrande and Dressler (1981, p. 5) refer particularly to issues of causality and time in the construction of coherent text worlds, and it is quite clear that such concepts need not be signalled overtly. In a text such as:

1. No milk in the fridge. Have gone to the shops.

most readers would assume that the writer (not the milk) had gone to the shops to buy some milk, although none of this is signalled directly by the grammatical forms of the text. Coherence is therefore often an implicit feature of texts and derives from the writers' assumptions that readers will have had similar experiences and are sharing the same social world. I have described it as writer-oriented largely because the assumption of coherence derives from the writer initially, although there are very good grounds for believing that readers also attempt to assign coherence to texts wherever possible. 'Intentionality' is signalled by writers through their manipulation of rhetorical devices. Writers typically intend their writings to have an effect on their readers, and they have to find appropriate ways of signalling these intended effects. There are a variety of ways in which such intentions can be conveyed ranging from such overt grammatical selections as the imperative: e.g:

2. KEEP OFF THE GRASS

to more indirect forms, e.g:

3. YOU ARE REQUESTED TO KEEP OFF THE GRASS

I have referred to these three standards of textuality as 'writer-oriented' precisely because they seem to refer to the selections made by the writer. However, it is clear that such selections will be meaningless without the readers' cooperation. Such cooperation is achieved primarily because language is social in its nature. Readers know how to interpret text because they know, through experience, how language works. Nevertheless, they make certain judgements when faced with a written text, and these are the features I have listed on the right of the diagram. Indeed, it is convenient to see these features in some ways as the converse of the features on the left. So, 'acceptability' involves a recognition on the readers' part that a given text is sufficiently well-constructed so as to be recognisable as a cohesive and coherent text. 'Informativity' can be related to the extent to which any given text has desirable effects on readers, in particular by making them aware of something that was not previously known. 'Situationality' recognises that the appearance of a text at a given time or in a given context will influence readers in their interpretation. For example, 'Keep off the grass' encountered in an art gallery will not be read as an injunction, but will be re-interpreted as having some other intended meaning.

The seventh of these standards is, perhaps, the one that is most problematic, and I have placed it between the other six precisely because it is a function of both writers and readers. 'Intertextuality' is a tricky concept because it recognises that all texts are created and interpreted in the context of other texts that have been experienced. That is, all texts contain 'traces' of previous texts. However, writers may select some of these deliberately (as, for example, in the case of quotations), whereas others may be the result of habit: so 'Keep off the Grass' and 'Keep Out' manifest features of intertextuality although neither is quoting the other. Equally, readers may pick up echoes of previous texts that they have read but which may not have been intended by the writer. For these reasons, intertextuality has to be considered a fundamental feature of all existing written texts, but one that needs to be treated with considerable caution.

Although de Beaugrande and Dressler's discussion of textuality is extremely interesting, it is essentially functional in that it states the circumstances under which a text will achieve meaning. They state:

> A TEXT will be defined as a COMMUNICATIVE OCCURRENCE which meets seven standards of TEXTUALITY. If any of these standards is not considered to have been satisfied, the text will not be communicative. Hence, non-communicative texts are treated as non-texts.
>
> (1981, p. 3)

This appears contradictory in that it seems to assert that there may be texts that are non-texts. In fact, de Beaugrande and Dressler do make their position clearer later in the book (ibid., p. 34) where they adopt the term 'presentation' to refer to a non-communicative text. Nevertheless, it is not at all clear what status a 'presentation' has as linguistic object since, if it is completely non-communicative, it would seem not to belong to the language. This kind of contradiction is inherent in any kind of definition that is constructed entirely in functional terms since it fails to recognise that objects may exist (and be seen to exist) independent of their function.

Halliday and Hasan (1976, p. 2) offer a slightly different definition, but one that is also conceived in largely functional terms, and one which produces similar kinds of problems:

> A text is best regarded as a SEMANTIC unit: a unit not of form but of meaning. Thus it is related to a clause or sentence not by size but by REALIZATION, the coding of one symbolic system in another. A text does not CONSIST OF sentences; it is REALIZED BY, or encoded in sentences.

If text is considered to be a semantic unit, it is not entirely clear what the minimum (or maximum) lengths of a text might be since, as we have seen, both single words and collected works can be treated in some sense as semantic units. Equally, their definition seems to suggest that texts are jointly constructed by writers and readers since the semanticity of a text is neither solely the property of a writer nor that of a reader. Later in their book, Halliday and Hasan indicate that texts are identifiable by the presence of certain formal cohesive devices. They argue that it is the 'concept of cohesion [which] accounts for the essential semantic relations whereby any passage of speech or writing is enabled to function as text' (ibid., p. 13). This is confusing in that I am not clear whether they are claiming that texts can exist *even though* they are not functioning as texts, although the drift of their argument would suggest that written symbols which do not function as texts are *ipso facto* not texts. This, though, seems counter-intuitive in that I may recognise a set of written characters as, say, a text in Chinese (or even in a language for which I do not know the name) but not be able to treat it as a semantic unit simply because I do not understand the language. Of course, they could argue that they are discussing a set of symbols which may, under certain circumstances, operate as a text for certain people, in which case it would seem almost anything could count as a text.

Halliday and Hasan do consider some of these problems and concede that a text may be of any length (1976, p. 294), but they continue to maintain that a text may be defined as a unit which is bound together by various types of cohesive devices: 'For most purposes, we can consider that a new text begins where a sentence shows no cohesion with those that have preceded' (ibid., p. 295). Interestingly, this insistence on the importance of (lexicogrammatical) cohesion has led Brown and Yule to criticise them by showing how a stretch of language may be constructed which manifests full cohesion but which is clearly not a semantic unit (1983, p. 197). Given that this stretch of language is being used as a text by Brown and Yule, it would be interesting to know whether Halliday and Hasan would also recognise it as such.

Although there are obvious problems with their initial characterisation, Halliday and Hasan do refine it so that their final definition is extremely subtle, involving both register and cohesion:

> The concept of COHESION can therefore be usefully supplemented by that of REGISTER, since the two together effectively define a TEXT. A text is a passage of discourse which is coherent in these two regards: it is coherent with respect to the context of situation, and therefore consistent in register; and it is coherent with respect to itself, and therefore cohesive.
>
> (1976, p. 23)

I shall be considering the concept of *register* in greater detail later since it is of considerable importance in understanding how texts achieve meaning in use. However, at this stage it is worth noting that this definition is also unsatisfactory since it fails to consider the possibility that a text may have been constructed with the intention of being coherent with respect to a given context of situation but which fails to persuade its readers that it is coherent. Also, it cannot account for those occasions when a text is fully coherent (see my example 1 above) but which manifests no obvious features of cohesion (van Peer, 1989). However, by introducing both cohesion and coherence as defining elements, they do manage to avoid the criticisms of Brown and Yule referred to above.

In their more recent book, *Language, Context and Text* (1985/9), Halliday and Hasan have re-addressed the problem, but their definition is remarkably similar in all essentials to the one developed in 1976. As with de Beaugrande and Dressler, they insist on a functionalist definition arguing that:

> We can define text, in the simplest way perhaps, by saying that it is language that is functional. By functional, we simply mean language that is doing some job in some context, as opposed to isolated words or sentences that I might put on the blackboard. (These might also be functional, of course, if I was using them as linguistic examples.)
>
> (1985/9, p. 10)

Although it is not entirely clear what they mean by the parenthetical sentence at the end, it would seem that functional definitions of text are not particularly illuminating. One reason for this has been succinctly expressed by Widdowson (1984, p. 125) in his claim that 'Texts . . . do not communicate: people communicate by using texts as a device for mediating a discourse process.' If we recognise that text is a product of the attempt to communicate, then we can construct a clearer definition and description of written text which does not need to take into account its success or failure to communicate.

In this book, text is considered to be that set of visual linguistic symbols which are capable of being employed in the construction of meaning. To elaborate slightly, it is necessary to distinguish linguistic symbols from other kinds of symbols. Although a passage of sheet music, or a set of mathematical formulae, may well constitute a visual text by analogy, I am only referring to linguistic texts. There will be occasions when other visual symbols insert themselves into linguistic texts (for example, pictures, graphs or figures of various kinds). When the text makes overt reference to such symbols they will be treated as part of the *co*-text. Where they appear to be present for decorative purposes, and no reference is made to them, then they are best considered as part of the *con*text. The use of the phrase 'capable of being employed' may seem to indicate a functional definition similar to the ones I have criticised above, but I should make it clear that my definition does not include any preconceptions as to the ways in which a text might be used in the construction of meaning. Isolated words on the blackboard, for example, become texts as soon as somebody pays attention to them whatever their original function may have been. Further, I have chosen this form of words to account for those occasions when we are confronted by a set of visual symbols that we *assume* derives from some natural language but that we do not understand. When this happens, we are inclined to consider that such symbols make up a meaningful text for some people, even though we are incapable of constructing meaning from them. Thus, we are still inclined to refer to them as 'text' even though for us they are meaningless texts and I am perfectly happy to recognise that my definition allows the existence of meaningless texts (cf. the discussion of schizophrenic texts in Chapter 3).

Further, this definition makes no presuppositions as to the potential or actual length of what may constitute a text. For our purposes, text may refer to the complete works of an author, a particular book, a chapter, a newspaper in its entirety, or news report, or even a sentence or part of a sentence. The important point is that it refers to any set of symbols that are being used as a mediating device in the process of making meaning within a given situation.

CO-TEXT AND CONTEXT

My definition of text necessarily suggests that it is best treated as an object of observation and comment. Given that texts may be of any length (including a single word) we need further terms to describe those elements which are not the object of immediate observation but which need to be referred to in discussion. Here we are faced with two slightly different kinds of entities. The first includes the surrounding linguistic elements which may need to be invoked in order to show how specific local interpretations depend on surrounding features of the text. These elements I shall refer to as *co-text*. This kind of reference, of course, becomes essential when we are discussing the grammatical and lexical relations which hold between different units of the co-text. One way of dealing with the apparent logical contradiction in this characterisation would be to refer to the notion of rankshift. Thus, any linguistic element can potentially be treated as a text (though typically, the word is likely to be the minimal unit within written text), although we also use text to refer to *any* longer stretch (e.g. sentence, paragraph, chapter, book, etc.) of which these smaller elements are textual units which are in a co-textual relationship with each other.

Co-text needs to be distinguished from *context*. Whereas co-text refers to the textual units which are an integral part of the larger text, but which are not currently the focus of attention, context refers to the relationships that may be contracted between the text and such extratextual features that are invoked to establish a particular interpretation.[3] I have discussed social context at some length in Chapter 3, but most readers are conscious of a rather more narrow range of contextual reference when they engage in the act of interpretation. These include such features as the relationship that a given text may hold with other texts of a similar, or different nature; the implied relationships between the writer and the reader; the intended (immediate) functions of the text; and the ways in which the text impinges on readers' construction of reality. Similar contextual considerations will be at play in the act of constructing a text, and the ideal is presumably for the contextual relationships which have been conceived by the writer to trigger off (by means of the text) identical relationships within the readers. Where this does not happen, or where these relationships are in conflict, meaning will not be achieved, or only achieved with difficulty.[4]

SOME PRACTICAL APPLICATIONS

These theoretical considerations can be clarified by looking again at the texts that were listed in Chapter 1 (here renumbered):

4 ADDITIONAL BENEFITS RIGHTS TO EXTEND THIS POLICY AND EFFECT NEW POLICIES BEFORE 19TH MAY 1993 (SEE MORTGAGE ASSURANCE OPTION PROVISIONS)

5 *Then t' Alleluias stick in t'angels' gobs.*
   When dole-wallahs fuck off to the void
   what'll t'mason carve up for their jobs?
   The cunts who lieth ' ere wor unemployed?

6 I enclose herewith the above mentioned policies together with accompanying documentation for your retention as they are not required in connection with your new mortgage.

7 Glad Abo went well. Re your recent PALA newsletter and books to review: I'd be quite interested in Nardoccio's *Reader Response to Literature* (if not already allocated) – I'm teaching a course in that area this year.

8 Symphony No 0? Surely some mistake! Well, no; originally designated Symphony No 2 Bruckner turned against this work in a fit of pique following criticism from the conductor due to give it its premiere.

9 GAS BOILER floor standing, balanced flue, 54,000
   BTU, Thorn, good working
   order £100. 0843 860929
   after 6pm

Although it is possible to treat each one of these examples as a text that is complete in itself, most readers would find such a treatment rather odd. Only Text 9 seems to be 'free standing'. To treat the other fragments as texts would suggest that they were being used for some other reasons than were envisaged in their construction. However it is quite clear, in my act of quotation, that I am capable of discussing them in isolation in order to make certain kinds of observations. To that extent, given that my intention is to use them as objects of reference (to do with linguistic form, supposed intention, etc.), they have become texts in their own right within the context of this book. Thus, it would be possible to demonstrate how, in Example 4, the particular layout allows us to treat the right hand column as the 'additional benefits' that are referred to on the left. Example 5 could be used to demonstrate certain kinds of cohesion and coherence. We might note the different kinds of lexical cohesion established between 'dole-wallahs', 'jobs', and 'unemployed'; the anaphoric reference manifested between 'their' and 'dole-wallahs'; the temporal cohesion/coherence demonstrated through the use of 'then', 'when'. And we could then leave these texts without any further reference to the roles that they might originally have served.

It would be otiose to labour this point, but it serves to underline how it is, in principle, possible to treat any unit of writing as a text. Although it could be objected that these exemplary texts are incomplete as texts until they have been discussed, and that they are therefore part of a larger text which involves them and my discussion of them (i.e. this book), such an argument risks re-introducing a functional definition of text which I have explicitly excluded. As visible linguistic signs that are capable of being used to make meaning, these fragments are recognisable as texts.

In discussing the existence of cohesion in Text 5 I needed to make cross-references between different parts of the text. In this way I was treating the referents as part of the co-text. I take this to be non-problematic. However, it is equally clear that there are elements within the different texts which refer (grammatically) to features which are not present within these frag-ments. For example, in Text 4 the reference to 'This policy' seems to be self-referring, and yet it is quite clear that the fragment is *not* a policy. Similarly, Text 6 alludes to 'the above mentioned policies', and yet the co-text makes no reference to such policies. It therefore seems reasonable to acknowledge that we *usually* use the term 'text' to refer to some unit that is perceived as grammatically complete. To this extent, we can agree with Halliday and Hasan (1976) that cohesion is a significant, and perhaps the most significant, grammatical element in the recognition of texts as mean-ingful while rejecting their apparent claim that it is the defining element of text.

Clearly, these fragments were not treated as texts by their original readers. Each one was embedded in additional text and (again with the exception of Text 9) for them to achieve their full impact, this co-text needs to be recovered. However, the mere recovery of such co-text will not in itself lead to successful interpretation of the larger texts. For this to be possible we need to refer to the likely contexts which have led to the production of the texts and which will be used in the construction of possible interpreta-tions. It will become apparent in trying to decide how to define appropriate contexts why the term is so slippery. With Text 4, it is reasonable to assume that the full text only makes sense to someone who has taken out a mortgage. However, in the act of taking out a mortgage, the mortgagee engages in a highly complex set of transactions involving the production of a considerable number of other written texts. These texts may be legitimately regarded as part of the context of this particular text, and it is clear that the meaning of this text depends on the meanings of the other texts that have preceded it. There is, though, no reason to limit our search for context there since the transactions that are involved in getting a mortgage depend upon a society which recognises the right of individuals to purchase their own homes. These rights will also be embedded in other texts, although no direct reference may be made to them. Similarly, the ability to negotiate a mortgage depends on a recognition that earnings and expenditure are in an unequal relationship such that payment has to be spread over a long period. This in turn assumes that some form of income will be available for the period of the mortgage. Thus, there is a vast complex of social relations that are invoked in the successful interpretation of this text, and they are social relations which are specific to this kind of transaction but also infect other transactions. While it may seem extravagant to claim that all these features are immediately inscribed in this text, advertisements for building societies always carry a disclaimer which suggests that ignorance of any one of them may lead to the loss of the purchased property.

Texts 6 and 7 are interesting in other ways. Both are from letters, and yet the differences they exhibit suggest that quite different kinds of contexts need to be established for their interpretation. Text 6 is clearly interactive in that it uses personal pronouns, and yet the use of certain terms suggests a distant relationship between sender and receiver. 'Herewith' seems redundant since, if the policies are enclosed, it adds no information. Similarly, 'together with' seems an unnecessary circumlocution for the simple conjunction 'and'. Such usages, however, are not merely random variations of style. Rather, they serve to indicate that the letter has the form of a quasi-legal document. By using terms and phrases that are frequently found in legal transactions, the writer is *placing* the text quite deliberately to indicate to the receiver that the meanings constructed are intended to have some kind of legal force. The context invoked here, then, is the particular transaction, but the particular transaction seen within the wider context of a particular set of legal practices and the language associated with such practices. Text 7, on the other hand, by virtue of its incomplete forms and exchange of personal comments, suggests a quite different context. The shared meanings are more private, although there is mention of a particular transaction which reaches beyond the text into a society where books are reviewed, where reviewers are allocated by somebody who (if only in this area) possesses authority, and in which the reviewer is supposed to have particular competences. Again, full understanding depends on considerably more than simply decoding the language since (indirect) reference is made to a range of external social meanings.

Texts 5 and 8 are interesting in quite other ways. The apparent intimacy of Text 8 has features which associate it with the personal features briefly mentioned in Text 7. However, when placed in its immediate context (that of a record catalogue), it becomes apparent that this text is 'imitating' features of intimacy in order to establish a persuasive tone which will encourage readers to buy the records on offer. Again, we can see that the notion of context expands from the more narrow confines of readers who are interested in music to that of advertising, and ultimately to a social context in which people are competing to sell different kinds of goods and services. Text 5 is perhaps the most difficult to place. Most readers will identify it as a stanza from a poem, and therefore assume that it is to be read in the context of other poems. However, its use of 'bad' language suggests that it has been designed quite deliberately to challenge familiar notions of what is appropriate subject matter for poetry. Thus, although it invokes the context of literature, it also inserts itself as a disturbing element within the collection of texts that are traditionally regarded as literary.

Text 9 might be considered the least problematic. But it also illustrates some of the points that I have been making most graphically. It is noticeably devoid of the kinds of grammatical features we expect in written texts, and yet it is not just a random collection of words. In order to interpret it successfully, its readers need quite detailed knowledge of the linguistic conventions of small ads. These include the occasions where they are likely to appear, the conventions governing abbreviations and ordering, which elements are descriptive and which are invitations, and the intended function of such ads. They further need to know that the activity of buying and selling that takes place through small ads is both related to, and different from, the kinds of buying and selling that takes place in society at large.

It should be apparent from this brief discussion, then, that context and text interact in ways that cannot easily be separated. Small ads only appear in certain physical contexts (e.g. papers, magazines, shop windows). In order to be small, they employ certain kinds of abbreviations (which may reasonably be regarded as features of text). And yet, it is the use of these features which allow us to recognise them as small ads, and distinguish them from the other kinds of advertisements which appear in the same contexts. Having recognised them as small ads, we also anticipate that the relationships between buyer and seller will be of a particular nature. Thus, it could be argued that the construction of text is determined by an anticipated (set of) context(s) in which the text will be read and used, while the successful interpretation of text depends on recognising which features of context are to be treated as salient.

A MODEL FOR DESCRIPTION

Throughout this chapter I have attempted to distinguish between the physical entity of texts and the functions that they may perform in given circumstances. I have made it very clear that I consider the contexts in which such texts may appear have significant effects on their likely interpretation, but I have suggested that these contexts are not an immediate feature of the text as text. Further, I have attempted to separate writer from reader by suggesting that the intended meaning of a given text may not be the one developed in the act of reading. I fully recognise that I have not been wholly successful and in my discussion of the small ad it must have been apparent that text, writer, reader, physical context and social context were all treated as integral elements in the act of making meaning. I have also criticised Halliday and Hasan and de Beaugrande and Dressler for introducing functionalist definitions where structuralist ones seem more appropriate and there might appear to be something of a paradox here. I believe this paradox to be intrinsic to any discussion of language. It is of course perfectly possible to discuss language as an object: i.e. to discuss it as though it were a semiotic system with a set of internally consistent rules which are independent of its users. This is to produce one kind of falsification since it ignores both what language does and the ways these 'rules' might have been developed so as to make it functionally more efficient. However, as soon as we shift our attention to the functional potential of language, we risk falling into another trap: that of treating the functions as though they were inscribed in the language rather than as properties of the people who are using language. I consider this to be another form of objectification, although it does have an advantage over the former of being able to produce much richer descriptions. If, on the other hand, we approach language entirely from the point of view of its (immediate) users, we risk losing sight of the extent to which language is in fact rule-based (even though we may concede that such 'rules' could be legitimately [re]described as conventions), and therefore how constrained users actually are as to what they can say by the lexicogrammatical limitations of the language. I cannot see any easy way out of these problems, but I would like to suggest that it may be helpful to recognise these different perspectives on language by adopting different terminologies to describe them.

In my discussion of the term 'text', I mentioned quite specifically that I intended to use it to refer to exemplary passages of writing. In this use, a text is an object of observation. My use of it as text is quite independent of the uses which were assumed in its construction. Of course, this does not preclude a discussion of its likely intentions, but *discussing* the construction of a text as, say, a letter is not the same as *using* the text as a letter. When I first read Text 6, I read it not as a text in this sense of the term, but as a communication relevant to my mortgage. It might, therefore, be useful to draw a preliminary distinction between *language-in-observation* and (to borrow a useful term from McCarthy and Carter, 1994) *language-in-action*. However, I believe it would also be helpful to have a further category to describe the social groups who typically employ language in characteristic ways since their social relations are not maintained exclusively by language but are frequently mediated by other forms of symbolic action.[5] Thus some recognition that they form a linguistic group but are not defined exclusively by their linguistic uses would seem appropriate.

Taking into account the comments I made in the last chapter concerning the pervasive effects of discursive practices, I shall try to capture the tripartite structure I have in mind through the following (Figure 4.2):

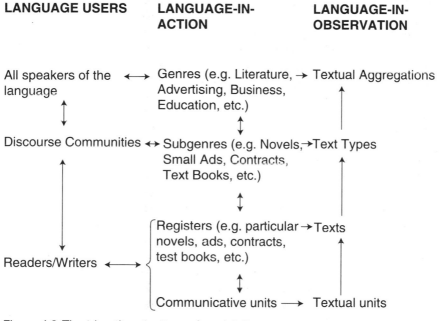

Figure 4.2 The tripartite structure of social discourses

Reading from left to right, I am suggesting that it is the society of language users which recognises or groups texts into genres and that genres are aggregations of texts which are perceived as performing broadly similar functions within this society. Of course, because genres develop to mediate the various discursive practices of a given society, they will contain traces of these various practices. They can thus never be 'pure'. Discourse communities are particular groups who generate and consume language for more restricted purposes giving rise to subgenres. However, people will belong to a variety of different discourse communities and their practices will also 'leak' across the boundaries. My examples represent the kinds of text types that may be generated by discourse communities. Reader and writers confront language use in specific individual situations and the relationship between them and the situations contribute to the specific meanings (or register) of the text. Finally, written texts are rarely produced or consumed at a glance so the units which are created or processed as part of the ongoing construction of meaning are treated as communicative.

In Chapter 3 I referred to a dynamic model of language use, and it is important to realise that the users of language and language-in-action are both dynamic. Readers and writers are situated within the society of language users and each time they contribute an act of writing or of interpretation they subtly alter their situation within this society and, by extension, the ways in which language has been used. Thus, we could redraw part of the figure as follows (Figure 4.3):

Figure 4.3 A dynamic model of language use

This dynamism is not present in our discussion of the right-hand column (except in a very indirect way) because we are talking about entities that have been removed from their communicative circumstances. Thus, although I can legitimately claim that a word is related to a sentence, a sentence to a text and a text to a text type, I am dealing with a hierarchical system rather than a dynamic one. The units are related by virtue of their grammatical properties (and similarities), rather than by what they do, and the text and its components are simply there. What I cannot legitimately claim is that a text or sentence is performing a specific communicative function (other than being the object of observation) because it is self-evidently *not* performing that function. Because of this logical contradiction, I prefer to reject functionalist definitions of texts and text-types, preferring instead to claim that they have the potential to perform certain functions in certain situations. This will become clearer in my discussion of relevance theory, register and genre, but at this stage I shall reiterate that the description of a text is logically distinct from the description of its function. Of course, we shall find that texts and text-types and indeed sentences have similar formal properties precisely because they have been constructed to perform certain functions, but we cannot make an illegitimate leap and claim that the co-presence of such formal properties allows us to predict how that text may be used.[6]

CONCLUSION

In this chapter I have discussed the nature of variation that typically manifests itself in the construction of written texts. Although there are a number of different and overlapping ways of describing such variation, I have argued that the most appropriate description for written language is variation according to register. I have deliberately deferred discussion of register to a later chapter, since it refers to texts in action and until I had established a clear definition of text such a discussion would be confusing. After considering the functional definitions of text offered by de Beaugrande and Dressler and Halliday and Hasan, I chose to reject them because they seemed to suggest that the functions of texts were self-inscribed. Instead I argued that texts are not in themselves functional, but are used (by people) to perform functions and that these uses are essentially unpredictable. I illustrated this by discussing various example texts. Although most people would reject the idea that these texts had been produced in order to be used for discussion in a linguistics textbook, the fact that I did use them in this way is a clear indication that they can serve that function. I therefore preferred to define text as any set of linguistic symbols which can be employed in the construction of meaning. This has the effect of rendering any stretch of language a potential text while it is being observed as such.

Nevertheless, it is clear that this characterisation produces its own problems because we do need some way of describing how texts are used in characteristic ways in given situations. I therefore produced a model which attempts to distinguish between three ways of talking about language involving users of language, language-in-action and language-in-observation. These interlinked at all levels, but whereas the first two were to be seen as dynamic models, the third was best considered as a static and hierarchical model.

FURTHER READING

The particular area of study we are investigating goes under a number of different names. In Britain, it is frequently referred to as *Stylistics*, although this carries the connotation that its central focus of study is (literary) style. It can also be called *Discourse Analysis*. In other areas of Europe it is variously referred to as *Text Linguistics*, or treated as a branch of *Semiotics*. This has meant that the titles of books are often opaque as to their subject matter. One excellent introductory book by Carter and Nash, though, has the simple title: *Seeing Through Language* (1990) and can be highly recommended.

Haynes (1989) *Introducing Stylistics* is also helpful as an introduction, but needs to be treated with caution. Although he does discuss written texts, he frequently refers to spoken text, and the techniques for analysing spoken language are not always appropriately applied to written language. He also, rather puzzlingly, uses examples drawn from comics to discuss features of speech. Comics are self-evidently written texts and I am not convinced that his observations are always fully justified. Nevertheless, his book is worth recommending if only because it contains a wealth of varied source texts.

An excellent book that explores many of the concepts discussed in this and the following chapter is *Language, Context and Text: Aspects of Language in a Social-Semiotic Perspective* by Halliday and Hasan (1985/9). It is, of course, written from the systemic-functional perspective developed within Hallidayan linguistics and, although it can be treated as a self-contained book, it is useful for readers to familiarise themselves with other works in this tradition and especially Halliday's (1994) *An Introduction to Functional Grammar*.

For those who wish to pursue these topics from an educational perspective, then the best book is McCarthy and Carter's (1994) *Language as Discourse*. It is from them that I have borrowed the expression 'language-in-action' and their views on how this is best described are always stimulating.

De Beaugrande and Dressler (1981) have produced an introductory textbook on text linguistics, *An Introduction to Text Linguistics*. Sadly, it is not quite as introductory as the title suggests. The opening chapters are clear and discuss the theoretical foundations of the subject in an extremely interesting fashion. However it soon plunges into considerable detail, and many students may find it rather daunting.

The distinctions I make between language-in-observation and language-in-action are very similar to those made by semanticists when they distinguish between sentence and utterance. I am wary of adopting this usage because all too often it implies that sentences have underlying (ideal) forms which are independent of the ways they are described. In my model of description I have deliberately placed social discourses at the top because discursive practices influence the ways we describe things (including sentences). In my view, then sentences can never exist (even as ideal forms) except as utterances. Thus, the distinction I am making is not between sentence and utterance but between different methods of describing utterances. However, readers who wish to pursue this topic would do well to read Chapter 1 of Levinson's (1983) *Pragmatics* and the relevant sections in Lyons's (1977) *Semantics*. For a corrective, they could also read Chapter 2 of Lecercle's (1990) *The Violence of Language*.

SOME QUESTIONS FOR CONSIDERATION

1 Consider the Texts 4–9 in the chapter above. Which, if any, of them might you consider to be exhibiting dialectal variation? For those which are not, how would you begin to describe the varieties that they exhibit?

2 a In what circumstances might you treat this sentence as a text?
 b In the above sentence, what features might you concentrate on in your discussion?
 c What is the function of 'this' as a co-textual element?
 d Is the sentence complete *as a text*?

3 a As language-in-action, what is sentence [a] above trying to do?
 b What effects does this have on your description of 'this'?
 c Would you want to treat [a] as complete as language-in-action, or does it seem to require some 'completing' element?

4 a As a language user, do you regularly encounter questions like these?
 b If not, where and when might you encounter them?
 c Do your fellow students have to answer these kinds of questions?
 d What implication might your answers have for defining a discourse community?

Chapter 5

Cohesion, coherence and register

INTRODUCTION

In Chapter 3, while discussing the ways in which language use was necessarily socially situated, I commented that writings are interventions in a continuing communicative process and are intended to have an effect within that process. In this respect they are rather like conversations, though with three significant differences. The first is that they are, in a sense, only one side of the conversation, and therefore have to imagine (or construct) an ideal addressee; the second is that they are planned but, in their finished state, show little evidence of their planning in the form of crossings out, etc.; and the third is that the texts themselves remain as a kind of residue after they have fulfilled their function, whereas in conversation what has been said (as text) has to all intents and purposes been lost after it has been spoken. These three features have a significant effect on the ways in which we view writings, and are influential in shaping the process of production. But the first two are crucial to our understanding of language variation since identifying appropriate readers and offering them coherent messages necessarily involves differentiating readers and messages and this can only be done by constructing texts in different ways.

In Chapter 4, I briefly discussed the kinds of variation that might be exhibited by various texts and suggested that these might indicate how the texts were intended to function within the discourse communities to which they were addressed. It is now time to consider how writers make specific selections from the language in order to make their contributions effective.

There are two intrinsic and interlinked difficulties in such an attempt. The first, which I discussed at some length in the previous chapter, is that the texts *themselves* do not communicate, although they are records of people's attempts to communicate. The second is related. We cannot climb into writers' heads and establish that they really did intend to communicate what our analysis suggests. So in all that follows (and particularly when I analyse other people's writings) my observations should be treated with a degree of scepticism. All that I, or anyone else, can really say is that I believe, on the basis of having used and constructed a significant number of written texts, that writer A constructed text B with the intention of achieving result C. I know (and no doubt my readers also know) that this is a dangerous assumption since there have been many occasions when I have written things which have been interpreted to mean something that was not part of my intention.

A useful starting point for this discussion is de Beaugrande and Dressler's first three standards of textuality (see above, Chapter 4). These are cohesion, coherence and intentionality. Writers have to persuade readers that what they are reading has a structure and a point. The structure can be achieved in two ways: either by signalling overtly the relationships that obtain between sentences by means of cohesion, or (more nebulously) by conjoining propositions and allowing readers to infer a relationship between them. To demonstrate intentionality, they have to persuade readers that they are the kinds of people who are likely to be affected in specific ways by the written communication.

COHESION

Cohesion can be seen as residing in the semantic and grammatical properties of the language. As we have seen, Halliday and Hasan (1976) have argued that texts achieve their status as communicative events through the use of cohesive devices. Although we have observed occasions where cohesion does not seem a necessary element in successfully achieving communication, it is undoubtedly true that it does help guide the ways in which units of text are to be understood in relation to each other. Cohesion is achieved in one of two ways. Either the presence (or absence) of an element which can only be understood by reference to some other co-textual element, or by repetition of an element with the same semantic range. The first of these is grammatical cohesion, and Halliday and Hasan have drawn up an exhaustive list of the devices which are cohesive in this way. Here I shall briefly discuss two of them to show how their uses may have a bearing on the ways in which writers construct their texts to achieve different ends.

Writers can indicate the relationships between clauses either explicitly or implicitly. Thus a cookbook may describe the same operation in any of the following ways:

1 Fry the onions and garlic. Add the rice.
2 Fry the onions and garlic and add the rice.
3 Fry the onions and garlic. Then add the rice.

In this instance the presence (or absence) of an overt cohesive device is unlikely to affect the interpretation significantly. However, when one has been selected it is clear that the writer is attempting to constrain the range of possible interpretations that are recoverable from the text. In these examples we can see a gradient of connecting relationships. In 1, the absence of any connective leaves the reader to infer the relationship between the clauses. In 2, a relationship is asserted, but its nature is left vague, while in 3, the relationship is overtly signalled. To cope with cases like 2 and 3 above, Blakemore (1987, pp. 124–5) distinguishes between 'logical connectives' and 'discourse connectives'. Thus in 2, the second 'and' is a discourse connective which relies for its interpretations on readers who understand that the rice is to be added after the frying. In 3, however, 'then' is a temporal connective which logically requires that something has preceded it. If we apply the same test to the following sentences:

4 Some connectives are vague. For example 'and' can mean many things.
5 Some connectives are vague. 'And' can mean many things.

The presence of 'for example' in 4 requires you to treat the second clause as an example of *something*. In 5, the absence of any connective presupposes a readership that is able to identify 'and' as a connective and therefore identify it as part of an example. Thus we can assume that the use (or non-use) of such cohesive devices will contribute to textual variety, and we might predict that such variety indicates different potential users. High usage of logically constraining connectives implies that the text is intended to be used by readers who are unfamiliar with the subject matter. Although this is intuitively appealing, empirical confirmation of this hypothesis does not yet (as far as I know) exist. And if we consider another example of grammatical cohesion, ellipsis, there is some counter-evidence. Texts 4 and 9 in the previous chapter both exhibit high degrees of ellipsis and to that extent are similar, but their potential readerships are both likely to be different and differently situated in relation to the two texts.

Another form of cohesion relevant to this discussion is lexical cohesion. Lexis is perhaps the most important way writers can indicate what their contribution is about. Therefore the ways in which lexical elements relate to each other is of fundamental significance. Again, Halliday and Hasan have interesting things to say about this, although they are unfortunately unable to offer clear methods of analysis, arguing that, When analysing a text in respect of lexical cohesion, the most important thing is to use common sense, combined with the knowledge we have, as speakers of a language, of the nature and structure of its vocabulary, (1976, p. 290). More recently, Hasan has attempted to distinguish between the textual presence of (lexical) identity chains and similarity chains. The former are 'held together by the semantic bond of co-referentiality' (1984a, p. 205) and are therefore text bound, while the latter are linked either through co-classification or coextension. A problem with these definitions is that it is not clear how readers can decide whether the lexical items are co-referential on the evidence of the text itself since it is only in use that this distinction becomes apparent.[1] Hoey (1991a, b), while acknowledging the values of Hasan's work, has pointed out that while it may account for one structural element within texts, it fails to show how the sentences themselves are related by lexical cohesion. He further refers to Phillips's work, which established that academic textbooks typically contained patterns of recurrent collocations and argues that its significance lies in demonstrating 'that there is an organisation to text that can be identified without recourse to any semantic analysis or intuition, an organisation that is solely the product of long-distance lexical relations' (Hoey, 1991b, p. 24)? It follows from this that we can argue that if extended non-narrative texts of the kind that Phillips analyses typically exhibit such patterns, this will be one way of formally identifying them *as texts*. Hoey builds on these observations to establish that texts of this kind exhibit complex interrelationships between lexical elements, but that one type, which he calls 'bonding' (i.e. a repetition of three or more items variously defined) 'accurately identifies related pairs of sentences in a text, and the net they combine to create accurately reflects the organisation of the text' (ibid., p. 193).

Of course, as Hoey himself recognises, the claim that lexical cohesion is part of the organisation of a text in that it shows how sentences (often at considerable remove from each other) are related to each other gives us no clue as to how the writer intends us to interpret the text. Nevertheless, the presence of grammatical and lexical cohesion will play a significant part in directing readers as to how sentences are linked both locally and at a distance, and will indicate what the text is about. To show how the text is to be 'used', however, writers have to establish coherence.

COHERENCE

Coherence, unlike the kinds of cohesion I have been looking at, is not a property of the text itself but is jointly constructed by writers and readers. However, it is writers who attempt to indicate the kinds of coherence they intend their readers to recover. Let us consider the following three sentences:

6 No milk in fridge.
7 Have gone to shops.
8 Therefore have gone to shops.

If encountered on their own, 6 and 7 would presumably be treated as simple statements. Sentence 8 would be largely uninterpretable since the presence of 'therefore' presupposes a cause. Thus when we read texts we assume that they are intended to perform some function, and are frustrated when they appear not to (as in 8). If we encounter 6 and 8 together, 8 now makes sense in that the logical relationship between the two has been filled in. However, the co-presence of 6 and 7 leaves readers to construct their own relationship. If we read these sentences on a piece of paper blowing about in the street we would, of course, be able to imagine a set of circumstances in which the communication was effective even though the text signals neither the participants involved in the exchange nor the setting in which it occurred. If, on the other hand, we came down to breakfast, noticed the absence of our partner and saw 6 and 7 scribbled on a piece of paper lying on the table, we would construct a set of meanings which probably matched the intentions of the writer. Thus we can argue that writers construct messages knowing that sentences perform functions (i.e. make statements, etc.), and that two or more sentences together imply that a 'meaning' relation will hold between them.[2] We can also assume that they will construct the message taking into account the circumstances in which it is intended to be read. And it is by dealing with all these considerations that writers attempt to establish coherence.

REGISTER

In order to account for the construction of coherence, we need a theory which links language to use in quite specific and complex ways and which is able to differentiate between and account for the presence of the particular choices which writers make. So far, I have illustrated much of my argument by referring to a very brief and artificially constructed set of texts. Let us now consider the following two (actually occurring) texts:

1 (a) Dear Tony and Jane,

Hello, there. I'm sure it was your turn to drop me a line, but I'll forgive you. I suspect you've been very busy. Or is it something I said? I hope not. Remember the rarer action.

2 (a) Dear Mr A. Bex

THREE STAR SERVICE CONTRACT

We are pleased to advise you that the annual inspection check of your CENTRAL HEATING BOILER is now due and we have arranged for our engineer to call on 11th March 1994 before 1:00 pm.

Most readers are likely to be persuaded that the first of these is the opening of a personal letter; that it is issuing a mild rebuke to the recipients but also probing the current state of social relations between the sender and the recipients. The second is also the opening of a letter, but it is both more formal (i.e. less concerned with establishing friendly social relations between the participants) and more immediate in announcing its practical intentions. Most readers will also assume that the relative informality of the former is intentional and therefore part of its meaning, just as they are likely to assume that the plunge into *media res* of the latter is also part of its meaning. Of course, it is easy to assert this, but consider the following invented texts:

1 (b) Dear Mr and Mrs Bex,

> I very much regret not having heard from you for some time, and am concerned that I may have offended you in some way. I was under the impression that you were to write to me.

2 (b) Dear Tony,

> Hullo there. You've probably forgotten, but we'd agreed to look at your boiler every year, so we're thinking of popping round on the 11th, probably in the middle of the day.

At one level these convey the same information as the original two letters. The relationships between the clauses and the clausal propositions are sufficiently similar to consider them as near paraphrases. But they are, of course, radically different in terms of lexis and clause construction which suggests that they assume quite different social relationships and therefore 'mean' differently. It is tempting to argue that these differences can be explained purely in terms of 'style' (cf. O'Donnell and Todd, 1980), but the concept of style is too vague to account for the various kinds of selectional processes that have gone into the construction of these letters. We need a fuller descriptive grammar of English which relates forms to functions in a principled and systematic way and which will allow us to account for the way these two letters mean different things at various levels.

A persuasive grammar which attempts to explain this has been developed by Halliday (cf. Halliday, 1994). While it would be impossible to survey this in any detail here, Halliday's account of _register_ is particularly interesting and important to my discussion. Register theory recognises that texts are multilayered in that they perform a variety of functions simultaneously. They are, necessarily, about something, but they also orient themselves to the readers in particular ways, and organise their information in ways appropriate to the medium selected and the contexts in which they occur. In the construction and interpretation of texts we pay attention to the elements in our language which are capable of encoding these various functions, and particular realisations of these three functions determine the register of the text under consideration. Halliday has worked out these ideas in some detail over the years, and developed and changed them slightly. The model I shall be taking as the basis of my analysis is that explained in Halliday and Hasan (1985/9), though I shall refer to other works where appropriate.

Their fundamental claim is that language is multifunctional in at least three respects. It represents the world in that it is referential; it indicates a relationship between text creators and text consumers; and it signals the medium of transmission. The ways in which it can perform these different functions are multifarious, and they overlap to a significant extent. In the first of my examples above the phrase *drop me a line* refers to the specific activity of *writing a letter to someone*. The someone is identified as being an entity in the world through the self-referential deictic *me*. However, the phrase has been selected from a range of alternatives which might include, *correspond with me*, *write to me*, *send me an epistle*, etc. to indicate an intimate relationship between the communicants. Further, the use of punctuation and graphemes indicates the medium of communication although, interestingly, the opening phrase *Hello there* is more likely to be encountered in speech (which again contributes to the sense of intimacy, since it implies face-to-face communication).

Halliday claims that these selections from the ideational (or representational), interpersonal and textual potentials of the language are realised in the field (what the text is doing), tenor[2] (the relationship between the participants) and the mode (the medium of communication), and particular combinations of field, tenor and mode reveal the register of the text. Thus, the register of a text is:

> a semantic concept. It can be defined as a configuration of meanings that are typically associated with a particular situational configuration of field, mode, and tenor. But since it is a configuration of meanings, a register must also, of course, include the expressions, the lexico-grammatical and phonological features, that typically accompany or REALISE these meanings.

> (Halliday and Hasan, 1985/9, p. 39)

Halliday continues by distinguishing between closed and open registers, referring to the coded messages that soldiers were allowed to transmit in the Second World War – a form of 'writing by numbers' in which the number of permitted meanings was highly restricted[3] – through to naturally occurring conversation where the number of meanings that might be transmitted is potentially infinite. Within the context of written language we should, by analogy, be able to identify a similar gradient between texts that are limited in the kinds of selections they make from the registerial potentials available within a given language, and those which are able to select much more freely. Further, by identifying the intersections that occur in different texts, we should be able to establish a typology of text types so that we can assign particular groups of texts to particular registers.

It would be interesting to test these claims by looking at two examples of texts that might reasonably be considered to be examples of closed registers.

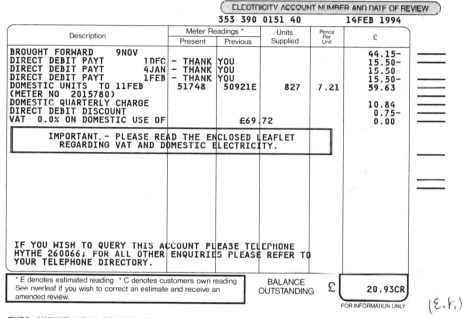

SEEBOARD

For enquiries, please contact your
Seeboard Customer Service Office
at the address below or your
local Seeboard Shop.

Vat Registration No. GB 587 7233 95

MILITARY ROAD
HYTHE KENT, CT21 5DB
☎ 0303 260066 ABOUT THIS ACCOUNT

MINICOM (FOR TEXT ONLY
TELEPHONES) 0303 232515

PLEASE RAISE QUESTIONS OF ACCURACY IMMEDIATELY
Telephone call queueing system in operation - please wait for an answer.
Bring this form with you or, if writing or telephoning, quote:-

ELECTRICITY ACCOUNT NUMBER AND DATE OF REVIEW

353 390 0151 40   14FEB 1994

Description	Meter Readings *		Units Supplied	Pence Per Unit	£
	Present	Previous			
BROUGHT FORWARD 9NOV					44.15-
DIRECT DEBIT PAYT 1DEC	- THANK	YOU			15.50-
DIRECT DEBIT PAYT 4JAN	- THANK	YOU			15.50-
DIRECT DEBIT PAYT 1FEB	- THANK	YOU			15.50-
DOMESTIC UNITS TO 11FEB	51748	50921E	827	7.21	59.63
(METER NO 2015780)					
DOMESTIC QUARTERLY CHARGE					10.84
DIRECT DEBIT DISCOUNT					0.75-
VAT 0.0% ON DOMESTIC USE OF		£69.72			0.00

IMPORTANT. - PLEASE READ THE ENCLOSED LEAFLET
REGARDING VAT AND DOMESTIC ELECTRICITY.

IF YOU WISH TO QUERY THIS ACCOUNT PLEASE TELEPHONE
HYTHE 260066; FOR ALL OTHER ENQUIRIES PLEASE REFER TO
YOUR TELEPHONE DIRECTORY.

* E denotes estimated reading * C denotes customers own reading
See overleaf if you wish to correct an estimate and receive an
amended review.

BALANCE OUTSTANDING £   20.93CR

FOR INFORMATION ONLY

(E.R.)

THIS AMOUNT WILL BE DEDUCTED FROM YOUR NEXT ACCOUNT ** DO NOT PAY

CALCULATION OF MONTHLY PAYMENTS FOLLOWING REVIEW

UNDER THE TERMS OF THE MONTHLY PAYMENT PLAN WE UNDERTOOK TO
REVIEW THE LEVEL OF YOUR PAYMENTS EACH YEAR. OUR REVIEW HAS SHOWN
THAT YOUR MONTHLY PAYMENTS WILL REMAIN UNCHANGED AT THIS TIME.

IF FOR ANY REASON YOU DO NOT AGREE WITH THIS PROPOSAL PLEASE LET
YOUR LOCAL OFFICE KNOW WITHIN TEN DAYS (THE ADDRESS IS SHOWN
ABOVE).

YOU WILL SEE THE TERMS OF THE MONTHLY PAYMENT PLAN OVERLEAF.

Figure 5.1 Invoice from Seeboard

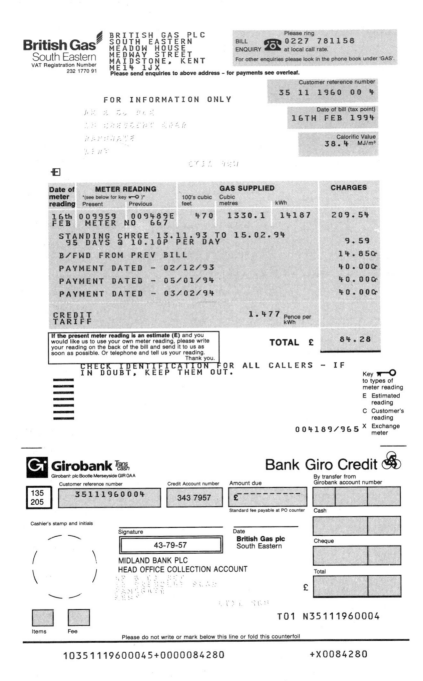

Figure 5.2 Invoice from British Gas

These texts (Figures 5.1 and 5.2) have a considerable number of features in common and they are the kinds of texts that are frequently encountered in our everyday life.[4] However, they are extremely complex, and very difficult to analyse.

MODE

Mode refers to the ways in which specific choices are made at the textual level bearing in mind the channel of communication. It will become apparent that the mere identification of texts as written tells us very little about how the choices available to a writer are actually realised. I have chosen to start my analysis with mode, since the most significant feature of both texts would appear to be the layout of the information on the forms. The top left hand corner, in both cases, carries an identifying name. Seeboard stands out because it has been printed in orange. British Gas is followed by a small logo. Although such elements fall within the realm of mode, it should be clear that this manipulation of textual features has consequences for the interpersonal relationships being constructed. Although the recipients are clearly identified (in a different type face) a little below the company names, there is no suggestion that these invoices issue from an identifiable person. Given that they are completely anonymous with respect to the sender, they become slightly more difficult to challenge on the part of the recipient. This produces asymmetric power relations between sender and receiver and demonstrates that realisations at the level of mode have consequences for the tenor of the communication.

The upper third of both forms also contains a quantity of small print with visual symbols. Perhaps the clearest element in both documents is the list of figures running down the right hand column. The layout has been arranged so that the eyes are immediately attracted to that column (the figures are clearly separated from the rest of the text), and by natural progression, to the figure at the bottom. This, of course, is entirely appropriate because it forces the reader to focus on the principal purpose of the invoice which is to refer to a commercial transaction between company and customer previously entered into by a contract.

Further features of mode that are worth investigating are the varying sizes of print and the different print faces that have been used. The forms have obviously been printed in advance so that the detailed customer information can be entered at a later stage. All the customer information that relates to the particular transaction occurs in upper case letters, and gives the appearance of having been entered from a computer printer. The use of upper case is interesting in that capitals are typically used for emphasis. Whether they are necessarily easier to read than lower case letters is uncertain, but it is a particular device that is commonly used in forms associated with this register. In so far as readers have learned to associate CAPITAL LETTERS with extra significance – and my choice of capitals here is quite deliberately done to encourage the reader to reflect on their significance, and to assess whether my evaluation of their use is correct – they will assume that capitalised text is more important than any co-text which is not capitalised. Further, they will notice this text as input from a machine which further reduces the identification of human agency, thereby making the whole transaction more impersonal.

It is also worth noting that both invoices use particular abbreviations. British Gas's STANDING CHRGE and B/FWD (cf. Seeboard's BROUGHT FORWARD) and Seeboard's DIRECT DEBIT PAYT are presumably employed to save space. These abbreviations are only realisable in the written medium (i.e. they are, as far as I know, *never* spoken), and they are neither particularly commonplace nor easy to interpret. Their presence (and interpretation), therefore, both depends on the context in which they appear, but also contributes to that context in important ways.

It might be argued that some of the features I have identified – and there are many more interesting features which could be scrutinised in a similar way – are more to do with general aspects of semiosis and cannot easily be included in a linguistic analysis of the texts under discussion. For example, it is difficult to decide whether the use of boxes to enclose various units of information should be considered as an aspect of mode, or is more suitably dealt with at some other analytical level. Boxes are certainly an aspect of the semiotic potential of the forms in that they signify in important ways. To the extent that they enclose information that is realised in linguistic form, they constrain interpretation of that language and therefore contribute to the message. However, to the extent that they do not, in themselves, manipulate the linguistic symbols employed, they are probably best seen as an aspect of more general semiosis.

Similar comments can be made about the other symbols employed. The telephone symbols, and the crossed ear, are clearly non-linguistic, although they draw the observers' attention to pieces of text. The reference to MJ/m^3 will be opaque to readers without the accompanying explanation that it is the 'calorific value'. Perhaps it is unnecessary to draw absolute distinctions here since the two elements exist in a symbiotic relationship in that pictorial, mathematical and linguistic symbols have the deictic function of cross-reference.

However, to the extent that such features are realised, or referred to linguistically, they have to be considered as part of the text and in this way, they are quite unlike road signs which typically only employ pictorial symbols. Given that language-as-substance occurs either as speech or writing, the manipulation of written symbols (including punctuation, spacing, colouring, size, etc.) correlates with, but is not identical to, the manipulation of the spoken word through such features as loudness, pauses, intonation, etc. We do not treat such graphological signs simply as aesthetic additions, rather they contribute directly, though possibly unconsciously, to the process of interpretation. They are therefore an integral aspect of the language used and thus contribute to the message.

TENOR

I have commented above on how certain features of the typographical layout contribute to the relationships between sender and receiver that are encoded in these texts. Careful consideration of the wording, however, suggests an uneasy ambiguity. If we concentrate on such features as method of address, forms of politeness and modality, it would seem that there are two slightly different addressees. The first, and the one that most of the black, upper case print is directed towards, is the particular recipient as customer; the second is what I shall call the 'recipient as member of the public'. These two addressees seem to be implied by both invoices, although they are realised in slightly different ways. The Seeboard invoice is addressed to MR & MRS A.R. BEX. This constructs a specific social identity for the two people mentioned as being married, and as being in a relationship in which A.R. BEX takes precedence over the other BEX. I have no way of knowing why Seeboard should make such an assumption, although its effect is to suggest a stable social relationship in which hierarchies and obligations are dutifully met.[5] The left hand column refers to payments made, followed by a polite THANK YOU, although the use of this politeness formula has been undercut in that it has been machine printed.

Other politeness formulae are also ambiguous in that they are typically embedded in directives. In the following example, taken from the Seeboard invoice:

IMPORTANT – PLEASE READ THE ENCLOSED LEAFLET
REGARDING VAT AND DOMESTIC ELECTRICITY

the effect of the PLEASE is negated by the preceding IMPORTANT. Similarly, the foot of the bill has the peremptory instruction DO NOT PAY, while the advice about the monthly payment plan is equally contradictory in tone. The first clause suggests that Seeboard will be undertaking an interactive activity. They 'review' and the customer responds to that review in some way. The ensuing clause contradicts this by suggesting that the customer has no control over the payments. Unpacking this shift in the relationships that are constructed by the text requires quite complicated clausal analysis and again we shall observe that some of the analytical procedures involved in showing how the tenor is realised will focus on elements of linguistic structure which also realise the field of the text. This, though, should not be a cause for surprise since, if field refers to 'what is happening, to the nature of the social action that is taking place: what is it that the participants are engaged in, in which the language figures as some essential component' (Halliday and Hasan, 1985/9, p. 12), then the construction of interpersonal relationships will be part of 'the social action that is taking place'. Although Halliday seems to distinguish between the ideational and interpersonal functions of language fairly sharply, I would suggest that he does so more for procedural purposes than because such functions can be easily separated.

The sentences under analysis can be segmented as follows:

Sentence 1

a) Under the terms of the monthly payment plan
b) we undertook
c) to review
d) the level of your payments
e) each year.

Sentence 2

a) Our review has shown
b) that your monthly payments
c) will remain unchanged
d) at this time.

1a) has the function of supplying essential background information for the reader and contributes to the meanings which will be processed in establishing the clause relations between this and the following clause. In thematising what might be assumed to be a *joint* contract involving monthly payments it is polite, and therefore selects from the interpersonal potential.

1b) has as grammatical subject *we* which identifies the sender. However, as my preceding discussion has demonstrated, the functionaries that this pronoun refers to are unclear. Equally, it is slightly ambiguous in that it could be an inclusive use of *we*, thus reinforcing the suggestion of an agreement entered into jointly.

1c) describes an activity, and is therefore best considered as part of the field.

1d) defines the payments as *your payments*, a usage that is repeated in 2b) *your monthly payments*. One effect of this is that what could have been previously interpreted as a joint activity is being subtly re-defined as something 'we' do to 'you'.

1e) with its time reference is again better dealt with under field.

2a) nominalises the process described in 1c) and therefore depersonalises it to some extent, although the presence of *our* still allows animate involvement. More interestingly though, the customer has been excluded to a greater extent. *Has shown* could be followed by an animate object, *us/ you*. In fact, it is treated as a reporting verb leading to the direct consequence expressed in 2c).

Although the text begins with the assumption that there is an equal partnership between sender and receiver, by a slow process of attrition first the receiver is excluded and then the sender. 'Your monthly payments will remain unchanged at this time' suggests that nobody has any power over this. It may be for this reason that the following sentence allows the receiver back in so politely. The conditional 'if' clause, the scope of 'any' reason, the reformulation of an apparent inexorable chain of events into a 'proposal', and the presence of 'please', all serve to re-establish a more friendly interpersonal tone. Running through this analysis, then, has been the suggestion that the tenor of this communication as addressed to the recipient as customer is highly ambiguous. At times s/he is perceived as a powerless agent, at other times as somebody to be treated politely. And this ambiguity is built into the communicative situation since it is part of our culture both that we should pay as required for services received, and that we should be cajoled into buying more.

The British Gas invoice is organised in a similar manner but contains rather less information. It is therefore more 'user-friendly'. Perhaps the most surprising feature is the machine printing of CHECK IDENTIFICA-TION FOR ALL CALLERS – IF IN DOUBT, KEEP THEM OUT. Whereas all the machine printed material in the Seeboard invoice seems to be specific information related to the particular co-text as invoice, this injunction from British Gas would appear to have a wider application in that it is only marginally related to the rest of the text.

FIELD

Identification of field would seem to be relatively straightforward. The social transaction being conducted is, in both cases, the transmission of information about the consumption of a utility over a given period together with the charge for its consumption. This might seem a circumlocution, in that most people would recognise these examples quite simply as bills or invoices. However, bills are typically statements of what is owed for goods or services received. My Seeboard invoice is clearly in credit, and there is a printed injunction under the balance outstanding: DO NOT PAY. Similarly, although the British Gas invoice shows that I owe them £84.28, the attached Bank Giro Credit has ———— overprinted under the section 'amount due'. Thus to call them 'bills' is slightly misleading unless we recognise that bills occur in a variety of forms and serve a variety of purposes.

Essential similarities can be seen in the headings above each column, although they are by no means identical. The British Gas invoice has clear entries immediately under each heading, whereas the Seeboard invoice has a confusing interruption listing payments before the columns are filled in. These features might be considered as part of the cohesive devices that operate in texts of this kind, and therefore realise the field in so far as they indicate the logical construction of the world being represented. However, since a significant amount of this information is supplied in numerals, it is difficult to analyse in terms of its linguistic properties.

This extended discussion of two rather innocuous documents has been undertaken to demonstrate the kinds of perceptions we bring to our analyses of the most everyday texts. I would agree that most people are so familiar with this kind of text that they do not read them in any detail. More usually, the eye moves straight to the figure at the bottom of the page and ignores the surrounding co-text. Occasionally, however, we do want to query, or to understand more fully, why an invoice has the information it has, and we therefore read it with some attention. It is at this moment that the specific realisations of the functions I have identified, and which contribute to the register of a text, come into play.

Further, it is worth remembering that these texts were constructed by people, and were constructed with quite deliberate purposes in mind. Because of the apparent automaticity of such texts, the presence of a human writer tends to be overlooked. But the writers of such texts, even if they compose them for machines, still have to make detailed choices both about design, typographical layout, address to the presumed readers and the ways of conveying the necessary information. Whether these two texts manage their function in the best way is an open question, but the fact that they are so similar suggests that their writers had a highly conventio-nalised format in mind when they set about the task.

Having said that, it is also clear that the two texts are not identical. They make different selections, albeit from a very narrow band, and these selections are not simply at the informational level – i.e. that one is a gas bill and the other an electricity bill; that the amounts owing are different; that the dates of the invoices are different and cover slightly different periods. There are also differences at the interpersonal level – I have suggested that the British Gas invoice is more 'user-friendly'. At the textual level (i.e. as realising the mode), I have indicated that the texts make different selections from the possible range of abbreviations. It might, therefore, be quite difficult to sustain Halliday's view that there are 'closed' registers. Rather, it would appear that each text can only realise it own register.

Nevertheless, particular texts might realise registers that are so similar we can identify common purposes behind them. However, if this is the case, we shall need to identify a higher level of analysis which groups texts into types and demonstrates what they have in common both in terms of their particular linguistic selections and in terms of their shared social purpose.

REGISTER: TEXT AND CONTEXT

A further claim is that given registers both realise and are constitutive of a context of situation (Halliday and Hasan, 1985/9, p. 45). That is to say, given a particular situation we are, broadly, able to predict the kind of language that will be employed and, conversely, given a particular text we can construct the likely context in which it will have occurred. These claims gain intuitive support from the observation of spoken interaction. For example, certain features such as a raised voice, the issuing of insults, loud overlapping of conversational turns will lead observers to assume that an argument is taking place. Similarly, the participants will generally be able to gauge when a discussion is turning into an argument precisely as such features become more prominent. Thus an argument can be defined *as an argument* precisely because of the selection of such features. Linguistic choices, then, constitute the kind of social activity that is taking place.

However, it is less clear whether written texts are quite so obviously rooted in such contexts of situation. Written texts are usually marked by the absence of the writer. Similarly, writers cannot easily predict the situations in which their texts will be read. Although they may take great care to signal the contexts of situation under which their texts should ideally be interpreted, such signals can only be suggestive rather than determinate.[6] Nevertheless, as I have suggested in the previous chapters, given that language is socially constructed, our knowledge of how language works in particular situations (including our knowledge of how we might use it) serves to constrain, if not determine, interpretation.

If we reconsider the letters quoted above, we can see that the writers have chosen markedly different ways of representing the world through the set of processes and agents involved in such processes (i.e. the ideational selections). They also construct different relationships between the sender and the recipient (i.e. the interpersonal selections); and adopt different ways of rendering the separate parts of these representations coherent with respect to each other (i.e. the textual selections). The representational elements can be rendered schematically as in Figures 5.3 and 5.4.[7]

Although not a particularly full analysis (and I acknowledge that the extracts are not of equal length), these figures show some interesting variations of field at the purely abstract level. Of the five verb forms in Figure 5.4, two refer to relational processes, two to material processes and one to a verbal process. In Figure 5.3, there is only one material process but three existential processes and three mental processes (possibly four if we consider the act of forgiveness essentially as something carried out in the

TEXT 1

SUBJECT	VERB	EXTRA ELEMENTS (1)	EXTRA ELEMENTS (2)
I = identifies one participant	'm = relates next element with initial one	sure = quality	
it = existential or dummy subject	was = existential verb referring to past time	your turn = a nominalised process that also identifies another participant	
	(to) drop = material action	a line = thing as goal	(to) me = participant as beneficiary
I = primary participant	'll forgive = performative verb as behaviour	you = person as goal	
I = (as above)	suspect = mental action as cognition		
you = secondary/ recipient participant	've been = existential verb referring to past time	very busy = action as attribute	
it = dummy subject	is* = existential verb	something = identified thing	
I = as above	've said = verbal action in past		
I = as above	hope not** = mental verb relating to feeling		
(you) = second participant	remember = mental verb relating to cognition	the rarer action = phenomenon involved	

* The question form has been inverted here since it is more to do with the interpersonal relationships established between the participants.
** A fuller analysis would indicate the negative polarity of this clause.

Figure 5.3 A schematic representation of Text 1

TEXT 2

SUBJECT	VERB	OTHER ELEMENTS (1)	OTHER ELEMENTS (2)
We = identifies one set of participants	are = relational verb, present tense	pleased = value	
	(to) advise = verbal process as report	you = identification of other participant(s)	
the annual inopootion check of your CENTRAL HEATING BOILER = participant as object	is = relational vorb	now due = attributo in tho present	
we = identification of participant	have arranged = material action in present		
our engineer = Identlflcatlon of further participant	(to) call = material action in the future	on 11th March 1994 = circumstance in which the action will take place	before 1.00 pm = further circumstanco in which the action will take place

Figure 5.4 A schematic representation of Text 2

mind of the forgiver). Further, the participants referred to in Text 1 as performing these processes are 'I' (five times) and 'you' (twice). Text 2, however, identifies 'we' twice, a further animate participant and a heavily nominalised activity. The text worlds constructed are therefore differentiated in that Text 1 seems to be primarily about the conveyance of feelings and ideas experienced by a particular participant, Text 2 is more concerned with material actions. This impression will be further confirmed if we analyse the noun phrases (NPs) used. The majority of NPs in Text 1 are pronouns with deictic reference to the participants in the exchange. Only four make reference to things, and one of these is realised by a general noun 'something', while another is part of an idiomatic phrase and is therefore obligatory in context: 'drop me *a line*'. Text 2, on the other hand, contains reference to two other participants one of which is realised by a complex NP containing a nominalised process (the annual inspection check = someone checks your boiler annually).

If we look at the verb phrases, we can observe a wide range of different processes in Text 1, while those in Text 2 seem more limited. Of course, to describe a verb as referring to a 'process-type' makes no prediction as to which particular verb has been chosen. Had Text 1 had, in place of *drop me a line*, *write me a letter*, the description of the two forms at the level of field would have been the same. However, these alternatives have effects on the tenor. Since the former is more informal, it indicates a more intimate relationship between the addressees.

If tenor is realised by the interpersonal potentials of the language, then it is important also to recover the forms of greeting used in these two texts. In Text 1, 'Dear Tony and Jane' contrasts with Text 2's 'Dear Mr A. Bex'. The selection of first names clearly implies a reasonably close relationship (although whether such an implication can be sustained will depend in part on the selections made in the co-text). 'Dear Mr A. Bex' is, to this reader at least, a slightly odd construction. The evident formality of supplying a title is slightly undercut by adding an initial. It could be argued that this is an element of mode which applies to the conventions of letter writing, but such conventions are themselves realised by particular linguistic selections which have an effect on the tenor of a text.

The subsequent phrases are interesting. Text 2 announces what the letter is about – to that extent it is a feature of field. However, the manner of announcement as a heading to the rest of the letter clearly establishes a formality of tone that is maintained throughout the letter. Tenor is typically realised through means of modality, and it is interesting to notice that the majority of the clauses in both texts operate as relatively simple statements. Text 1 shifts its modality between clauses to some extent. The choice of the adjective 'sure' suggests epistemic certainty, but this is followed by 'suspect' which carries overtones of epistemic doubt. Broadly speaking, though, we could claim that the attitudes toward the messages, and the ways in which these attitudes are conveyed, are mediated in rather similar ways. However, there are some interesting lexical choices which also operate to establish relationships between addressee and addresser. The selection of the set phrase 'We are pleased to advise you' contains an expression of politeness, 'pleased', followed by a non-finite performative verb which carries a number of potential functions ranging from warning: 'I advise you not to do that' through to a simple informing function. In this case, given that a particular relationship has been established already, and given that the recipient knows that it is a stock phrase used in business letters, it would seem to be primarily a focusing device.

Text 1, on the other hand, maintains its level of intimacy with the greeting 'Hello, there'. Although, as I have commented above, this might seem a more appropriate form for a spoken greeting, it establishes a conversational tone which is maintained throughout the text by such features as verb contractions (again, typically associated with speech, and noticeably absent in Text 2), and idiomatic expressions.[8] The one phrase that is apparently inconsistent with this analysis is 'Remember the rarer action'. However, once this has been identified as a quotation that is presumed to be familiar to the recipients, the element of intimacy is re-established.

Thus far, we have established marked dissimilarities in terms of register both at the level of field and at the level of tenor. In terms of mode, they might at first sight appear to be fairly similar. Their medium is identical. In the original, both were typed although Text 1 was typed on a less expensive machine than Text 2. Their layouts were remarkably similar, as were the spaces between the initial greeting and the subsequent co-text. Given that I have already commented on the function of the heading in Text 2, I shall make no further comment here, although it can usefully be analysed under mode as well. Thus it would seem that mode is the primary identifying feature of letters, and we would have to reject the notion of a 'register of letters' for the same kinds of reason that we rejected the notion of a 'register of invoices'. We could choose to re-classify them as examples of the registers of friendship and of business (cf. Matthiessen, 1993, p. 274), but we are then presented with other kinds of problems. Friendship and business are carried on through a variety of linguistic practices which operate in quite different contexts of situation. If, though, we recognise that registers are *particular* configurations of field, tenor and mode, we have an apparent solution since we could argue that whereas the field and tenor manifestly differ, the mode is remarkably similar. Thus, we could claim that there is a register of personal letters and a register of business letters each of which is realised within these two example texts.

This is a neat solution but difficult to sustain, partly because of the indeterminate nature of the term 'mode'. Halliday argues that mode

> refers to what part the language is playing, what it is the participants are expecting the language to do for them in that situation: the symbolic organisation of the text, the status that it has, and its function in the context, including the channel . . . and also the rhetorical mode, what is being achieved by the text in terms of such categories as persuasive, expository, didactic, and the like.
>
> (Halliday and Hasan, 1985/9, p. 12)

As stated, this seems rather a ragbag of categories and overlaps quite considerably with features of field which 'refers to what is happening, to the nature of the social action that is taking place' (ibid.) and tenor which 'refers to who is taking part, to the nature of the participants, their statuses and roles' (ibid.). It is difficult to see what clear dividing lines there might be between 'what part the language is playing' (mode); 'what is happening' (field); and 'the nature of the participants, their statuses and roles' (tenor). Equally, it is quite unclear how the concept of 'rhetorical mode' is to be defined and whether it should be clearly differentiated from the other features of mode so described.

In fact, the whole concept of register is somewhat undefined and has given rise to a variety of different interpretations both as to the status of the different categories and the elements which should be included under each one. Butler has commented that

> much of what Halliday claims in his most recent work rests on our acceptance of the validity of the field/tenor/mode distinction and the functional components hypothesis. Because of lack of rigour in giving criteria, we cannot be sure of the validity of either.
>
> (1985, p. 88)

There is little evidence that Halliday has clarified his position in the ten years since this statement was made, although a number of Hallidayans have made significant contributions to the debate.[9] In this chapter I have tended to use mode in two slightly different ways. The first of these refers to the (visible) forms which may be deemed appropriate in one kind of writing but not in another. For example, contractions and abbreviations clearly 'stand for' full grammatical and lexical forms, but their use varies quite considerably across different texts. By extension, all other visible features of written language which contribute to the meanings of a text are also included under this head (e.g. the specific layouts of letters, poetic stanzas, timetables; features of typography; handwriting versus printing, etc.) including punctuation which self-evidently is an important indicator as to the ways in which phrases and clauses are related.

However, even with this more limited definition of mode, it remains unclear whether register analysis is more than a very useful tool for establishing how specific texts manage to achieve meaning. The claims that are sometimes advanced (cf. Halliday, 1978) that texts can belong to a register seem fundamentally misconceived since the way in which register has been conceptualised suggests that it can only relate individual texts to their contexts of production and reception. As we have seen above, even the two invoices differ in significant ways and the two letters are so different that register analysis fails to capture what they may have in common *as letters*.

CONCLUSION

In this chapter I have looked at some of the resources that writers have at their disposal to construct messages that are both cohesive and coherent. Cohesion concerns the ways in which texts can refer to themselves and is typically achieved through the use of grammatical devices. However, another important cohesive element is lexical repetition. This is achieved in a variety of ways but Hoey has demonstrated convincingly that non-narrative extended texts show characteristic 'clusterings' of lexical elements. Coherence is a property that is not in the texts themselves, but is signalled by texts. Writers try to construct texts which are coherent in respect of themselves by signalling the ways in which their clauses may be related, and which are coherent within a given context of interpretation. Context here refers both to the circumstances in which the text is to be read, and to the people who are intended to read it. One theory which has tried to describe how this coherence is achieved is register theory. Register theory has sometimes been used as a means of establishing a typology of texts, so texts can be said to 'belong' to a register. By analysing four different texts using a simplified model of register theory, it appeared that the theory was very successful in showing how particular local coherence was achieved, but was less satisfactory in showing how or why similar texts are perceived as performing similar functions and are therefore treated as the same kind of text. Part of this failure was because of a lack of clarity in defining certain key concepts, but part of it resided in the nature of the theory itself since if a particular register is a configuration of field, tenor and mode, then no two texts will ever manifest the same configuration. Register analysis, then, can only explain how a particular text achieves meaning in a given context and cannot, in itself, show how texts are related. For this we need a more general analytic category.

FURTHER READING

Many of the ideas that have been developed in this chapter are dealt with in various ways by the authors I mentioned in the 'Further reading' section of the last chapter. Halliday and Hasan's *Cohesion in English* (1976) is a comprehensive list of the kinds of cohesion that may be present in a text. At times, though it reads more like a descriptive taxonomy than a full theory of how cohesion works. Their description of lexical cohesion is always interesting, but they founder on the rock of collocation. While it is undoubtedly true that we do feel that words share semantic fields and are therefore likely to co-occur in predictable clusters, the size of the fields and the nature of the clustering can only be mapped by large-scale computer analysis. Such analysis is beginning to bear fruit and readers are advised to consult Sinclair's *Corpus, Concordance, Collocation* (1991) for an introduction to this kind of work. Also relevant to this area, if only tangentially, is Carter's *Vocabulary* (1987b). I have referred to Hoey in some detail and his *Patterns of Lexis in Text* (1991b) is a clearly written account of his research. Although lexical clustering clearly does contribute to the structure of a text, lexical elements undergo subtle shifts of meaning with each reappearance. This point is mentioned by Halliday and Hasan, but a fascinating study of such changes in scientific texts occurs in Phillips's (1988) 'Texts, terms and meanings'.

The concept of register is particularly associated with Halliday and readers are advised to consult Halliday's (1978) *Language as Social Semiotic* for a clear exposition of what he intends by the term and/or the more recent Halliday and Hasan (1985/9) *Language, Context and Text*. Others working in the same tradition have refined the theory in various ways and shown how it might be applied. Two useful collections of papers are Ghadessy's (1988) *Registers of Written English* and his (1993) *Register Analysis: Theory and Practice*. The latter contains a slightly sceptical view by de Beaugrande: '"Register" in discourse studies: a concept in search of a theory.'

SOME QUESTIONS FOR CONSIDERATION

Sole

With such a superb fish, it is important not to get your 'soles' mixed up. Dover sole is the true sole and is not related to lemon sole, which isn't! It has a most wonderful flavour and needs little in the way of added ingredients. Dover sole is unusual among flat fish in that its flavour intensifies and is at its best when the fish is two or three days old.

(Susan Hicks, *The Fish Course*, London: BBC, p. 156)

1 In this passage what kinds of cohesion can you identify?
2 Do you notice any lexical repetition?
3 How would you describe the cohesion of 'fish', 'dover sole' and 'lemon sole'?
4 What coherence relations exist between the first two sentences?
5 In sentence 3, 'It' could refer anaphorically to *either* 'dover sole' *or* 'lemon sole'. Which of the two do you think it does refer to and why?
6 What kind of book do you think this extract comes from and what consequences does this have for the kinds of coherence relations it has both with itself and with its potential readers?
7 How would you describe its attitude to its readers, and what evidence can you find to support your views?

Chapter 6

Interpreting the language

INTRODUCTION

In the preceding chapter I concentrated on the resources available within the language which enabled writers to construct texts that were cohesive and coherent. I argued that cohesion was largely a textual property whereas coherence was something that had to be assumed by writers. Nevertheless, writers could construct messages with the reasonable expectation that readers would identify and interpret the linguistic signs in the ways they had intended. For example, where two sentences co-exist readers would judge that they were meant to be related in some way even if that relationship were not overtly signalled. Lexical choice and the coherence relations between sentences would tend to establish what the text was about and how writers were approaching this 'aboutness'. However, texts typically are intended to convey messages within particular social and physical spaces, therefore a fuller theory was needed to show how writers could signal these kinds of relationships. I considered register theory in some detail because it seemed most adequate to this task. However, I noted a lack of clarity in the use of key terms, particularly mode. Nevertheless, when applied to any particular text a registerial analysis does seem to capture the motivations behind different writers' selections from the lexicogrammatical range of English. However, because each text is a unique intervention into a continuing communicative activity, register theory can really only show how individual texts create a social space for themselves. If we want to account for the ways in which texts are perceived to be of the same kind in that they are fulfilling similar social purposes, we need a higher level of analysis.

When I refer to texts being used for the same kind of communicative activity, I am necessarily talking about reader perceptions. Writers cannot force their readers to interpret their work in given ways, so it is now time to consider the processes involved when readers confront a text and construct their interpretations of it.

THE COOPERATIVE PRINCIPLE

A recent and convincing theory of interpretation has been developed by Sperber and Wilson (1986) and is called Relevance theory. This theory was originally developed from work done by Paul Grice, who was interested in the ways in which interlocutors were able to develop agreed meanings from language that was often indirect. Grice suggested that conversationalists typically acted cooperatively, and their cooperation could be represented by positing four principles which 'participants will be expected to observe' (Grice [1968] in Davis, 1991, p. 307). These he referred to as the four maxims of quantity, quality, relation and manner.

The maxim of quantity requires interactants to provide as much, and no more information, than is needed for the purposes of the exchange; the maxim of quality enjoined interactants to be truthful by supplying only such information as they had adequate evidence for; the maxim of relation obliged interactants to be relevant; while the maxim of manner referred to the need to 'be perspicuous' by being brief, avoiding ambiguity and obscurity and constructing expressions in an orderly manner. Of course, Grice was well aware that conversationalists did not necessarily abide by these maxims. People can lie, or can quarrel. But he argued that by assuming some such contractual arrangement, a great deal could be learned about how we construct meanings on those occasions when the maxims were deliberately exploited.

His central claim is that the *flouting* of a maxim (except in those cases when a conversationalist sets out to mislead, or when two maxims clash) will be recognised by the interlocutor so that s/he will make an extra processing effort to establish the additional meanings implied (and intended) by the speaker. These additional meanings arise from a set of formal derivations that Grice called *conversational implicatures*. The significant feature of Grice's formulation was that it helped describe the kinds of inferencing processes that typically take place in all conversational interaction. Furthermore, it formalised these processes in a way that related them quite specifically to linguistic behaviour. The point about conversational implicatures was that they could be distinguished from other kinds of implications 'that are inferred solely from logical or semantic content' (Levinson, 1983, pp. 103–4).

Grice demonstrates the kinds of implicatures that might be derived from exchanges that can be assumed to be observing the maxims by considering the exchange (Grice, [1968] 1991, p. 310):

A: I am out of petrol.
B: There is a garage round the corner.

A has every reason to believe that B is being as informative as is required and that the information is based on sufficient evidence. Clearly the response is brief. Thus three of the maxims of cooperation have been (to all apparent purposes) fulfilled. Assuming that the maxim of relation is also being observed, then A has every reason to infer that the garage is a filling station with petrol for sale, and not a car repair depot. This conclusion is said to be implicated by the response since it is not explicitly stated. Levinson refers to this kind of implicature as a *standard implicature* (Levinson, 1983, p. 104) since there is no reason to believe that any of the maxims have been flouted although it is self-evident that the response was an indirect one.

Grice's claim that such implicatures are 'conversational' rather than 'conventional' depends on his argument that such implicatures are attached to the particular conversational exchange. That is that they are *defeasible, non-detachable*, and *calculable*. By defeasible, he means that the implicature (which is constructed by the addressee) can be denied by the speaker. In the above example, then, it is open to B to cancel the implicature by adding that the garage is closed.[1] This is quite unlike a logical implication which cannot be similarly cancelled. By non-detachable, he means that the implicature is attached to the moment of utterance and is not part of the semantic meaning of the sentence. Had A said 'My car has broken down', B could have offered the same response, although here the implicature derived would be that the garage repaired cars whether or not it also sold petrol. Third, it is calculable in that the inferencing sequence which leads A to assume that s/he can obtain more petrol can be demonstrated.

Grice further developed his ideas so as to show how the deliberate flouting of the maxims could be used to produce 'a conversational implicature by means of something of the nature of a figure of speech' (Grice, [1968] 1991, p. 311). In this section of his argument, he is particularly interested in the ways in which listeners may derive inferences which are quite far removed from the semantic meanings of the sentences uttered, considering such tropes as irony, metaphor, tautology, etc.

There are particular problems with Grice's work which are of immediate concern. The first of these I have already mentioned. It is not at all clear that the canonical situation of conversational exchanges is always cooperative. Frequently, conversationalists are in unequal relationships such that one speaker wishes to impose interpretations on another. In such cases, it always possible for the weaker partner to develop two concurrent sets of inferences from the exchange: that which s/he assumes that stronger partner wishes to impose and that which s/he derives from the unequal relationship: e.g. that the partner is trying to argue him/her into a corner. This is not a trivial objection since such inferences may well be drawn according to the same kinds of principles that Grice adduces in support of the Cooperative Principle. Given that the implicatures are non-detachable from the utterance, then particular choice of lexis, or complex syntactic structures may give rise to implicatures that are not those necessarily intended by the speaker.

In spoken interaction, implicatures can be stated overtly by the addressee and therefore cancelled (where appropriate) by the speaker. This is not possible with written texts. (Although writers can, of course, judge a range of possible implicatures and cancel them by using some kind of disclaimer such as 'Though this seems to suggest . . . , nevertheless . . .'.) Thus, it would seem that written texts may well give rise to a range of implicatures that were not intended by their writers. This might be more likely with certain kinds of texts. Academic textbooks are a case in point in that their 'dense' style and use of complex syntactic structures may lead to a range of unintended implicatures. Consider, for example, Fairclough's introduction to his book, *Language and Power* (1989, p. 4): 'My aim has been to write a book which is accessible to students and teachers in higher education, but also to a variety of people in other spheres . . .' Here he seems to be accepting implicitly that there are degrees of accessibility and that some textbooks are (un)necessarily obscure in the ways I have outlined. However, one possible implicature that may be derived from this utterance is that Fairclough is 'writing down'. Such an implicature follows the Gricean rules of defeasibility, non-detachability and calculability. Conversely, other textbooks may signal (to some readers) that they are primarily designed to demonstrate the superiority of their authors. When readers come to this conclusion, it is by a process of inference which derives entirely from the utterances within the text. The conclusion may, therefore, be regarded as an implicated conclusion of the same type as other implicated conclusions.

In fact, I doubt whether Grice would regard this as consonant with his theory, and there are genuine problems with the way I have posed it. It could be argued that such a conclusion refers to the 'manner of saying' rather than the 'content', but I shall be arguing later that these are not so easily separable as may appear, and that a reaction to a way of saying will have corresponding effects on the interpretation of what has been said.[2]

A second problem, mentioned by Sperber and Wilson (1986, p. 37), concerns the issue of calculability. Although it is frequently possible to calculate how a particular interpretation has been reached, there is nothing in the theory which predicts why that interpretation, rather than any other which might have been selected using the same principles, was the one chosen at that particular moment. In other words, calculability is not only *ad hoc* (which is allowed by the theory), but is also always *post hoc*. Although there is some dispute about the role of prediction in pragmatic theory (cf. Chametsky, 1992), Grice is certainly not able to show how a given interpretation *must* occur in a given situation.

A third problem relates to the maxim of relation. Grice admits that relevance is a particularly difficult concept to define, and Levinson points out that almost any contribution to an exchange might be perceived by some interactants as relevant (Levinson, 1983, p. 111).

Underlying each one of these particular problems is the more general problem of mutual knowledge. Levinson (ibid., p. 102) has commented that the Cooperative Principle 'may describe a philosopher's paradise'. This, in fact, does seem to be the case, but not merely because conversationalists do not always follow the maxims. Indeed, Grice does not assume that they do. The paradise that Grice has unwittingly constructed is of a world in which conversationalists not only behave predictably for most of the time (e.g. when they are not lying, etc.), but have access to the same information at the same time. There seems to be the underlying assumption that what is relevant to speaker A will also be relevant to speaker B; that what is offered by speaker B as an utterance which is intended to have *n* implicatures will have just those implicatures for speaker A and no others; and that both speakers have access to the same kinds of knowledge and the same ways of representing such knowledge in language.

RELEVANCE

It was this problem that Sperber and Wilson investigated more fully in their ground-breaking book *Relevance Theory* (1986). Although they built on Grice's work in significant ways and, in particular, developed the theory of conversational implicature, they first had to base their work in a coherent theory of communication. The interesting difference between Grice's work and that of Sperber and Wilson's was that whereas the former assumed that conversationalists were essentially cooperative, the latter seem to suggest that they are fundamentally selfish. Interpretation, for Sperber and Wilson, is typically seen as a cognitive activity performed by the listeners for their own benefit. I shall come back to this later because it has important implications for the study of discourse as a socially constructed mode of behaviour, but much of what they say is very persuasive.

Sperber and Wilson locate verbal communication within a more general theory that assumes all ostensive acts of communication are produced with the intention of having some effect on their audience. In other words, we do not communicate involuntarily. This is not the same thing as claiming that we do not observe involuntary actions and treat them as acts of communication. Clearly we do. However, such acts are not under the control of the producer and are therefore not *intended* to be communicative. Sperber and Wilson identify linguistic communication as a special type of ostensive communication. Ostensive communication may occur in a number of different forms, e.g. by pointing, by waving, the use of traffic lights or fire alarms, etc. Many of these acts partake of the nature of a code in that their interpretation is both restricted and conventional.[3] Verbal communication, however, is not carried out by means of a code since language does not have a one-to-one relationship either to the objects it refers to, or to the propositions that are being made about such referents. Rather, a linguistic message is an incomplete representation of a speaker's thoughts that needs to be fleshed out by the hearer.

Such thoughts can never be recovered in their entirety, simply because speakers and hearers do not share mutual knowledge. Indeed, Sperber and Wilson establish that the notion of mutual knowledge is a logical impossibility within any theory of communication both because it can never be demonstrated and because the attempt to demonstrate it leads to infinite regress. However, if speakers do not possess mutual knowledge, they must share some common ground if communication is to be successful. This common ground is described as a shared cognitive environment in which various assumptions may be made mutually manifest.

The concept of a shared cognitive environment is importantly different from shared knowledge. As Sperber and Wilson argue:

> The total shared cognitive environment of two people is the intersection of their two total cognitive environments: i.e., the set of all facts that are manifest to them both. Clearly, if people share cognitive environments, it is because they share physical environments and have similar cognitive abilities. Since physical environments are never strictly identical, and since cognitive abilities are affected by previously memorised information and thus differ in many respects from one person to another, people never share their total cognitive environments. Moreover, to say that two people share a cognitive environment does not imply that they make the same assumptions: merely that they are capable of doing so.
>
> (1986, p. 41)

It is this intersection of environments that is crucial to the theory of relevance, and it is likely to have particular repercussions when we come to consider the role of written texts as acts of communication precisely because the degree of intersection between writer and reader is likely to be significantly reduced. In particular, writers cannot assume shared physical environment and will therefore have to modify their use of deixis, but even more importantly, they can neither check, nor respond to checks, as to how their contribution is being received (i.e. to what extent a shared cognitive environment is being maintained) which has a corresponding effect on the ways in which they construct their texts so as to maintain a 'text world' which can be subsequently situated in the phenomenal world of the reader.

In the canonical dyadic situation which Sperber and Wilson use to illustrate their theories, two people may be said to share a cognitive environment to the extent that a given set of assumptions are manifest to both. Thus, if I were sitting in the garden with my partner, various physical features of the garden would (probably) be manifest to each of us, although we might entertain completely different assumptions. Where she might be receiving pleasure from the scents and colours, I might be irritated at the prospect of mowing and watering. The intersection of cognitive environments in this case would be minimal. Following Sperber and Wilson's example, if we were sitting close to each other and the phone were to ring, it would be manifest to me that the phone was ringing, it would be manifest to my partner that the phone was ringing, and it would be manifest to both of us that it was manifest to both of us that the phone was ringing. Thus, the ringing of the phone would be mutually manifest (Sperber and Wilson, 1986, p. 42). Mutual manifestness is an important element within Sperber and Wilson's theory, since it underpins two central elements within their theory. First, the act of speaking (or writing) makes mutually manifest some communicative intention; and second, what is said (or written) makes mutually manifest a set of assumptions.

I have suggested that, while sitting in the garden, I am entertaining a set of assumptions. This requires some clarification since the set of assumptions that I am holding will not be of equal strength and some of them will be below the level of consciousness. Given that it is not raining, I will entertain the assumption that it is not raining, although such an assumption may not be manifest to me at the time. By the same token, such unlikely assumptions as that we are not involved in a nuclear war, or that the sea has not flooded the garden, are also available for recall should the occasion arise. Sperber and Wilson, therefore, seem to suggest that the range of assumptions that are possible for human beings are equivalent to their total knowledge of the universe, whereas the range of assumptions that are manifest are those that are actually held in consciousness at a particular moment. When an act of communication occurs, manifest assumptions are likely to be altered in significant ways. New assumptions may be brought to mind which either confirm or deny existing assumptions, or existing assumptions may be strengthened and therefore become more salient. The ringing of the telephone, in my example above, would have the effect of cancelling the (unconscious) assumption that the telephone was not ringing while making manifest the assumption that the telephone, in fact, is ringing. Similarly, if my partner were to turn to me and comment that the grass needed cutting, then that assumption that I already hold relatively weakly would be strengthened.

I have commented above that Sperber and Wilson claim speech is necessarily an incomplete representation of a speaker's thoughts. It follows from this that speakers cannot make their own assumptions directly observable for hearer interpretation. All they can do is provide a stimulus which will have an effect on listeners' existing assumptions. I shall discuss the ways in which language may supply clues to the likely set of assumptions that are being made manifest by a speaker later. At this stage, we need to consider in slightly greater detail the immediate role of speech in verbal communication. Sperber and Wilson (1986, p. 49) claim that speech is a particular form of ostensive communication that comes with a guarantee of relevance. The claim here is quite simple: people do not speak unless they assume that what they have to say will have some effect on (will be relevant to) their audience. This is an underlying principle. Conversely, audiences assume that what is said to them will be relevant *in some way or another*. Thus, when somebody speaks to me two assumptions are made immediately manifest: 1) that somebody is speaking; and 2) that their speech is in some way relevant to me.

It will be apparent from this that the computation of relevance depends entirely on the audience. Speakers cannot know for sure what is present in listeners' minds, nor can they represent their own thoughts directly, therefore they cannot guarantee the relevance of what they are saying. However, it is reasonable to assume that they would not start speaking unless they assumed that what they had to say would be relevant.

However, if the assumption of relevance is an intrinsic feature of verbal communication, it needs to be shown how listeners assign relevance to what they hear. I have explained above that our cognitive environments are made up of a range of assumptions held with different strengths. This environment may usefully be described as the context within which verbal communication is processed. Relevance is achieved through alterations to this context by making manifest new assumptions or influencing the strengths with which existing assumptions are held. Sperber and Wilson, therefore, define relevance as a set of assumptions which have contextual effects within a given context (1986, p. 122). They further refine this definition by developing the notion of *optimal* relevance in the following way:

a) The set of assumptions {*I*} which the communicator intends to make manifest to the addressee is relevant enough to make it worth the addressee's while to process the ostensive stimuli.
b) The ostensive stimulus is the most relevant one the communicator could have used to communicate {*I*}.

which leads them to the principle of relevance, which is that 'every act of ostensive communication communicates the presumption of its own optimal relevance' (ibid., p. 158).

This is an interesting formulation in that it accounts, in part, for the roles in the speaker–hearer dyad. Speakers are typically assumed to be finding the most appropriate ways in which to transmit their assumptions, while hearers assume that what they are being told will be optimally relevant to them. Although this has overlaps with Grice's view of the Cooperative Principle, it is significantly different in important ways. In particular, it does not assume that conversationalists are necessarily being cooperative (although they may be), since the principle of relevance will apply even in non-cooperative exchanges. Further, it does not assume that speakers know and follow the set of maxims identified by Grice (or any other set that may be postulated by other theorists) since the principle of relevance 'is a generalisation about ostensive–inferential communication . . . [which] . . . applies without exception'. Further, 'Communicators do not "follow" the principle of relevance; and they could not violate it even if they wanted to' (ibid., p. 162).

There is something slightly worrying about this claim since it renders the theory essentially unprovable and therefore vacuous. The force of this axiom seems to lead to the conclusion that any act which fails to be relevant to any of its observers is, by definition, not a communicative act. While understanding why Sperber and Wilson wish to cast their net so wide, it leaves certain kinds of texts (and particularly written texts) in an ambiguous state. Private diaries, which are intended to have as their sole audience their writers, just manage to preserve their status as ostensive–inferential communication, as do those kinds of texts which are written to be ignored (Hickey, 1992). The kinds of graffiti found scrawled on bus shelters are less obviously captured by Sperber and Wilson's characterisation since they may have been produced with no obvious communicative intention, and may lead to no contextual effects in their readers' cognitive environments. Nevertheless, they have all the apparent hallmarks of verbal (and here 'verbal' refers to writing as well as speaking) utterances and might therefore be considered to be examples of ostensive–inferential communication.[4]

Where Sperber and Wilson are convincing is in their development of Grice's notion of conversational implicature. They point out that Grice seems to assume that it is possible to distinguish between explicit speaker meaning and those forms of verbal indirection which lead hearers to assume that there is some (calculable) additional meaning. Explicit speaker meaning may be regarded as the thoughts of the speaker encoded directly into language. Sperber and Wilson argue that the code model of communication is quite simply impossible. Although language can represent the assumptions of a speaker, it can only represent them incompletely. This is not the same as arguing that language is not, to some extent, a code. It is, however, a code which provides clues as to the speakers' meanings rather than full representations of them:

> Verbal communication is a complex form of communication. Linguistic coding and decoding is involved, but the linguistic meaning of an uttered sentence falls short of encoding what the speaker means: it merely helps the audience infer what she means.
>
> (Sperber and Wilson, 1986, p. 27)

It remains to be seen, then, the extent to which language is capable of encoding information and the kinds of inferencing procedures which audiences typically engage in when interpreting utterances.

Answers to these questions depend in part on the characterisation of the mind. Sperber and Wilson adopt a modular view derived from Fodor (1983) in which there are input systems which process incoming data and convert them into conceptual representations and central systems which integrate these conceptual representations. To achieve such integration, conceptual representations need to possess logical properties which enable them to be compared with each other according to the same criteria. Typically, then, to convert an utterance into a conceptual representation requires the recovery of the proposition (and any attitudes to that proposition) expressed by the utterance together with its logical form. Thus, to adapt an example from Sperber and Wilson (1986, p. 73), the utterance

1 She may have carried it in her hand

enters into a logical relationship with the following sentence:

2 She may have held something in her hand (by implication)

and, under given circumstances, express the proposition that:

3 Jane (at some time specified in the past) carried a cat in Jane's hand

but with the speaker's attitude towards this proposition being now deleted.

The recovery of logical forms, propositions and attitudes is not a straightforward matter since they are not always directly encoded in the language.[5] But if the utterance is to be converted into a conceptual representation of what the listener thinks the speaker meant such recovery is necessary, and it is carried out by means of pragmatic inferencing.

Such inferencing is pragmatic because it will be affected by the set of assumptions that are currently held by the hearer. The recovery of 'cat' as the anaphoric co-referent for 'it' depends entirely on the physical circumstances in which the utterance took place, or on what has previously been said, and the set of assumptions that these have given rise to. So, even if the speaker had been suffering from a cold, and pronounced the word 'cad', the listener would still have recovered 'cat' if there were sufficient clues to suggest feline animal rather than human male animal.

In the interpretation of utterances, then, a considerable amount of pragmatic inferencing is required. I have indicated that listeners assign logical form, fill out incomplete propositions and identify speaker attitude. They also assign reference and resolve lexical ambiguity. If I come across a note on the table asking:

4 Get some bread from the bank

I engage in a complex process of disambiguation which involves knowing that 'bread' is a 1960s slang term for 'money'; that money is held by financial institutions and not at the side of rivers. I supply a referent for '*the* bank' rather than assuming that I can get money from any bank; and I interpret 'some' as referring to a given amount. I also identify the imperative as a request to make the proposition 'I have money' a true proposition (in the immediate future); and assign it an appropriate logical form such that the assumption I now entertain can enter into logical relationships with other assumptions I may hold.

This description of the processes I may go through to construct an interpretation of this text, however, fails to explain why I should arrive at just this interpretation and not the myriad of others that may be derivable from the same utterance. As with Grice's theory, this would seem to be a *post hoc* explanation. Sperber and Wilson deal with this issue under the principle of economy of processing effort. They argue that interpretation is assigned when the contextual effects achieved by entertaining the new assumptions inferred on the basis of the linguistic signals are consistent with the underlying principle that the communicator intends such assumptions to be relevant. In the example given above, I could entertain a range of assumptions (and, in fact, did so in describing the process of disambiguation). However, the assumption that the instruction might refer to some time next year, although not specifically excluded from my reading, is not consistent with my assumption that the message is intended to be relevant to me at the moment I read it. Equally, I could entertain such assumptions as that banks are only open from 9:30 to 4:30 on weekdays, that they are closed on bank holidays, that I will need a chequebook and possibly a cheque card, and some of these may actually be entertained weakly, but the effort of processing such assumptions contradicts the assumption of *optimal* relevance (Sperber and Wilson, 1986, pp. 167–71).

To summarise: as a reader, I identify linguistic signals. In the act of reading them, I presume that they are intended to be relevant in that they represent a set of assumptions that the writer wishes to make manifest to a(n) (particular) audience. Given that I cannot recover the assumptions directly held by the writer,[6] I treat the linguistic signs as clues to her assumptions. Nevertheless, they can only affect the assumptions that I hold. Thus they are relevant to me to the extent that they have some contextual effects on my assumptions. Given that they could, in principle, have an infinite number of effects on my assumptions, I select precisely that interpretation which has the most immediate and salient effects.

Certain extremely important consequences follow from this view of verbal communication. The first is that speakers can never be strictly relevant in the *non-technical* sense of the word. In the construction of a verbal message, all they can do is to produce a set of utterances which, to a greater or lesser extent, they assume will communicate a given range of assumptions to their audience. The second consequence follows from the first. The assignment of relevance is undertaken exclusively by the audience, and will occur as a result of the modifications of existing assumptions that are triggered by the new assumptions entertained as a consequence of the utterance. A third consequence is that a particular utterance is unlikely to lead to the same kinds of contextual effects in different hearers. In fact, given the way Sperber and Wilson have formulated their theory, it is logically impossible for two people to interpret utterances in identical ways.

If we wish to reinsert this theory of communication into a more socially based theory (and it should be obvious that Sperber and Wilson's theory is posited on a type of individualism in which minds are forever solipsistically enclosed), we need to understand more fully how utterances are constructed both from the formal constituents of a language and how they are interpreted according to a supposed set of social norms. Sperber and Wilson's theory of language is not always fully explicit, although they do go further than Grice. They suggest that there is a level at which the formal properties of language are processed in the interpretation of utterances, and these formal properties are realised by features of the grammar and semantics of all natural languages. However, they argue that formal operations will not, on their own, lead to interpretations of particular utterances. Blakemore (1987, 1988, 1989, 1992) has explored the ways in which certain logical features of the language as system constrains interpretation of particular utterances, although she acknowledges that particular interpretations still require a large amount of pragmatic interpretation. Interestingly, if we compare the following two sentences:

5 She came with John and she came with Bill.
6 She broke her leg and she went to hospital.

the choice of conjunction indicates the same logical relationship between the clauses: i.e. that the two events described are connected in some way. However, given a particular intonation pattern and a stress on 'and' in sentence 5, the audience is likely to assume that she came with two men at the same time. An interpretation of 6, on the other hand, is likely to lead to an interpretation which assumes that the visit to the hospital occurred both *after* and *as a result* of the break. This suggests that we do process the logical properties of grammatical words, but that we also engage in pragmatic enrichment before assigning an interpretation to them.[7]

Similar pragmatic enrichment occurs with the semantic properties of language. For example, many semantic textbooks (e.g. Hurford and Heasley, 1983) suggest that the 'meaning' of lexical items can be broken down atomistically into sets of features which enter into systematic meaning relationships with each other. Thus, 'bachelor' entails having never been married (thus excluding divorcees), being in a position to get married (thus excluding Roman Catholic priests), being adult (thus excluding children), and being male. Thus, a statement such as:

7 Although she's married, she's really a bachelor girl.

would seem to violate a number of formal semantic features. It is contradictory, in that it is impossible to be married and unmarried; it refers to a female rather than a male; and it refers to a female child. The introduction of 'really' also suggests that the claim is not intended to be treated entirely as figurative. And yet such an utterance is quite likely to occur, and quite easy to interpret.[8]

Sperber and Wilson deal with this apparent mismatch in an interesting way. They argue that 'the linguistic description of an utterance is determined by the grammar, and does not vary with the interests or point of view of the hearers' (1986, p. 175). If we accept this, we are obliged to agree with them that language is 'a grammar-governed representational system' (ibid., p. 173) which exists independently of the purposes to which it is put.[9] In this respect it is like other (vocal) animal languages. A characterisation such as this which sees language as a device for representing concepts which are stored in the mind/brain in a logically consistent set of forms satisfactorily accounts for the code-like nature of the device, but says nothing about the uses to which this code is put in communication.

However, what is unique about human language is the uses to which it can be put. As Sperber and Wilson argue:

the fact that humans have developed languages which can be used to communicate is interesting, but it tells us nothing about the essential nature of language. The originality of the human species is precisely to have found this curious additional use for something which many other species also possess . . . the result has been that something widely found in other species has undergone remarkable adaptation and development because of the new uses it has been put to.

(1986, p. 173)

While accepting the broad thrust of this argument, I shall be claiming in the following chapter (and I have already foreshadowed in Chapter 4) that the kinds of development and adaptation that language has undergone is such that the very nature of the code has been changed in important ways. In particular, I shall be arguing that the linguistic description of an utterance is not merely incomplete but is also essentially wrong if it fails to take into account the ways in which the social uses of language are also encoded in the grammatical systems of any given natural language. If I am right, it would seem that the purely logical and semantic features of the code have not only undergone their own kinds of adaptation but have also been supplemented by other coded features which signal utterance meaning within particular situations.

Of course, Sperber and Wilson do not ignore these features in use, but they associate them with the inferential features of interpretation rather than with language-as-code. Certainly, some of the elements they investigate require precisely the degree of inferencing they suggest. Lexical disambiguation of polysemic words clearly does depend on context in important ways and the context of their interpretation is established by complex operations which include taking into account the co-text and the presence of various kinds of deictic elements.

INTERPRETATION IN ACTION

To demonstrate how Sperber and Wilson's theory may work in practice, let us consider the following sentence from *Relevance Theory* (1986, p. 172):

> 8 Language and communication are often seen as two sides of a single coin.

At first sight, this is fully explicit. However, a close analysis will reveal considerable indeterminacies of meaning which are only likely to be resolved by detailed inferencing. Further, the kinds of interpretation that I shall construct will probably be different in some subtle particulars from that constructed by other readers of the same text, and yet different again from that constructed when it is read in the context of this text rather than the text from which it was taken.

Although I cannot give a full account of the various thought processes that took place when I originally read it, I can sketch out some of the inferences that are developed in the act of reading (according to a relevance theoretic perspective) which enable this utterance to become optimally relevant to me. However, I should stress that the description I shall be offering is flawed in one very significant way. It assumes a linear reading in which disambiguation occurs in a left to right chronological sequence. In fact, a lot of the inferences that readers develop happen so rapidly that they may be considered to be simultaneous whereas others may be held in suspension until the full form of the sentence has been established.

Typically, I recognise that 'language' and 'communication' are relatively indeterminate. I therefore assign them provisional meaning until the sentence is complete. This provisional meaning derives from the encyclopedic entries I have of the terms. An encyclopedic entry might be likened to a mental dictionary which lists all the possible meanings that can be associated with a given word shape.[10] I then notice that the verb phrase is present tense indicative in mood, but passive in voice. I further notice the presence of an adverb which specifies indeterminate frequency. These choices are likely to lead to the (incomplete) propositional form:

> 9 An unspecified but given number of people see language and communication as two sides of a single coin.

I now disambiguate 'see'. Although it is perfectly possible to use the visual organs to see language (as in reading) and to see communication (as in watching the TV), my mental dictionary also has an entry for 'see' as *think of*. Further, this use has become so familiar that I no longer consider it to be metaphorical. However, the final phrase 'two sides of the same coin' requires far more complex processing since it employs a metaphor that, although very familiar, is not quite 'dead'.

Sperber and Wilson invoke the Gricean notion of conversational implicature to explain how this kind of trope is likely to be processed. Whereas it would have been open to the authors to state that 'Some people consider language and communication to be comprised of the same material entity' – and notice that in rewriting it like this, I am offering a particular interpretation – they have chosen a completely different form of words. My lexical entry for coin includes the information that coins are material entities that achieve value through exchange; further that they are conventionally circular and that they therefore only have two sides. It also includes the information that they come in many different sizes; have different names and denominations; are frequently made of a metal alloy; devalue; have designs on them, etc. And yet I am not likely to call all this information to mind. Instead, I am likely to follow something like the following sequence:

10 (Some people often consider that) language and communication are two sides of a single coin.

Identifying the relational verb *be*, I construct a proposition for the embedded clause which asserts the identity of language, communication and coins. This is not explicitly stated in the original formulation, but is a premise that I can reasonably expect the authors intended to make manifest to their readers. It is therefore an implicated premise. As Sperber and Wilson state, 'An implicature is a contextual assumption or implication which a speaker, intending her utterance to be manifestly relevant, manifestly intended to make manifest to the hearer' (1986, p. 194).

However, the entries in my mental dictionary contradict this identity. I can halt the processing effort at this point, and assume that such people who identify language, communication and coins are mad (in which case, the claim fails to achieve relevance for me), or I can continue the processing effort by assuming that language and communication are like coins only in some unspecified ways. I therefore call to mind those elements (in my mental lexicon) which are held in common between language, communication and coins, and end with the implicated conclusion that:

11 (Some people often consider) that language and communication are like coins in that they are both used for exchanges of value; that value does not reside in the coin itself but in the act of exchange in

> the same way that language, until it is used in communication, has
> no value; that coins have material substance as does language, but
> that the material substance is only symbolically related to the value,
> etc.

Indeed, my processing could continue so as to include the ways in which
language and communication are quite unlike coins, but to do this would
contradict the principle of economy.

There is still one problem to be resolved in establishing a full interpretation, and it is not one that yields any obvious solution. The word 'often' has
an ambiguous range, so that two possible interpretations can be reached
with equal validity:

either

12 A given number of people (always) see language . . .

or

13 A given number of people (frequently) see . . .

I assume that the adverb is to be conflated with the (unmentioned) agents
and therefore adhere to the first interpretation. The inferential processes at
work here are roughly as follows:

14 If x is often done, then some people often do x.

15 Given the nature of x, it is more likely that people will be consistent
in their behaviour.

16 Therefore, I assume that x is always done by some people, but never
done by others. Thus, although x is often done, it is always done by
the same people.

You will notice that the structure of my argument, although rational, is not
necessarily underpinned by strict logic. Indeed, step 2 is purely empirical
and depends on my knowledge of the world (which may be faulty).
However, following the principle of optimal relevance, I have derived
those assumptions which have the greatest contextual effects in the context I have constructed for myself and there is nothing in the language
which contradicts such assumptions. Other readers, whose experience of
the world leads them to assume that humans are inconsistent in their
behaviour may well come to the second of the interpretations offered
above.

I shall be applying similar principles to subsequent interpretations of
written texts. If Sperber and Wilson are correct, all I can do is to demonstrate some of the processes involved in reaching *my* interpretations of the
texts under discussion. Others, with different knowledge, may engage in
different processes, and reach different interpretations but this is a necessary consequence of relevance theory. In this particular instance having

achieved an interpretation in which the words used have maximum contextual effects, I have established the relevance of this particular utterance for me.

A BROADER VIEW OF THE INTERPRETIVE PROCESS

However, certain very important elements in my interpretation of this utterance are missing from this description, and it is not entirely clear whether the relevance theoretic account can deal with them. The first relates to the grammatical form of the sentence. I have noticed that it includes an agentless passive, and that the scope of 'often' is ambiguous. I am clearly able to construct an incomplete logical and propositional form for the sentence, but I am led to the conclusion that, at this stage in their argument, Sperber and Wilson do not wish to identify the logical subject of the sentence. This assumption is still consistent with the principle of relevance, but I also entertain further assumptions, among them one that identifies the use of the agentless passive with a particular style of academic writing. This assumption is triggered by the linguistic elements of the sentence, but is in many ways detachable from the particular sentence. It is not clear whether, within the theory outlined here, this information is part of my encyclopedic knowledge or whether it is part of my more particular knowledge of the ways in which language is used in given situations (i.e. part of my linguistic knowledge). If it is the latter, then Sperber and Wilson need to build into their account a clearer discussion of the ways in which particular linguistic constructions trigger particular assumptions about language functions. Further, I also notice that Sperber and Wilson use the expression 'two sides of a single coin'. I am more familiar with the expression 'two sides of the same coin', therefore I entertain some vague assumptions, and they are very vague, about the use of this unfamiliar expression. In some ways they are also conflicting, since I cannot decide whether Sperber and Wilson are manipulating a set expression for as yet unknown reasons, or whether they are merely using a slightly different dialect. In either case, it is my linguistic knowledge which gives rise to these assumptions and therefore it is linguistic knowledge which contributes to the identification of function. The point of these speculations is to suggest that Sperber and Wilson are not entirely clear as to how the functional nature of language is to be considered as part of its 'meaning'.

Of course, they do not neglect it altogether. In their discussion of speech act theory (1986, pp. 243–54), they distinguish between three different kinds of utterances, each of which have been of interest to speech act theorists. The first, those which include explicit performative verbs, they identify as 'institutional' speech acts in that the presence of the performative is essential for the speech act to be realised. The second, and the more common, are those which contain no such verb, but whose utterance may reasonably lead the hearer to assume that some speech act is being performed. They give as an example (ibid., p. 245)

17 The weather will be warmer tomorrow.

and assert that the recovery on the part of the hearer that this is a prediction depends on the assumptions entertained by the hearer. Given that it is open to the speaker to make this assumption manifest by supplying an appropriate performative verb, and given that she did not supply such a verb, the assumption that it is a prediction 'is not *essential* to the comprehension of [the] utterance' (ibid.).

The third type is associated with the choice of mood, and relates to utterances which direct (typically using the imperative), ask (typically using interrogative forms), and which assert in such a way as to commit the speaker to the truth of the assertion. Sperber and Wilson admit that this area of their theory needs considerable elaboration, but again it is not entirely clear how far it is possible to separate the conventional interpretation of an utterance in context from the form in which such an utterance has been made. Knowledge of language is as much knowledge of how language is used in particular circumstances as it is of the possible interpretations that can be assigned to particular grammatical structures. Thus, to revert to the sentence:

9 (a) Language and communication are often seen as two sides of a single coin.

I do not simply process this in isolation, but treat it as part of a continuing communicative process which derives from what has been written before and, to some extent, predicts what is likely to follow. The choice of the agentless passive suggests that this assertion should not be attributed to the authors. However, if it is not to be attributed to the authors then its mention is probably so that the authors can rebut such an assertion and offer an alternative of their own later in the text. Although it would be impossible to unpack all these meanings from this sentence, they are assumptions that derive partly from the syntactic form of the utterance and partly because I am familiar with the ways in which such forms are typically associated with more general (argumentative) functions.[11] In fact, I would go further and argue that the choice of syntactic form is a particular rhetorical choice which signals its intended function and that this function is part of the meaning of the utterance in context. However, to demonstrate this more clearly we need a richer description of the relationships between linguistic forms and functions than Sperber and Wilson offer.

However, I have still not exhausted the assumptions that haunt my mind in the interpretation of this sentence. Somewhere, I remember that Saussure employs a similar image (though in a completely different context) when he refers to meaning and substance as being like two facets of the same sheet of paper.[12] This piece of information, however, is activated remotely, and may be said to be part of my encyclopedic knowledge. The term *encyclopedic* is useful here since it suggests metaphorically that we have memory stores of clusters of information. The ways in which memory is clustered is a matter of considerable dispute among psychologists, and the ways in which it is activated by language is even more obscure. But it would seem at least possible that I am accessing two slightly different kinds of information here. The first might be called *intertextual* information in that it relates quite specifically to a linguistic expression, and therefore, by extension to a previous text (and ultimately to a previous body of texts). The importance of this kind of information is that it helps contextualise expression within a history of usage, thereby making indirect reference to previous voices who have contributed to the same (or similar) discourse(s).[13] The second is less specific and relates more to my general knowledge of the world.

It is, perhaps, rather difficult to demonstrate how this more general knowledge is activated by the text I have chosen, but let us consider a complete text to explore the kinds of processes that may be involved in its interpretation (see Figure 6.1).[14]

If, following Sperber and Wilson, the first task is to use the linguistic input system as a means of assigning propositional and logical forms to the sentences, then there are severe problems because the flyer only contains one grammatical sentence. Nevertheless, most readers will have little difficulty in deciding that this is an announcement of a particular event due to take place at a specific place on a stated date. This is nowhere obviously stated, and it is not easy to see how such information is recovered. Brown and Yule (1983, p. 234, see also Carrell and Eisterhold, 1988) distinguish between 'bottom-up' and 'top-down' processes of decoding, whereby 'bottom-up' refers to the kinds of activity involved in parsing sentences word by word to establish their grammatical relationships and 'top-down' refers to the construction of coherence by establishing the meaning relations that hold between sentences in the production of textual meaning. Although these distinctions are useful for limited analytical purposes, it is quite clear that we engage in both processes simultaneously and that each is likely to affect the other.

If we follow Sperber and Wilson, and agree that our global task in processing written text is to establish an interpretation that is relevant to us as readers, then faced with the kind of text represented in Figure 6.1, the amount of 'bottom-up' processing we can engage in is severely limited, predominantly consisting of recovering a semantic representation of the lexical items. Indeed, in this case, we might argue that the recovery of the ellipted syntactic forms depends entirely on 'top-down' processing. But this activity depends on our recognition that this text has been designed to perform a communicative function similar to those performed by other

ΑΡΙΣΤΟΤΕΛΕΙΟ ΠΑΝΕΠΙΣΤΗΜΙΟ ΘΕΣΣΑΛΟΝΙΚΗΣ
Aristotle University of Thessaloniki

9th INTERNATIONAL SYMPOSIUM
OF
THEORETICAL & APPLIED LINGUISTICS

April 3-5, 1995

Department of Theoretical & Applied Linguistics
School of English
Aristotle University of Thessaloniki
Greece

Organizing Committee:

Michalis Milapides	(chair)
Eliza Kitis	(vice-chair)
Niovi Iliadou	(treasurer)
Paschalina Groutka	(secretary)
Lena Agathopoulou	(member)

Mailing address:

540 06 Thessaloniki,
Greece
Phone: +31 99 7457
99 7479
Fax: +31 99 7432

Official languages: English and Greek

For more information contact the Organizing Committee

Figure 6.1 Announcement of the 9th International Symposium of Theoretical &
Applied Linguistics

texts that have been realised using similar forms. Another way of putting this would be to say that grammatical choice and genre are in a symbiotic relationship with each other such that neither has precedence. In the construction of a given text my linguistic choices are constrained by the genre with which I want it to be associated and, conversely, my recognition of a given generic type depends on identifying the presence (or absence) of certain linguistic forms.

Having recovered a set of syntactic forms for this announcement, I search my mental lexicon to establish appropriate meanings for the vocabulary items displayed. I have a very sparse entry for 'symposium'. It collocates with Socrates and Greek philosophy (which is reinforced by other references to Greece in the text); it has overlaps with *conversazione* which, in turn, link it with *conversation*. Since it is, for me, a semi-foreign word, I select the most likely synonymous entry to be *conference* and I make this decision partly on the basis of my encyclopedic knowledge.

Again, exactly how encyclopedic knowledge is stored in the mind/brain is a matter of dispute. Recent theorists have developed theories from artificical intelligence which assume that memory is packaged into units which consist of stereotypical representations of locations and events (Anderson and Pearson, 1988; Cook, 1990; Turner and Cullingford, 1989). These stereotypical representations include a set of default elements which are assumed to be present unless they are specifically excluded by the text. Thus, my stereotypical representation of a conference will include a group of people gathered together (usually in an academic setting), listening to a person delivering a talk and this matches neatly with my mental representations of symposia and conversazione/conversations.[15]

CONCLUSION

I have outlined some of the significant features which seem to be involved in the process of interpretation since it is quite clear that we do, typically, interpret written texts in idiosyncratic ways. We therefore need some cognitive model which indicates how such interpretation takes place, and I have suggested there are good reasons for thinking that Sperber and Wilson have developed a persuasive account of the cognitive processes involved. I have also suggested that their model is based on a theory of language that is deficient in that it seems to ignore the ways in which given social functions are directly encoded within the language system. In my discussion of a sentence from their own work, I have tried to indicate how some of the linguistic choices persuade me of the social spaces which this text has been designed to fill. Put baldly, these choices *show* me that Sperber and Wilson have written an advanced textbook. This conclusion goes beyond the limits of the model they propose.

Sperber and Wilson seem to suggest that linguistic form is essentially some kind of algorithm which can be solved in its own terms and then applied to particular occasions of utterance. Their argument rests on the assumption that the interpretation of utterances (typically, though not in all cases; cf. their discussion of speech act theory) depends on two different kinds of knowledge: linguistic knowledge and social knowledge. I would suggest that they are setting up a dichotomy here which cannot easily be sustained in quite the ways they suggest. I have already indicated how, historically, language adapts its forms to perform particular social functions, and also how language use necessarily has a social context. Although I agree with Sperber and Wilson that interpretations are necessarily individual, I have argued that meanings are socially constructed. In the following chapter I shall be showing in more detail precisely how different uses of language serve to constrain the potential range of (individual) interpretations. In particular, I shall be suggesting that our assignment of texts to genres enables us to understand how differently constructed texts that seem to say 'the same thing' propositionally, can actually mean quite different things in use.

FURTHER READING

Following the principle of relevance as described, I have necessarily constructed my own interpretation of Sperber and Wilson's theory. I cannot pretend that this interpretation is what they had in their minds when they wrote the book, nor can I assume that it will be the same interpretation that other readers may achieve in their reading of it. Readers are therefore strongly urged to read *Relevance: Communication and Cognition* (1986) for themselves. Various writers have extended the applications of relevance theory in interesting ways. Blakemore (1993) and Pilkington (1994) have both applied it to the analysis of literary texts, while Ziv (1988) has suggested that it should be buttressed with the principle of rationality. My own critique, that it needs to be supplemented with a more socially based account of language use, suggests that *Relevance* is the first, rather than the last, word in an interesting debate that will continue for some time. A book which explores relevance theory and relates it to a more semantically based view of language is Blakemore's (1992) *Understanding Utterances* which can be highly recommended as an introduction to the theory.

SOME QUESTIONS FOR CONSIDERATION

1 I may want to include rather more on the issue of socially constructed meaning by making reference to Law cases, for example: also the anthropological literature.

Re: relevance theory: it would be worth finding studies which demonstrate how subjects are pressured into interpreting texts in ways contrary to the evidence so as to suggest how propaganda (e.g.) succeeds. The point being that the first interpretation etc. may often not be the one that is used when conditions of social pressure persuade readers that another interpretation will be more appropriate. If this means more 'relevant', then we are stretching the term too far.[16]

1 Can you construct an interpretation for either of these texts?
2 To what extent was your interpretation dependent on reading them in this context?
3 To whom do you think these texts were directed?
4 Are they likely to have a different 'meaning' for the intended recipient?
5 Can you imagine what that meaning might be?
6 In the light of your answers to these questions, to what extent do you think that the 'social setting' has influenced the linguistic form of these texts, and what evidence can you find to demonstrate this?

Chapter 7

Genre

INTRODUCTION

In Chapter 5 I indicated that register analysis was a useful way of describing how a particular text functioned as a communicative event, but could not be used to classify groupings of similar events. Although I noticed a number of overlapping features in the invoices and the letters that I analysed, there was nothing that clearly indicated that they were the same kind of communicative acts. I observed that some, but not all, aspects of mode were shared between them but suggested that mode was too vague a concept to be applied rigorously. The question now arises as to why we should need a way of grouping communicative acts. There are three possible answers to this. First, people just *do* describe writings as being of a particular kind. They refer to such things as diaries, advertisements, letters, etc. which suggests that they have an intuitive recognition that these are different from each other in significant ways. As Miller observes, generic names are 'cultural artifacts' (1994, p. 69) and therefore an understanding of such artifacts will teach us more about how societies speak to themselves. Second, it invites us to focus more closely on language variety as a phenomenon in its own right as both necessary and the sign of a healthy society. And third, it contributes to our understanding of what would otherwise be a very puzzling use of language: parody.

PARODY

Let us consider the following text:

> The other day I turned up at work and was amused to note that myself and all my workmates had arrived wearing exactly the same clothes! Then I suddenly remembered. We are all uniformed police officers.
>
> <div align="right">P.C. Swinton-Perry
Isle of Man
(<i>Viz</i>, Issue 36)</div>

From the point of view of 'language-in-observation' there is nothing remarkable in this. It is cohesive and coherent as a text. If we now apply register analysis, we would be able to identify it as a letter. It shares certain features of mode with the earlier letters I analysed. Obviously the field is different. One could characterise this as the 'telling of an amusing story'. As for tenor, the selections it makes from the interpersonal level suggest a degree of intimacy with its intended audience, although the mention of rank in its closing address is slightly incongruous. Thus far, there is nothing untoward in our perception of it as a letter. However, most readers would be suspicious of such a classification, for although it seems like a letter, the story it tells is too fantastic to be believable. But if it is *not* a letter, how can we re-classify it? The most satisfactory way would be to argue that it is a parody of a letter. But to reach this conclusion we need to go beyond the analysis of individual letters and recognise that letters as a class – in this case, letters to the press – fulfil particular social functions which are being undermined by this example.[1]

This type of grouping is typically referred to as a *genre*. A genre, then, is best seen as an aggregation of communicative events that fulfil a common social function. But if genres are communicative events, they cannot be composed of texts *as such* nor can they be analysed in terms of the formal features shared by a set of texts (even though the texts themselves may be representative of the same genre). To do this would be to fail to capture what genres actually do.[2] An example of this kind of failure occurs in Bhatia's work. Following Swales (1987; 1990), Bhatia (1993, Chapter 4) discusses the variability that is likely to occur between abstracts, research articles and student reports, but asserts there is likely to be sufficient similarity between them to support the idea that there is a genre which can be called *academic introductions* (ibid., p. 100). He further claims that these similarities are best seen in terms of (rhetorical) *moves* which can be represented schematically as in Figure 7.1.

If we analyse 'Agents of ice' using this formula (see Appendix, p. 171), we will find that it conforms to all of Bhatia's rhetorical moves. The first paragraph clearly contains steps 2 and 3 of move 1. 'Teenagers cause winter' operates as a topic generalisation, while the ensuing sentences can be treated as 'reviewing items of previous research'. The reference to such well-known names as Fahrenheit, Celsius and Kelvin might be deemed to be a way of claiming centrality. The following paragraph realises step 1D in the second move in that it argues it is continuing a tradition of research into a stated problem; whereas paragraph three in part realises step 1A. The remainder of the article realises move 3 by announcing the principal findings both discursively and by means of statistical tables. The article concludes with a set of notes containing references to other works. Certain other features, of which Bhatia makes no mention but which are increasingly common as markers

Move 1   Establishing a territory

Step 1   Claiming centrality
            and/or
Step 2   Making topic generalisation(s)
            and/or
Step 3   Reviewing items of previous research

                                    Declining
                                    rhetorical-effort

Move 2   Establishing a niche

Step 1A   Counter-claiming
            or
Step 1B   Indicating a gap
            or
Step 1C   Question-raising
            or
Step 1D   Continuing a tradition

                                    Weakening
                                    knowledge
                                    claims

Move 3   Occupying the niche

Step 1A   Outlining the purposes
            or
Step 1B   Announcing present research
Step 2   Announcing principal findings
Step 3   Indicating article structure

                                    Increasing
                                    explicitness

Figure 7.1 A schematic representation of the rhetorical moves in academic introductions, after Bhatia (1993, p. 83)

of academic respectability are the provenance of the authors (stated next to their names) and the appearance of the article in a well-respected geographical journal.

It could be argued, then, that all the surface features of the genre have been adequately met. However, it is quite clear that few readers would treat this as a serious research article. Exactly why not is rather puzzling. Part of the answer must lie in the hypothesis advanced which is so preposterous that it cannot be taken seriously. Further evidence can be derived from the ways Fahrenheit, Celsius and Kelvin are referred to, although it would be quite possible to argue that the writers have failed adequately to control one relatively minor aspect of academic style by introducing *ad hominem* arguments. Certainly, the list of references that appears in the notes is so bizarre that it cannot possibly be taken seriously.

However, these arguments only hold if we have already decided what genre the writing should be assigned to and what the typical functions of such a genre are deemed to be. The article fails as a geographical research article simply because, when checked empirically against the works of other geographers, it cannot be verified. Once it has been re-classified as a parody, then it will be read in a totally different way.

Nevertheless, parodies must parody something, and in this case the article must be read as a parody of other geographical articles (and, by extension, some of the work performed by other geographers). This suggests that the forms and functions of genres are related to each other in very direct ways, but it also suggests that readers approach written texts with expectations that have been formed by their recognition of, and ascription to, the text's genre. Rose has argued that

> The overall function of [the] devices used by the parodist is to assimilate 'Text B' into 'Text A' as its second code, and (after fulfilling other functions, such as the evocation of the expectations of the reader) to ironise, criticise, or refunction Text B in some comic fashion.
>
> (1993, p. 79)

But the point about the parodies we have been considering is that there is no prior text, there are merely prior texts, which can in some way or another be considered as representing some kind of genre.

GENRE

The concept of genre has been a matter of considerable discussion and research over the last few years (for further references see the 'Further reading' section at the end of the chapter). In the course of my discussion so far various informal hints have appeared as to how it may be possible to classify different genres. On the one hand, we have observed the use of particular generic names (e.g. invoices, letters) to describe groups of texts which seem to have similar features and to be performing similar functions. On the other, we have noted the existence of texts (parodies) which apparently manifest registerial selections which suggest that they belong to a particular text type but which, equally manifestly, perform quite radically different social functions. It would seem, then, that genres operate at the interface of social function and text type in quite interesting ways. Their existence is evidence of the discursive practices of a particular society, but because they can only ever be realised by individual texts which are to some extent heterogeneous they are always subject to change and modification and to that extent abstract constructs. Indeed, Threadgold (1988, p. 355) has suggested that the relationship of particular texts to the genres which they instantiate is best seen as a dialectic of the kind Register/Token:Genre/Type 'in which the type is only ever instantiated as token, mediated by an intertextual semantic frame'.

In considering how such mediation might take place, we need a clear understanding of what kind of object 'an intertextual semantic frame' might be. I have argued in Chapter 4 that intertextuality is janus-faced in that it is partly a construction of writers and partly a construction of readers. Writers have, at the back of their minds, previous texts that they are imitating. And they choose to imitate such texts precisely because they have observed a shared intention between the text they are composing and the anterior texts they are imitating and a supposed success in achieving that intention by the anterior texts. However, they cannot guarantee that their text will achieve a similar success, partly because their texts are new instantiations (and therefore shift the boundaries of the genre however slightly) and partly because they cannot be sure that their readers will perceive precisely the same similarity as they intend (cf. the chapter on relevance theory above). To this extent, genres are interactive formations constructed by writers and readers. Nevertheless, language and language use are not random, and writers have to assume that the intertextual references they make will be recognised. However, there still remains the problem in deciding which elements of anterior texts are selected so as to indicate membership of a genre.

Hasan (Halliday and Hasan, 1985/9, p. 63ff.) has argued that genres are typically realised by a set of obligatory elements (ibid., p. 66) each of which carries a meaning potential within the exchange. These obligatory elements seem to have been characterised as moves in an exchange largely because Hasan is considering spoken language. It would, however, be perfectly possible to characterise them as simple rhetorical sequences as Bhatia has done. These she refers to as realising the Generic Structure Potential (GSP). An important point here is that the presence of each of the obligatory elements suggests that the completed text has become a member of the genre which it realises. Should the text be aborted, or should any of the elements be omitted, then the genre has not been realised, although we may still recognise that the text has entered into the framework of a particular genre. This captures the important insight that texts are always immanent in that they unfold in real time both in their writing and in their reading (Lemke, 1988, p. 162; Martin, 1992, p. 503).

Hasan suggests that texts are always embedded in some 'contextual configuration' (CC) (Halliday and Hasan, 1985/9, pp. 55–6). It would seem from her description (and from that offered by Halliday, ibid., p. 46) that CCs exist prior to the language which realises them. She argues that:

The CC is an account of the significant attributes of [the] social activity. So, it is not surprising that the features of the CC can be used for making certain kinds of predictions about text structure. These are as follows:

1 **What** elements **must** occur;
2 **What** elements **can** occur;
3 **Where must** they occur;
4 **Where can** they occur;
5 **How often** can they occur.

(ibid., p. 56)

Her examples are taken from exchanges at a shop in which the offering of goods and services can be taken for granted and they lead her to construct a complex network of features which realise the genre of shopping. However, it is not entirely clear what interrelationship is supposed to obtain between CCs, GSPs and particular language usages. Hasan seems to acknowledge the problems of her analysis when she claims (ibid., p. 103): 'If the CC has these values, then these elements will appear in any text embedded in this CC; if these elements appear in any text, then these values of the CC can be inferred from it.' As she recognises (ibid., p. 104): 'It is true that the definition is circular, since the GSP itself was defined as the verbal expression of a CC; but the circularity lies in the nature of the relationship between language and reality.'

The problems with Hasan's formulation have been discussed by Ventola (1987) where she points out that the ways in which the GSP has been constructed is over-constraining. Ventola's own research suggests both that there were iterative elements which Hasan failed to take into account, and that some of the obligatory moves were not necessarily realised. However, even were Hasan's claims well-founded, there would be problems in accounting for parodic texts. I have suggested, above, that parodic texts are successful precisely because they realise the typical features of a register which might be associated with a particular genre, but that they are perceived as parodic precisely because they subvert the typical functions of that genre. Such recognition depends not merely on the CC as outlined by Hasan but on a more personal orientation towards the text undertaken by individual readers. A further criticism is that Hasan's formulation does not easily account for the ways in which genres adapt and change over time. Again, we need to take into account the ways in which individuals are socially situated such that they may want to try to change the social functions of particular genres.

A successful description of any given genre needs, therefore, to include a component which shows how groups of texts realise similar linguistic elements and a social component which indicates how such elements realise common social practices. Swales (1990, p. 58) has attempted the following definition of genre:

> A genre comprises a class of communicative events, the members of which share some set of communicative purposes. These purposes are recognised by the expert members of the parent discourse community, and thereby constitute the rationale for the genre. This rationale shapes the schematic structure of the discourse and influences and constrains choice of content and style. Communicative purpose is both a privileged criterion and one that operates to keep the scope of a genre as here conceived narrowly focused on comparable rhetorical action.
>
> (1990, p. 58)

Although this is persuasive, the definition has been drawn so tightly as to exclude certain communicative events from realising a genre. If we consider the example of invoices, as previously illustrated, then we would be inclined to agree that they conform to the first sentence above. However, it is difficult to ascertain who the 'expert members of the parent discourse community' might be. At one level, we might conceive them to be the issuers and recipients of the invoices. However, it is quite clear that some of the information supplied on the invoices is of a technical nature which is unlikely to be easily accessible to the customer. If we therefore redefine the 'expert members' as being the accounts department of the company, we are faced with a slightly different problem in that the 'communicative event' has become asymmetric in its communicative potential between the sender and the addressee. Indeed, if the invoices were to be challenged, further experts from the law would be brought in to argue as to the precise meanings of the invoice. Thus, it would seem that genres are not necessarily as discrete as Swales's definition suggests.

One of the problems underlying Swales's definition is his concept of a 'discourse community' which I have discussed in some detail in Chapter 3. I argued that people typically belonged to overlapping discourse communities and had multiple and variable memberships. This has, to some extent, been recognised by Swales (1993, pp. 695–6) in his more recent work where he claims that a 'rhetorical community persists by instantiation and by engagement, rather than *existing* through membership and collectivity'. If we take the notion of instantiation seriously, then we would have to acknowledge that each individual's contribution would, at any particular moment, redefine the internal dynamics of the rhetorical community, and it would follow that genres were never one hundred percent stable.

Bhatia has argued:

> Swales offers a good fusion of linguistic and sociological factors in his definition of a genre; however, he underplays psychological factors, thus undermining the importance of tactical aspects of genre construction, which play a significant role in the concept of genre as a dynamic social process, as against a static one.
>
> (1993, p. 16)

which suggests a similar position to the one that I have just offered. However he runs the risk of locating genre formation too much in the individual. It should be apparent that the dynamic nature of genres cannot be *simply* explained in psychological terms. Although individual contributions always have the potential to influence the ways in which genres adapt, this adaptation is a response to fresh social pressures rather than to the whims of individuals. Indeed, the development of a genre may frequently signify a reconstitution of the relationships that are supposed to obtain between the addressors and addressees of particular messages which is highly significant. A central claim of this book then is that the formation of genres is the way by which societies manifest their discursive practices in language. It follows that a genre is always a record of a particular practice but that it will be shot through with traces of the other discursive practices a given society engages in.

To the extent that this is true certain consequences follow in our attempt to classify different genres. The first has already been mentioned above: that no text can in itself manifest a particular genre. The second might seem more damaging to my theory which is that genres can never be described in discrete terms. The boundaries between them are always indeterminate and subject to shift. However, this is perhaps inevitable since the act of classification is in itself a social act (cf. Zimmerman, 1994). As we shall see later, when we come to discuss the problem of literary genres, classifications are likely to change over time as societies redefine their relationships to groups of texts. This can be seen most clearly in the case of letters. What may have been conceived as a private communication can, by virtue of being published, enter the public sphere and ultimately be regarded as part of a particular author's literary *œuvre*. The letters will, indeed must, retain traces of their private nature but they will be read for different reasons and will therefore be reclassified accordingly.

It would be interesting, therefore, to observe how it is that a variety of texts which manifest different kinds of linguistic features can be legitimately regarded as realising the same genre. In order to show in some detail how this occurs I have chosen as central examples *letters* and *advertising* and make a brief mention of *recipes*. Broadly speaking, we might assume that letters are typically addressed to a single recipient. They are therefore personal in their orientation. This is an important point since it helps us to make an initial distinction between private and public genres.

PRIVATE VS. PUBLIC GENRES

Private genres can be characterised as those which are intended to be interactive between specific individuals. In the example of the letter from the gas board given in Chapter 5 (p. 94), it can be argued that the informational nature of the communication takes precedence over the personal relationship. This is not necessarily the case with private communications. Indeed, quite frequently private communications can be treated as examples of what Jakobson (1960, p. 37) has referred to as the *phatic* function of language. Their primary aim is to maintain the channel of communication. This is perhaps most obvious in the case of Christmas and birthday cards which typically contain a printed message (selected because it is thought to be in some way appropriate to the addressee) and a brief handwritten greeting which contains minimal information. Private written genres would include notes to oneself (e.g. shopping lists) and messages scribbled between students during lectures or left pinned to noticeboards in shared flats, etc. Diaries are interesting examples of a private genre in that they serve the double function of recording events and feelings that have recently occurred as well as reminding the writer of events that are due in the future. Although they may appear to be non-interactive (in that the writer and intended reader are the same individual),[3] they are interactive to the extent that the reader has undergone various transformations since the original act of writing.

An interesting example of two texts (although in their totality, they may well be treated as a single text in that they are part of an ongoing exchange) which realise a private genre occur in Figures 7.2 and 7.3.

Their occasion was an overnight stay by a friend. Figure 7.2 contains a variety of features which mark it out as private. The most obvious of these is the fact that it is handwritten. However, it is noticeable that only one clause contains a subject; that there are two abbreviations ('v. tired' and, perhaps less significant, 'ok'); that the clauses are relatively simple in structure; and that there is a peculiar mixture of formal and informal lexis (e.g. 'churlish' and 'pinch') at the end. Such features suggest a degree of intimacy between the writer and reader. Perhaps more important, there are certain elements which can only be understood within the given context. The NPs: 'the front bedroom', 'the movie', 'the morning' all have deictic determiners that would make no sense to a reader who was unfamiliar with the configuration of the house, the activities I was engaged in, or the time referred to. Thus the sense of intimacy is reinforced by reference to a common context. There is direct reference to a 'here and now' situation[4] which can only be understood by the participants in the exchange.

Figure 7.3 is more interesting because it demonstrates the interactive nature of the exchange far more overtly. The addressee and addressor are identified simply by their initials. This is clearly a feature of writing. There is a similar use of abbreviations and reduced forms ('don't', 'I'm') which may be considered to be more typical of the spoken mode, and a marked lack of punctuation in the original message coupled with the use of symbols such as the slash and the arrow. However, the interesting feature is the way the annotations are appended to the original message. The interactive and personal nature of the exchange are made clear and the

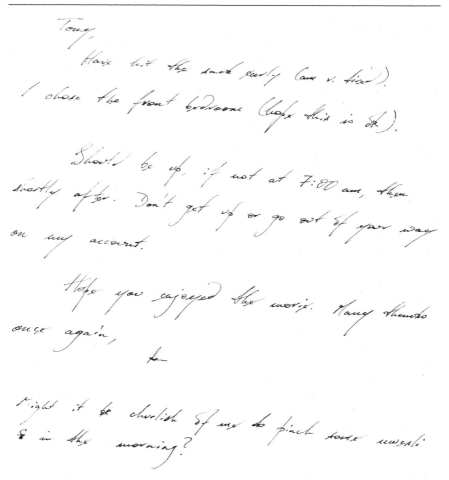

Figure 7.2 An example of a text in a private genre

final text has some features of a conversation. In particular, the injunction 'STOP!' only makes sense as a move if it is interpreted as an interruption. However, this is strictly impossible since the text which is being annotated preexisted the interruption. Thus, although it operates in some ways as a conversational move, it has to be interpreted as part of a written exchange. McCarthy (1993, p. 180) has argued that 'written text is no less interactive than spoken text, that terms such as "spoken" and "written" can often be misleading'. While conceding the general point that *all* written texts are necessarily interactive, in that it is difficult to conceive of a piece of (completed) writing that is not intended to be read, it is important to distinguish between the immediacy of the interaction that is intended. It may be only such kinds of notes as I have been analysing, i.e. those which

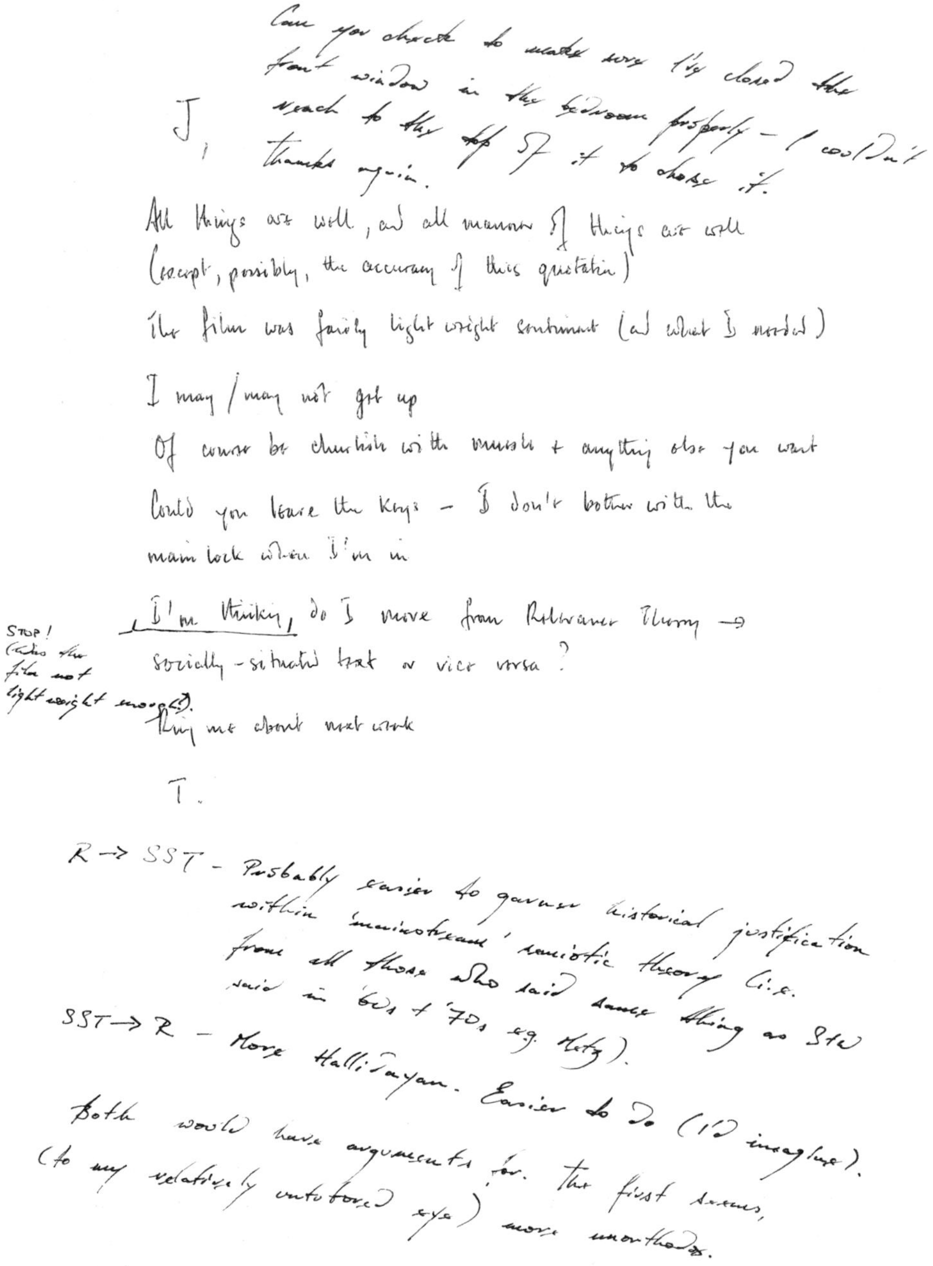

Can you check to make sure they closed the front window in the bedroom properly — I couldn't reach to the top of it to close it. thanks again.

J,

All things are well, and all manner of things are well (except, possibly, the accuracy of this quotation)

The film was fairly light weight sentiment (as what I needed)

I may / may not get up

Of course be churlish with muesli + anything else you want

Could you leave the keys — I don't bother with the main lock when I'm in

STOP!
(was the
film not
light weight enough).
I'm thinking, do I move from Relevance Theory → socially-situated text or vice versa?

Ring me about next week

T.

R → SST - Probably easier to garner historical justification within 'mainstream' semiotic theory (i.e. from all those who said same thing as SW said in '60s + '70s, eg. Kitty).

SST → R - More Halli-Sayan. Easier to do (I'd imagine).

Both would have arguments for. the first seems, (to my relatively untutored eye) more unorthodox.

Figure 7.3 An example of a text in a private genre

depend on their immediate context for successful interpretation, that are interactive in ways that are directly analogous to conversation. However, even in these texts, there are a range of distinctive features (including the graphic substance) which mark them out as *written* texts. Nevertheless, it does seem reasonable to suggest that a distinctive feature of the genre of notes is their high incidence of markers which derive from spoken forms, and it may be that such features distinguish them from other forms of 'immediate' written communication, such as office memoranda.[5]

Such immediate notes obviously have some of the features of private letters. However, there are good reasons for classifying them as a separate genre in that they are far more tightly tied to an immediate context. I have suggested that they share some of the features of conversation and this they share with private letters.[6] However, such letters are situated differently in that the addressees and addressors are at some distance from each other. For this reason, we would anticipate that the deictic elements would be more explicit. If we reconsider the personal letter referred to in Chapter 5, this is indeed what we find. A slightly fuller version appears as Figure 7.4.

```
                            Antiochou, 12,
                            Thessaloniki, 546 33

              July 6 1994


Dear Tony and Jane,

Hello, there. I'm sure it was your turn to drop me a line, but I'll forgive
you.  I suspect you've been very busy. Or is it something I said ? I hope
not. Remember the rarer action..

I assume all is well with you, and that this little letter reaches you in
Ramsgate, which is no longer your new address.

Are you both still working in Canterbury or have you moved on to fresher
pastures ? You could do worse. I see Tony's ex-postgrad students
occasionally and they always speak warmly and send even warmer greetings.
I'll be passing through (Canterbury) and staying for a day or two round
about August 15, if you're going to be around. I'd love to see you both
again.
```

Figure 7.4 A fuller version of Text 1

One of the important differences between this and the notes above is the additional information supplied. The address of the sender is given in the top right hand corner, together with a date. The name of the sender (not shown) is preceded by a handwritten closure, 'Love and kisses', while the names of the recipients are spelled out in the conventional opening greeting. These are specific deictic devices which help to locate the communication in time and space, and their presence, although not obligatory, serves a double function. They offer the recipients a checking function, allowing them to confirm that they are indeed the intended addressees, and offer sufficient identity of the addressor to enable the exchange to continue. The presence of the date is interesting in that, although (in this kind of communication) it may seem unnecessary, it takes into account the potential vagaries of the postal service by offering a way of judging the time between transmission and reception.[7]

The second paragraph carries specific reference to a place, and the third contains both a place and a date. These are necessary features for similar reasons. Although it would have been possible for the writer to have produced vaguer locutions (e.g. *Are you still where you were?*; *I'll be passing through later*, etc.), they would have affected the nature of the exchange. The degree of specificity is prompted precisely because the writer wishes to ascertain particular information in return and that nothing can be assumed to be the case. However, there are also a number of features which indicate a degree of shared knowledge. The (unidentified) quotation from Shakespeare is likely to have a particular resonance, and the reference to 'Tony's ex-postgrad students'. While it could be argued that such references will be relatively transparent to other readers (and therefore on the margin of the personal and the public), there is one particular phrase that has a very particular meaning in this context and that would be quite opaque to an 'eavesdropper'. 'I suspect you've been very busy' is, on the surface, a simple concessive claim. However, both the sender and the recipient will recognise this as an example of intertextuality in that when we were students together I had an irritating habit of prefacing a number of my (argumentative) statements with 'I suspect'. Thus, the creation of intimacy has been constructed by a number of different methods, not all of which are recoverable through linguistic analysis alone.

A further point that will become relevant when we come to distinguish between different types of letters is the frequent shift of topic and the high degree of modal expressions even in the small extract quoted above. The writer moves from a positive assertion as to whose turn it is to write, through to a personal reaction expressed with modal 'will'. This is followed by an assessment of the situation (in which 'suspect' has the epistemic modal force of 'may') and a checking question which introduces a further possible reason. And all this occurs in the space of five clauses. Although the majority of these clauses have 'I' as their grammatical subject, the rhetorical sequencing constantly shifts the reader's attention from the speaker to the things that are being spoken about.

The point of the above discussion was to demonstrate that the boundaries between genres are not always particular clear. The private letter, because it *is* private, shares a number of features with the private note. However, we recognise it as a letter because it has been invaded by a number of more public discursive features and particularly those which signify the temporal and spatial distance between the interlocutors.

It might be objected at this point that one of the primary ways we identify private letters is that they arrive through the letterbox, are usually stamped and are enclosed in envelopes. However, these features are not *in themselves* sufficient as identifying markers. The physical nature of a postal transmission does not, in itself, constrain the linguistic features we select when we sit down to compose a letter. In the act of writing, we follow certain conventions because we wish our interlocutors to recognise the kind of transaction that is taking place. And in following these conventions, we consciously or unconsciously construct our text according to the generic norms that we associate with such a transaction.

This can be illustrated most graphically by considering the growth and development of a relatively new genre: the email. The name itself is significant, since it is a shortened form of electronic mail. 'Mail' as a descriptor suggests that it shares some similarities with postal communication, and it is interesting to note that, just as we can post or send a letter so we can post or send email messages. However, some emails are on the border between the public and the private. Although messages between individuals are likely to be composed according to the nature of the transaction being conducted (i.e. they may be business transactions or more private messages), those that are sent to public networks and are redistributed through 'listservs' have a peculiar status. Although they carry an address string which indicates their provenance, this can be in the form of a code that is quite opaque to the recipients. My messages, for example, start with the string 'arb1'. There is, therefore, the potential for a degree of anonymity. Further, because they are being mailed to vast quantities of people (sometimes numbered in thousands), the likelihood of the sender knowing even a small percentage of the recipients is quite remote. However, a characteristic of news groups is that their members are likely to have common interests and, often, deeply held convictions about such interests.[8] A further feature of email though is that communication is almost instantaneous. In this respect, it is similar to telephone communication. The interaction within a newsgroup is therefore socially ambiguous. On the one hand, the interlocutors are bound by shared interests (sometimes of an esoteric nature) and may be regarded as intimates in the same way that members of a club are intimate. On the other, they are frequently far removed in space and have never met each other. Given the immediate nature of the communication, there is the impulse to respond immediately to messages and to interact as though speaking personally on the telephone. However, senders are also to some extent protected by a degree of anonymity.

Not surprisingly, the ambiguous nature of such communication has fostered some considerable discussion as to the appropriate ways of composing messages and, in particular, to developing a form of 'netiquette'. Some suggestions involve the exploitation of the symbols available on the keyboard and can therefore be said to be peculiar to the development of this particular genre. For example, the use of brackets, dashes and colons[9] can be used to express satisfaction with a 'smiley' face [(-:] or dissatisfaction with a frown [)-:]. Equally, certain lexis has developed a specialised meaning. 'Flaming', for example, refers to the expression of extreme anger, and can be used in a way that is non-insulting. However, these conventions are still in the making and are being formed interactively between the people who use the network and the possibilities that have been opened up by the network as a means of communication.

Some of the flavour of the developing nature of the conventions used in email communication can be gained from the following quotations from *Zen and the Art of the Internet*:

> The first thing to understand about Usenet is that it is widely misunderstood. Everyday on Usenet the 'blind men and the elephant' phenomenon appears, in spades. In the opinion of the author, more flame wars (rabid arguments) arise because of a lack of understanding of the nature of Usenet than from any other source. And consider that such flame wars arise, of necessity, among people who are on Usenet. Imagine, then, how poorly understood Usenet must be by those outside!
>
> Usenet is not a democracy: A democracy can be loosely defined as 'government of the people, by the people, for the people'. However, as explained above, Usenet is not an organisation, and only an organisation can be run as a democracy.
>
> (Kehoe, 1992)[10]

As this quotation makes abundantly clear, the development of the genre of email, although manifested in linguistic form, depends on the nature and community of its users.

If we now reconsider the letter from the gas board (Figure 7.5), it will be apparent that the public nature of the discourse takes precedence over the private, although some elements of the private remain. The recipient is clearly identified but the social identity offered is peculiarly impersonal. Mr Bex is certainly an individual, but he is an individual identified both formally as male, and publicly (rather than intimately) through the use of the last name, as is the sender, although interestingly the letter is unsigned. This suggests that the sender is transmitting his message as a functionary of the gas board rather than as an individual. This is further confirmed by the use of the plural personal pronoun 'we' in the first sentence. The use of capitals draws attention to the subject of the exchange. The first paragraph supplies a deictic 'now' which conveniently links the date of the letter with

British Gas

South Eastern

General Manager
MICHAEL HUSBAND

British Gas plc
(South Eastern)
RAMSGATE DISTRICT
BOUNDARY ROAD
RAMSGATE
KENT CT11 7ND

MR A BEX
14 CRESCENT ROAD
RAMSGATE
KENT
                    CT11 9QU

Telephone 0843-595588
Fax 0843 596261

22nd February 1994

Dear Mr A Bex,

THREE STAR SERVICE CONTRACT

We are pleased to advise you that the annual inspection check
of your CENTRAL HEATING BOILER is now due and we have arranged
for our engineer to call on 11th March 1994 before 1.00 pm.

If this date is not convenient, please call us on the above
number and ask for Customer Enquiries to arrange an alternative
appointment.

British Gas are always at the forefront of new technology. Our
Service Engineers now carry the latest precision equipment,
called the Performance Tester, to use during the annual visit
to your gas appliance.

This allows our Service Engineer to carry out accurate checks
on your gas boiler so that we can tell how safely and
efficiently it is performing. If it is working well, we may not
need to disturb any parts.

When the annual visit is completed, we will leave you with a
comprehensive check-list showing exactly what has been done, and
the reassurance that your gas appliance has a clean bill of
health.

If you have been considering the purchase of a new gas
appliance, or you wish to discuss any of our range of service
products our service engineer will be happy to assist you during
the visit.

Yours sincerely,

Alan Firmin
Customer Officer

Figure 7.5 A fuller version of Text 2

the date of the intended visit, while the second paragraph is cohesively linked to the first through the use of 'this'. It can be seen then that these two paragraphs serve to focus very precisely on the nature of the transaction in a variety of ways. The topic is introduced through a heading and is then maintained and given greater detail within the first clause. This topic is further firmly situated within time and space through particular deictic devices. The continuation in the second paragraph is directly linked to the preceding one by grammatical cohesion, and the verbal forms, which are both imperatives, and the presence of the politeness marker 'please', reaffirm the potentially interactive nature of the exchange. There are, thus, features which we might assume to be typical of letters, although in this case some of those which we observed in the private letter have been replaced by others which still mark this letter out as personal but which nevertheless move into the more public sphere. This is perhaps most obvious in the ways in which the letter seems to contain three broad topics. I have commented above on how it may be typical for private letters to shift frequently between topics. In this way they share some of the features of conversation. The letter under consideration does, indeed, move between topics but they are far more carefully managed. The first topic is clearly concerned with the intended visit. This is expanded in a way which offers extra information which is only tangential to the customer, although it clearly has publicity value. The first sentence of the third paragraph, 'British Gas are always at the forefront of new technology', is initially confusing. It has no obvious relationship with the previous paragraphs, and it is only as the paragraph proceeds that readers can establish a clear link. The deliberate fronting of such a sentence, however, enables the writer to assert something positive about the corporate nature of the company, and thus has some elements that we will observe later when we consider advertising texts. Clearly, the introduction of such apparently extraneous material has a function and it is reasonable to assume that its presence is evidence of the invasion of features from another genre which is more centrally concerned with successful marketing. Thus, we can see how the larger social discursive practices within a society can have an effect on the composition of texts which ostensibly belong to genres which are only marginally related to such practices.

PUBLIC GENRES

I have commented that the kind of business letter we have been analysing is interesting in that it contains elements both of the personal (since it is privately interactive) and of the public (in that it contains features of the world of business and marketing). We are, therefore, beginning to establish a way of identifying a particular genre (i.e. that of letters) and the sub-genres that it contains according to the specific communicative purposes of the interaction. If we consider a further subgenre, that of the problem page, our insights can be further refined. The problem page letter is particularly interesting in that the letters it contains present private problems for public view and demand some kind of response from the 'agony aunt'. It is therefore highly interactive. The problems displayed are necessarily personal and usually of a sexual nature, although there are also a number of magazines which contain pages devoted to medical and financial issues. In general, unlike the other letters we have looked at, these tend to be anonymous although there are good grounds for arguing that they are genuine letters. A brief example from *Cosmopolitan* (November, 1994, p. 243) will serve as an illustration:

> i'm [sic] a 20-year-old student and think that I may be becoming obsessed with my appearance. I'm attractive but not perfect, and this makes me increasingly depressed. I'm constantly striving for my ex-boyfriend to re-accept me. We have sex occasionally but he is insensitive and often eyes up other women, which makes me feel unattractive. Without my make-up, I've had comments from strangers about how ugly I look.

The high incidence of personal pronouns indicates the personal nature of the communication very clearly. It is noticeable that the majority of the sentences start with 'I' and that they are all self-referential. The rhetorical structure of the communication thereby forces the reader to concentrate on a single topic (i.e. the writer's self-perception). However, the use of reduced forms, the relatively brief clauses typically joined by simple conjunctions and the use of such lexis as 'eyes up' indicates a degree of informality associated with a conversational interchange. These, though, are mixed with more formal lexis (e.g. 'striving'), an expansion of the verb phrase ('he is') and the fronting of the adverbial 'without my make-up'. Thus, the letter wavers between the intimate and the formal in that the writer seems to be conscious that it will be on public display even though it is discussing a highly personal issue.

Interestingly, this impression of uncertain control is reinforced by the absence of either a name or a provenance, which is quite unlike the other letters we have so far investigated. Given that readers cannot confirm the existence of the writers of such letters, some have claimed that they are fictions designed to increase the circulation of the magazines in which they appear. However, anonymity is a necessary protection for people who are in other ways insecure and, if we accept such letters at face value, it is not entirely surprising that we should find a mixture of public and private styles in such letters.

Further evidence of the genuineness of such letters can be derived from two further sources. First, problem pages invariably include some such instruction as the following:

If you have a problem, write to Irma Kurtz, The Agony Column, Cosmopolitan, National Magazine House, 72, Broadwick Street, London W1V 2BP. Irma regrets that she cannot answer your letters personally.

(Cosmopolitan, November 1994, p. 245)

It can be argued that the foregrounding of an address is significant. It indicates clearly that the printed examples have been composed as letters and will therefore arrive bearing salutations, origin and name of sender even though these may have been subsequently deleted. However, further and more important evidence is supplied by the nature of the printed replies. Kurtz's reply to the letter quoted above starts, 'Your boyfriend will never be "ex" until you stop sleeping with him. And you will never get over him until he's well and truly "ex".' This bears features of a genuinely interactive exchange. By thematising 'your boyfriend', Kurtz uses an interesting rhetorical device to redefine at least part of the problem. Similarly, the relexification of 'have sex' into 'sleeping with him' can also be seen as a way of formalising the exchange to some extent, and thereby giving the response greater authority. But certain elements of the original letter have been retained in ways that suggests a conversational exchange. The relative informality of ' "ex" ' and 'well and truly' and the use of a reduced form 'he's' indicate a degree of intimacy.

These observations, then, suggest that the composition of letters is not merely constrained by the general conventions appropriate to the genre, but is also affected by the typical interaction entered into in the act of writing. We are therefore some way into understanding how genres may contain within them subgenres. So far we have looked at letters that are both private and personal, that are private but identify the recipient as engaged in a particular discursive activity within the larger society, and that are public but are concerned with matters that are of an intimate and personal nature. We have also noticed that such letters signal their differences by means of specific choices at the lexical, grammatical and rhetorical potentials of the language.

Such variations seem also to occur in other types of letters. An interesting subgenre consists of 'Letters to the Editor'. Broadly speaking, letters to the press comment on some aspect of news that has either been reported in the paper and/or previously mentioned in the letters column. The interesting feature of such letters though is that they can adopt various forms. An example, from the Independent (2 November 1994), is given below:

Trains that take the motorway route

From Ms. Amanda Mackenzie Stuart

Sir: Lady Bridges reports that 'rare and beautiful sight' of a double-decker freight train loaded with cars passing through Ipswich station,

and asks whether this is an endangered species (letter, 1 November).
I fear she may be right. A short time ago, I overtook a train travelling up
the M40 on the back of a large truck. Is it possible that even trains now
prefer to travel by road?
Yours faithfully,
AMANDA MACKENZIE STUART
Oxford
1 November

This compares interestingly with the following from *Isle of Thanet Gazette*
(28 October 1994):

In pursuit of peace

A dream came true at Albert Hall.
The marching, the singing lightened my heart
And the finale when the poppies fall,
Made it an occasion apart.
I listened to the singing and joined in the songs,
Felt sad when they recalled the heroes of war,
Listened to the voices of youth,
Trying to recreate days gone before.
The rousing tunes, the marching,
Brought joy to my heart,
Filled me with compassion for the young men,
Who'd fought and lost from the start.
Oh God. let us have no more wars,
Let us live in happiness and peace.
Young men using their strength for good.
And injury, bloodshed and hatred

Ruby Griffiths, Chapel Road, Ramsgate

The first of these is clearly intended to be humorous. However, it is also part
of a contribution to a continuing discussion initiated by the government and
reported in the newspaper as to the relative merits of different kinds of
transport. The continuing nature of the discussion is clearly indicated by the
reference to a previous letter in the same correspondence column. The
discussion is then continued by an observation that, in itself, would be of
little interest unless it had contextual effects on the debate as a whole. That
it is humorous is obvious, but the humour has a particular function within
the overall set of exchanges. A further interesting point is that the letter is
constructed not merely as a comment, but in narrative form. By and large, a
significant proportion of letters to the editor relate a narrative which is
designed to shed further light on, or to introduce, a topic for discussion.[11]
   In terms of its linguistic realisation, this letter is marked by full clauses,

no verb reductions and complex modal constructions ('I fear she may be right', 'Is it possible . . .') that suggest an educated writer. The second is altogether different. Not only is it in the form of a poem (something that is comparatively rare in national newspapers), but it is also marked by uncertain control of tense sequencing (cf. 'fall' in line 3, presumably in the present tense in order to preserve the rhyme); repetition of 'stock' phrases ('lightened my heart'; 'brought joy to my heart'); uncertain focus on an addressee – it is not entirely clear whether the poem is intended to be read as a report of an event and the feelings aroused, or as a prayer – and uncertain rhetorical sequencing (e.g. a 'dream' is mentioned in the first line, though precisely what the dream was is never made clear). There are, of course, other stylistic infelicities to do with scansion and rhyme schemes that are outside the scope of my discussion here and it seems highly likely that the last word or line has been omitted. The combination of these features suggest a relatively uneducated writer. Nevertheless, they are acceptable because they appear in a local newspaper with limited circulation. The potential readers will be members of a narrow geographical area whose interests will be focused on local issues and, by extension, on local people. The communicative event, then, takes precedence over grammatical correctness and stylistic felicity.

On the face of it, then, there would seem to be very few features in common between the various examples of letters I have subjected to analysis. It therefore seems somewhat surprising that we should be able to classify them all as examples of a single genre, and it would certainly suggest that the boundaries of a genre are wider than have been suggested in most studies carried out to date. One way of resolving this problem, as I have suggested, is to reclassify texts within genres according to the nature of the social interaction they are fulfilling. This will allow us to acknowledge that there is a broad genre which we can refer to as *letter-writing*, but that it contains a variety of subgenres. I have indicated that the features which distinguish letters from other genres are a salutation aimed at the addressee, the presence of time deixis, a close which identifies the sender and an address. In the case of 'problem page' letters, we have observed that these may not necessarily be printed. Nevertheless, there are good grounds for assuming that they were included in the original composition. Their absence is intended to protect the anonymity of the sender. In other letters to the press, it would seem that the formal salutation 'Dear Sir' may be omitted in the printed form, although again, it is reasonable to assume that there was some kind of salutation in the original. However, normally we would expect to find some mention of the name and address of the sender usually printed at the bottom.[12] We can also expect to find some considerable variation both in topic and rhetorical organisation of letters depending on the kind of publication in which they appear. This, of course, is obvious if we consider the kinds of letters that may be sent to specialist journals.

But it also seems to be true even of letters that are directed to more general outlets. These differences are a function of the intended readership of the journals or newspapers and may be said to indicate the different discursive relationships that hold between the writers and readers of such letters (and, by extension, such publications).

We can illustrate these differences with the following (Figure 7.6):

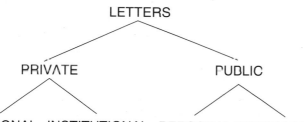

Figure 7.6 The broad genre of letter-writing

in which the personal letters will contain a higher frequency of interactional features designed to indicate closeness (if not intimacy) between the addressor and addressee, while the institutional will tend to more formal styles of presentation. We can also predict that private institutional letters will contain more overlapping features with public institutional letters, while private personal letters will be more similar to public personal letters.

THE CASE OF ADVERTISEMENTS

Following on from this discussion, it is worth looking at the following example of what, on the surface, appears to be an exchange that would fall under the category of a public personal letter:

CRUFTS ON WHEELS

Dear Rhoda, My hobby is breeding and showing dogs. I travel all over the country with my dogs and thoroughly enjoy it. The only problem is my car. Inside it really whiffs – even when the dogs aren't there! Man's best friend is man's worst pong. What can I do about the doggie phew?

You need the Supreme Champion in pong killers Neutradol Car Deodorizer. It comes in a gel sachet or concentrated spray and it's made with natural ingredients. It also works more effectively than any other product of its kind; destroying odours instead of just covering them up. Neutradol Car Deodorizer works on all kinds of in-car pongs and is particularly effective on lingering odours like doggie-smells. You'll find it at your nearest good garage or accessory shop. Try it and your car will smell like a car again – not a dog-basket.

(*Sunday Mirror Magazine*, 6 November 1994, p. 55)

Features which we have typically identified as belonging to the genre of letters are clearly present. There is a greeting although, rather surprisingly, there is no identifier for the sender. However, this could (just) be explained by assuming that unpleasant odours are a matter of such embarrassment that the writer wishes to remain anonymous. Also, elsewhere on the page, there is an address to which readers can write should they wish to know more about car odours. Nevertheless, most readers would have little hesitation in assigning this text to the genre of advertisement.[13] Hasan (Halliday and Hasan, 1985/9, p. 115) mentions a similar case and refers to it as a 'pretend-genre'. This is not a particularly helpful description since, once we have decided that we are reading the text as an advertisement, the genre is no longer pretend. On the contrary, we have identified the text as realising a quite specific genre. Nevertheless, we are still faced with the problem of explaining what it is that this text shares with other texts that we regard as advertisements, and why we should have classified it in such a way.

I have suggested in the preceding section that letters vary according to the functions that they are performing in relation to their intended audience. We can use the same insight to explore the multiplicity of advertisement types. However, we would be inclined to recognise that advertisements have one overriding aim which is to sell goods and services. The different types of advertising texts are therefore likely to vary according to the perceived differences of the potential consumers of the various goods and services being advertised. One of the tasks of a successful advertising campaign is to target a section of the population in such a way as to suggest that they have common interests which can best be met by buying the product on offer. Advertising will, therefore, tend to be parasitic on those genres which are associated with such potential customers. Thus, the kind of advertising manifested by the text above is presumably directed to those readers who both enjoy reading problem pages and who also consider unpleasant smells as something of a personal problem.

Nevertheless, this analysis fails to take us very far since it gives no indication of what the 'Dear Rhoda' letter shares with other advertisements. Clearly, if we wish to identify advertisements as a genre then we would anticipate that they would each contain a set of features which proclaimed their common identity as advertisements. As with letters, advertisements occur in a bewildering variety of forms, ranging from the typical brief (usually postcard sized) announcement in shop windows through to the vast billboards that stand by roadsides. On the surface it might seem that there is little such text types have in common such that readers are capable of identifying a shared function. However, if we recall the distinction made in the last section between public and private genres, we can begin to make sense of both the heterogenous nature of advertisements and also what they have in common.

The idea that advertisements may be viewed as 'private' may seem counter-intuitive at first sight. One function of advertising is to draw the goods and services on offer to the attention of as wide an audience as possible. However, advertisements in shop windows are self-evidently quite restricted in the number of potential readers they are likely to attract. Equally, advertisements in the local press (or in specialist magazines), although likely to be seen by a significantly larger readership, will still only be read by a small proportion of the literate population. A further consideration is that such readers are self-selecting to a far greater extent than the readers of billboards. We can extrapolate from this to suggest that the linguistic realisation of different types of advertisement will be directly affected by the discourse community created by the intended interaction. In the case of shop window advertisements, we can assume that the goods and services on offer are aimed quite selectively at the local community and, perhaps even more narrowly, to the patrons of the shop. This narrowing of potential readership means that such advertisements are highly likely to manifest some of the features which we associate with private genres. In fact, this is what we find. It is not unusual to see such advertisements in handwritten form with slips of spelling, abbreviations and deictic features which point to external circumstances which may be known only within the local community. A typical example (taken from a shop window) is reproduced below (Figure 7.7):

Figure 7.7 An example of an advertisement in a shop window

We can observe that, not only is it handwritten, but the lineation is clumsy. The individual lines each contain unrelated pieces of information. The heading, which might seem superfluous, is presumably included both to draw the readers' attention and to indicate that the transaction indicated is the sale of, rather than a request for, something. The goods on offer are mentioned with a minimum of detail, but followed by a persuasive claim which indicates that such a bed has the desirable quality of being in 'good condition'. The ensuing lines are interesting in that they offer an explanation for the sale. In more public advertisements such explanations would be unnecessary (although they may occur when shops need to clear outdated stock). Here, though, they suggest the private, personal nature of the transaction (cf. my comments on types of letters) in that the advertiser is revealing 'intimate' details which are not normally of any importance in a straight sales transaction. Finally, the figures at the foot are not preceded by an area code, thus suggesting that the sale is likely to take place within the limited geographical area bounded by a local telephone number.

Other features of this advertisement which are significant are the initial deletion at the head. This kind of correction may occur in a private letter to a friend but is much less likely to a more formal, public communication. Similarly, the misspelling of 'neaded' would probably be silently corrected had the advertisement been placed in the local press and appeared in print. Also, there is the interesting rhetorical progression which allows lines four and five to refer both to each other and to line six. A rewrite of this advertisement which fills in the missing grammatical elements might be roughly as follows:

1 (I have something) FOR SALE
2 (It is a) 3ft BED (which is in)
3 GOOD CONDITION
4 (I am selling it because the) ROOM (it occupies is) NEADED
5 (For this reason I am offering it) FOR QUICK SALE
6 (This is also why it is only) £10
7 (If you are interested you should telephone) 580285

Interestingly, though, these missing elements have to be supplied by readers and they can only be supplied if such readers are familiar with the generic conventions appropriate to such advertisements.

The kinds of small advertisements that are found in the local press are likely to manifest similar features, both because they tend to be aimed at a similarly restricted audience and because they are constrained in the same way by considerations of size.[14] The following example may be taken as typical:

LEATHER flying jacket, black,
vgc, £40. Boys Booster bike,
vgc, four-six, £30 – Thanet
01843 848650

Successful decoding of such an advertisement requires a great deal of specialist knowledge. Because the majority of us already possess such knowledge, it may be difficult to appreciate exactly what is involved in constructing (and interpreting) this text appropriately. However, if we re-write it in as full a form as possible the tasks become more obvious:

1 (We have a) **LEATHER** flying jacket for sale.
2 It is black.
3 It is in very good condition.
4 We are offering it for sale at £40.
5 We also have a Boys Booster bike for sale.
6 This is (also) in very good condition.
7 It is suitable for a boy aged between 4 and 6 (?)[15]
8 We are offering it for sale at £30.
9 If you are interested, you should phone Thanet 01843 848650.

What happens in the advertisement (as with the shop window advertisement illustrated above) is that the transitivity and modal choices that would typically be realised by the presence of verb phrases have been deleted, and have to be inferred by readers. Also, some of the lexical elements have been either removed or reduced to an abbreviation. We might also claim that there has been some (optional) re-ordering of the elements in that the adjective which describes the leather jacket occurs after the noun phrase rather than being an integral part of it.

Nevertheless, none of the likely readers of this advertisement are likely to be confused as to its intention even though it has not been realised in full grammatical form. If we are searching for an explanation as to why this is the case, then we would be obliged to argue that grammatical choices are to some extent constrained by the type of interaction intended. Although readers recognise this as a small advertisement for a number of reasons (e.g. it occurs on the page which carries other, similar, advertisements), they still need to be familiar with the conventions of the genre in order to interpret it correctly. This familiarity, though, is the possession of a set of readers and producers who are engaged in buying and selling using a particular medium which requires brevity of expression and the particular generic choices selected are therefore a function both of the larger social discursive practices of commercial exchange and of the more intimate kinds of exchange which might take place between interactants who have recognised common interests.[16]

If we now compare these two advertisements, we can notice a common rhetorical organisation in the ways that the information has been presented. In both cases, the goods and services offered for sale have been thematised by being placed in a prominent position. In the case of the printed advertisement, there is graphological thematisation in that it has been given a prominent typeface and is in upper case letters. The goods are subsequently described in evaluative terms as being, in some sense, worth having. Next, the price is given and finally the source of the information is mentioned. Interestingly, the 'Rhoda' advertisement follows a very similar format. The product is named in the reply almost immediately. Although the enquirer is thematised (and this follows the conventions appropriate to 'problem page' letters), far less attention is paid to the (imaginary) enquirer than is given to the name of the product. It is mentioned twice, and on both occasions it has upper case initial letters which has the effect of foregrounding it. Information is given as to its specific qualities, and its availability. What is missing is any mention of the product's price. But this can be explained in two ways. In the first place, the manufacturers cannot control the price of the goods in the various outlets in which it can be bought, but, perhaps more importantly, the issue of cost is of less central concern than it is to the producers and readers of small advertisements. For the writers of small advertisements it is imperative that they are not pestered by an excess of potential customers who are subsequently not interested. It is therefore in their interests to state clearly how much the goods will cost. For the readers, it is important to know how much the goods are likely to cost, given that they have probably already decided to buy these, or similar, goods anyway.

These observations seem to be confirmed by the following advertisements for sanitary protection. The first (Figure 7.8) appeared in *Just Seventeen* (26 October 1994), a magazine self-evidently aimed at younger (women) readers.

The advertisement, therefore, needs to take this assumed readership into account. Some of the text is written over a picture of a face of a young woman. It leads with the name of the product (which is repeated in various ways eight times within the co-text). This is followed by a persuasive claim that is, at first sight, somewhat mysterious. The mention of 2,400 days is clarified in the ensuing text that appears beneath the picture, which is followed by yet further persuasive claims that are more precise. These claims are related to the heavily modalised information: 'Periods may not be the most important thing in life but they are something you'll probably have to deal with about five days a month for 35 years.' These clauses clearly have an informative, rather than persuasive, intention. This is entirely appropriate to an advertisement for younger readers, some of whom may not yet have started their periods and others of whom may be ignorant about their frequency and occurrence. However, the high degree of modalisation is presumably intended to indicate that the information is only approximate. Nevertheless, it also has the effect of reinforcing

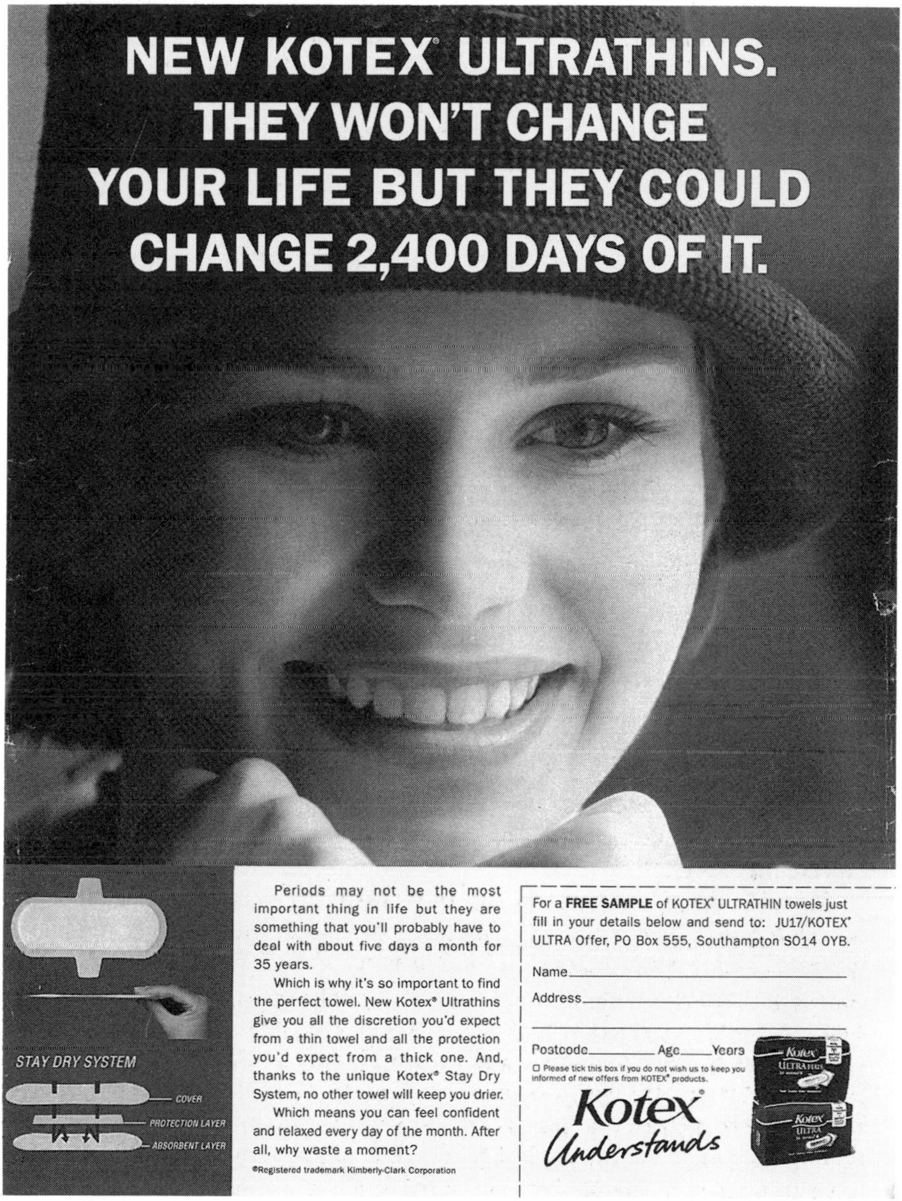

Figure 7.8 Advertisement for Kotex (© M S George Limited)

a conversational style already evident through the choice of set phrases ('the most important thing in life' which rhetorically and lexically relates to the phrase above 'change your life'), reduced verb form ('you'll') and informal lexis ('have to deal with'). The box at the bottom right corner indicates where the product can be obtained. Thus three of the four features I have identified above as belonging to the genre of advertisements are realised.

The Carefree advertisement (Figure 7.9) is constructed in similar ways. The name of the product is foregrounded by being presented within a visual display (a section of which has been inserted into the initial text) and is repeated four times. The list of irritants which heads the advertisement may, at first sight, seem rather surprising. However, it serves two slightly different functions. Formally, it is presented as a full clause although it lacks a finite or non-finite verb. It is therefore rhetorically connected to the list in the co-text: 'The time of the month. The state of the weather.' Semantically, as a list of features which are likely to lead to becoming 'hot and bothered' (and therefore sweaty), it relates to the function of the product which is 'designed to keep your underwear fresh and dry'. However, it also constructs a set of readers who are perceived as drivers which is entirely appropriate for the intended readership of *Cosmopolitan* (November 1994) where it appears. The spine of the magazine proclaims 'Smart Women Carry Cosmo' and presumably one of the attributes of smart women is that they drive on motorways.[17] The persuasive claims are clearly made, but it is not made clear where the product can be bought. We can, however, reasonably assume that anyone who was reading the advertisement would be aware of the outlets which typically sold sanitary protection since, unlike readers of *Just Seventeen*, they would already have started their periods.

I have chosen advertisements for sanitary protection for analysis because, although advertisements have precise customers in mind they are often likely to be read by readers who have no interest in the products on offer. The two I have investigated both appear in magazines with a largely female readership and there is a reasonable assumption that the majority of readers will use some form of sanitary protection.

Thus it makes sense to refer to this group as a discourse community. However, in discussing these advertisements something interesting has occurred in that I (and my readers) have become (temporary) members of this discourse community. As such, I cannot pretend to the specialist knowledge which women readers may bring to these advertisements, but I can participate to the extent that I understand how advertisements work *as a genre*. The same applied to my analysis of the small advertisement where I was confused by the reference to 'four-six'. My interpretations, then, are constrained by my awareness of how advertisements typically work within our society and I can recognise advertisements as such even though I may

Hot days.

Jams, contraflows,

brutish drivers.

All leading

to an experience

for which

I was totally

unprepared.

My knickers felt

fresh on.

How long does a fresh pair of knickers feel fresh?

The answer of course is it depends. On the time of the month. The state of the weather. Where you are. What you're doing. Or whether you're wearing Carefree Panty Liners. Carefree are designed to keep your underwear clean and dry.

EDGE-TO-EDGE ADHESIVE
LINER STAYS SECURELY IN PLACE
COTTON-SOFT COVER

Not only when you're having a period but also for those periods in between.

And because Carefree are slim, soft and secure they won't show, they won't rub and they won't fall out.

By changing them as often as you like, you'll keep your knickers feeling as fresh as when you put them on.

CAREFREE PANTY LINERS.
KEEPS PANTIES CLEANER FRESHER LONGER.

Figure 7.9 Advertisement for Carefree

have no interest in the goods and services on offer. Advertisements, then, can be seen as a generic realisation of a particular discursive practice within our society (that of buying and selling) and I, as a member of that society, am capable of identifying this function and treating even these advertisements as communicative acts.

THE CASE OF RECIPES

The recipe is another genre which seems to have a variety of potential realisations. The basic recipe is well represented by the following:

Cheese-stuffed eggs

cooking time   about 8 minutes

you will need for 4 servings:

4 eggs	3 oz. grated cheddar cheese
salt and pepper	1/2 teaspoon made mustard
1 oz. butter	8 small rounds buttered brown bread

1 Hard boil the eggs and cut in half lengthwise. Trim egg bases so they stand firmly.
2 Scoop out yolks and sieve.
3 Blend with salt, pepper and butter.
4 Mix in cheese and mustard; spoon filling into egg whites.
5 Place on bread rounds and serve with a crisp green salad.

(Patten, 1980, p. 69)

The construction of this is interesting. Although I have described it as a 'basic' recipe, it can only be clearly understood by readers who have some elementary knowledge of cookery. This is indicated most obviously by the lexis (all of which is taken from the semantic field loosely concerned with food preparation) and the abbreviation 'oz'. However, there are some interesting features of cohesion by ellipsis in which the elliptical element has various coreferents. This can be seen by the following rewrite:

1 Hard boil the eggs and cut $\emptyset_1$ in half lengthwise.
2 Scoop out yolks and sieve $\emptyset_2$.

The first instruction depends on readers being fully aware of how long it takes to hard boil eggs. Understanding the second instruction, though, requires knowing both that 'sieve' is a verb and that the sieving applies *only* to the yolks and not to the eggs as a whole. Although relatively trivial knowledge, it is in its way specialist and can be said to assume a particular readership. Formally, this recipe leads with three informative headings, one of which addresses the readers directly. The ingredients to be used are presented in list form with an appropriately reduced grammatical form (cf.

the absence of possessive 'of'). The instructions are each fronted by a verb in the imperative (and share this feature with other instructional genres). There is significant ellipsis not only of pronouns (as mentioned above) but also of articles. Indeed, the only two articles are the deictic specifier 'the' to refer to the eggs already mentioned and the indefinite article in '*a* green salad'. The use of the former may be said to act as a focusing device to select one only from the list of ingredients, and this is perhaps confirmed by the absence of any further specifying devices. The use of the latter can be explained by the green salad being an optional extra.

Chermoula

A Moroccan Marinade for Fish

Every town, even every family has a special combination for this marinade in which every type of fish big or small, whole, filleted or cut in chunks, is left to absorb the flavours. Different herbs are used – parsley instead of coriander, spices in varying proportions, onion instead of garlic – so you may feel free to use the following list of ingredients as a guide and suit your taste.

It is marvellous and I strongly recommend it, but not for a fish with a delicate flavour.

The following measures make a rather large quantity but it keeps well for several days if covered by a thin layer of oil.

1 large bunch fresh coriander, very finely chopped	1 tablespoon paprika
	1 very good pinch cayenne
1 large bunch parsley, very finely chopped	Juice of 1 or 2 lemons, or 150 ml (1/4 pint) vinegar
6 large cloves garlic, crushed	300 ml (1/2 pint) olive or
1 tablespoonful cumin	other oil
1 teaspoon coriander	

Beat all the ingredients well together. Scale, gut and clean the fish if necessary and marinate for at least an hour [you may leave it overnight]. If the fish is large, put some of the marinade inside as well.

(Roden, 1985, p. 204)

Although this is clearly recognisable as a recipe it has some interesting differences as well as similarities with the first one. The most obvious similarities are the presence of an informative title, the list of ingredients and the set of (unnumbered) instructions. Although there is slightly less ellipsis, it is noticeable that the list of ingredients conforms to type by omitting 'of' and by offering similar abbreviated measurement forms. However, this list is also less precise in that it is not at all clear to me (as a relatively inexperienced cook) how large 'large' bunches of coriander and parsley are likely to be, nor exactly what might be intended by '1 very good pinch cayenne'.

The differences are perhaps more significant in that they clearly construct a slightly different readership than that constructed by the former. Not only are the readers assumed to be more familiar with the practicalities of cooking, they are also assumed to be interested in the relationships that hold between cooking and culture and between reader and writer. The initial paragraph is only marginally related to the set of instructions that follows, although the potential variation in ingredients is obviously important. What Roden does do, though, is suggest a mutually shared interest in the activity by introducing a number of interactive forms which are designed to suggest a degree of intimacy. The modality of the phrase 'you may feel free' and the overt appeal to the readers' own tastes suggest (in her own words) a 'guide' rather than instructor. And the ensuing sentence, with its evaluative statements, indicates the personal nature of the communication.

These examples, then, tend to confirm the claim that variety within a genre is a function of the writers' relationship both to the subject matter of the text and to the potential readership. However, they also seem to indicate that there are certain obligatory elements which enable the text to function as a realisation of a particular genre. In this case, we would expect to find the name of the dish, a list of ingredients and a set of instructions for a text to count as a recipe. We would, further, expect the ingredients to be listed in a particular form (typically in columns), with reduced grammatical forms, absence of articles and the presence of abbreviations for quantities. Similarly, we would expect the instructions to be realised through a high incidence of imperative verb forms and (possibly) a considerable degree of ellipted coreferential items. The way these elements are embodied within their co-text will vary quite considerably. We have noticed that Patten introduces no material that is extraneous to the activity of preparing and cooking the ingredients whereas Roden is more expansive offering us a cultural context in which such a marinade is typically prepared. The communicative purposes behind these differences are largely transparent. Patten's book is a very basic one, designed for those who are not yet particularly skilled although even her text takes some knowledge of cookery for granted. She needs to supply a minimum of information that is likely to distract from the activity she is describing. Roden, on the other hand, is introducing a new and relatively exotic cuisine to readers who are assumed to be competent cooks (and interested in cookery) but who want to know more about the dishes she is describing. In the act of analysis, we are able to examine how the two texts both realise and signal these different purposes, while also recognising what they have in common such that we acknowledge them to be instances of the same genre.

CONCLUSION

If we are to draw these observations together in an informative way, it would be to suggest that genres have a real existence and that they serve to orient the reader towards the text in particular ways. Such orientation can never take place in a vacuum. In the act of reading, readers make predictions as to what type of text they are dealing with. They do this primarily because they are familiar with previous texts which manifest similar selections of language (or, in a negative sense, similar ellipses and abbreviations). To that extent, we can claim that writers' linguistic choices overtly signal how their texts are to be read and that genres are properties of text. However, this formulation would be slightly misleading on two counts. The first is that readers are always capable of rejecting (through recontextualisation) the intended readings. To some extent this has happened in the course of my discussions of the various genres I have been looking at. In transferring those texts into this text, I have subverted their original and intended functions in order to recontextualise them as objects for linguistic study and invite you, the readers, to view them in my way. This leads on to the second objection, which is that generic interpretations are always joint functions of readers and writers. They are only ever realised in use. Thus, genres should be seen as collections of text types which serve a common function. I have chosen the verb 'serve' quite deliberately, since texts do not possess functions intrinsically so much as signal the ways in which they are intended to be used. Their use, however, is a function of individual readers operating as members of a given society.

I have suggested above that social interaction is rarely a unitary activity. Although it is a convenient fiction to assume that individuals are students, academics, children, parents, taxpayers, economic animals, voters, etc., it is also true that they manifest these various social roles *at the same time*. At any given moment, one such role may predominate. However, although the other roles may be in temporary abeyance, they are not completely absent. These various roles are mediated through and constituted by (though not exclusively by) language. A genre, therefore, represents a set of texts which invites readers to orient themselves towards a particular social role or set of social roles. Because social interactions are rarely entirely discrete,[18] we would expect variations within genres to reflect both the particular subset of readers that are being addressed and the particular role(s) adopted by the writers.

In the analyses offered above, I have suggested that it may make sense to refer to 'letters' as a distinct genre although given the huge variety of purposes for which people may write a letter, it has been necessary to posit various subgenres to account for such variation. Advertisements are also directed to a vast potential readership, but their function within our society is relatively constant. Their defining characteristics as a genre are therefore more salient, although there remains significant variation between different kinds of advertisements. Recipes, another genre, also have a limited social function and their potential readership is further limited. We would, therefore, anticipate rather less variety within the genre. However, we have noticed that recipes typically include the 'giving of instructions' and therefore necessarily overlap with other genres which purport to be instructional. Academic journal articles are socially situated within an even narrower *milieu* (although there are significant differences between academic disciplines) and have a correspondingly more limited range of (linguistic) variation thus allowing Swales and Bhatia to treat them as distinct subgenres with recognisable features. But they too are likely to share features with, say, textbooks because they are part of a collective set of discursive practices. Therefore the boundaries of genres and subgenres are not, and cannot, be fixed precisely because they represent communicative activities within the larger society of which they are a part. They are, by their very existence, in communication with other communicative acts. Nevertheless we would expect genres to be sufficiently distinct as to be recognisable, and the existence of parody suggests that this is indeed the case.

It is now time to relate these observations to my earlier chapters. It should be obvious to my readers that the various texts that I have analysed are unlike each other in a number of respects, and yet I have little doubt that most readers managed to construct successful interpretations of all of them. This unlikeness is, quite literally, eloquent proof that written texts are not all constructed using a single language variety (variously characterised as Standard English). It is also obvious that the varieties we have observed have developed (and changed) historically. The contemporary letters have many features in common with the one from the eighteenth century quoted earlier in the book; the contemporary small advertisements share some, but rather fewer features with the one I introduced in the questions to Chapter 2. One of my complaints in the first two chapters was that by failing to study language variety we failed to understand how language might be used as a means of social representation. We observed this happening in my examples by distinguishing first between private and public genres which imply different kinds of social relationships, and then by seeing how letters, advertisements and recipes all appealed to slightly different social constituencies (although they may all be represented in the same person). Further, we noticed that our interpretations of any particular text would always be that which was most immediately relevant to ourselves (cf. my own 'uses' of the sanitary protection advertisements), but in the construction of that interpretation we would be guided by our experience of other texts we had encountered. However, we would be guided not solely on the basis of textual form, although this would play its part, but on our experience of what given texts actually seemed to do. And finally, but briefly, we observed that genres, as communicative events, indicated what kinds of activities were regarded as important within a society.

APPENDIX

Agents of ice

Gary L Gaile, Department of Geography, University of Colorado, Campus Box 260, Boulder CO 80309, USA and **Dean M Hanink**, Department of Geography, University of Connecticut, Storrs CT 06268, USA

Teenagers cause winter. This long-lost fact was initially revealed at the turn of the 18th century to Gabriel D Fahrenheit, who developed a scheme of measuring temperature based on age. Fahrenheit realised that not only is temperature related to age, but that teenagers actually control climate. Over the centuries, Fahrenheit's age-climate control theory has been viewed mercurially, but his scale has lived on, challenged only by the metric of IC Celslus, who, being 5/9 the scholar Fahrenheit was, felt life and temperature began at 32 (note that teen temperatures are cold in Fahrenheit, but warm in Celsius), and by Chastity Kelvin who believed in absolute frigidity.

In order to test the hypothesis that teenagers cause winter, data from the 1980 US Census has been subjected to unerring statistical analysis. The variables used to measure age and temperature respectively were '% of the population 5–17 years old' which includes most teenagers and many who aspire to the status and 'mean January temperature' (in Fahrenheit, coincidentally). The data were collected for all central cities of Standard Metropolitan Statistical Areas in the US and a robust unilateral sample of 68 cities was taken (Table 1). The results are conclusive: an inverse relationship ($r = 0.87$) between teenagers and high January temperatures, therefore teenagers cause winter. Despite the high correlation (R^2 0.755, significance level = 0.0001), the predictive power of the model is not perfect. Additional minor determinants of climate, e.g. solar energy, are not included because this would just confuse everybody.

Initial critics of our research have argued that the correlation is simply due to the fact that the elderly tend to move to sunnier climes upon retirement, thus accounting for the skewed age distribution. Such criticism is an attempt to cover up perhaps the most nefarious conspiracy in climatic history. Age is not just related to climate, teenagers actually control climate and have through time immemorial caused winter.

How and why do teenagers cause winter?

Evolution indicates that humans evolved in the equatorial regions. Why did they move from such a central location? It is probable that early teenagers had a rapport with their parents similar to the rapport that exists today. It is surprising anyone lived through it. Survival, indeed, was the name of the game. To survive the identity crisis (complicated not just by ego, but by speciation), teenagers fled north and south from equatorial regions. They soon learned to cause winter in an attempt to discourage their parents from following them and bringing them back home. The ice ages caused by teenagers were quite effective in limiting both the mobility and the life expectancy of adults.

Now that teenage control of climate has been proven with certainty, it is important to look at the evidence for causality and motivation. Causality is indeed

Table 1 Age-temperature relation of US cities

City	% pop. 5–17	Mean Jan. Temp	City	% pop. 5–17	Mean Jan. Temp
Abilene	19·9	43·7	Dubuque	24·0	17·7
Akron	20·9	26·3	Ft Lauderdale	16·1	66·8
Amarillo	20·2	36·0	Ft Myers	16·6	63·5
Anaheim	20·5	54·5	Gainesville	17·0	57·0
Anchorage	22·0	11·8	Las Vegas	20·5	44·2
Anderson	22·4	28·2	Los Angeles	19·7	54·5
Appleton	22·3	16·9	Melbourne	19·5	61·8
Asheville	19·7	37·9	Miami	18·2	67·2
Athens	18·8	44·5	Ocala	20·1	57·0
Austin	19·2	49·7	Racine	23·0	22·3
Battle Creek	22·0	22·3	Raleigh	19·0	40·5
Bay City	22·8	23·1	Richland	22·4	32·2
Benton Harbor	23·1	24·2	Rochester MN	21·7	12·9
Billings	21·0	21·9	Rock Island	22·4	20·2
Binghamton	21·2	22·0	Sacramento	19·6	45·1
Bismarck	22·0	8·2	St Cloud	23·2	8·9
Boise	21·4	29·0	Salinas	19·9	50·0
Bradenton	15·7	61·3	San Angelo	19·8	46·4
Bristol	21·6	24·8	San Diego	18·6	55·2
Brockton	22·9	29·2	San Francisco	17·5	48·3
Burlington	21·1	16·8	Santa Barbara	18·1	53·2
Canton	21·5	26·3	Santa Cruz	17·4	48·8
Cedar Rapids	21·6	20·4	Santa Rosa	19·3	46·1
Charleston WV	19·6	34·5	Sheboygan	21·5	24·5
Chicago	21·2	22·9	Sherman	19·6	41·7
Cincinnati	21·6	31.1	Syracuse	21·5	21·8
Colorado Sp.	21·4	32·9	Tallahassee	18·9	52·6
Cumberland	21·2	29·0	Tampa-St Pete	17·2	60·4
Danbury	23·3	24·8	Tucson	19·7	51·1
Davenport	21·6	22·9	Tuscaloosa	20·0	45·0
Dayton	21·4	28·1	Waco	19·3	47·0
Daytona Beach	16·3	58·4	Wausau	22·9	12·4
Decatur	21·2	28·3	W Palm Beach	16·2	65·5
Detroit	22·4	25·5	Yakima	22·3	27·5

Correlation: R = 0·869, α = 0·0001, R^2 = 0·755, F = 203·6
Regression: Temperature = 180·3 – 7·04 Age, Standard error = 0·49

difficult to wholly determine, although particles of evidence have surfaced in diverging areas. It is well known, for instance, that teenagers often try to 'act cool'. It is also known that they frequently leave the refrigerator door open. There are even some reports that teenagers have illicitly been importing 'snow' from Colombia. They are always ordering ice in their drinks and taking coolers to their sporting events. They have grown long hair as natural protection (it is interesting to note that baldness comes with age, perhaps indicating early sucess of teenage genetic engineering). They (and a few adults who'd like to be younger) are the only ones who actually go out and play in the snow. Most nefarious of all, during the summer months they actually 'soak up rays' very casually, thus depriving the earth of its source of heat.

Indeed, if we go back to the earliest teenagers, the Eskimos, we find that they abandon their elderly in the name of preserving their natural environment. In the tropical areas of the world, humans 'grow up' fast and may even be said to completely miss their teenage years as they progress directly to adulthood with the onset of puberty, thus explaining the lack of winter in these parts.

The seasonal migration of teenagers to Florida indeed signals the end of winter in the northern areas they inhibit. It is important to note that the leaders of the teenage cult migrated from colder climes upon reaching maturity, e.g. Jerry Lee Lewis and Dick Clark moved from the cold to Los Angeles[1] as did Hugh Hefner when he came of age. Indeed, some teenage heroes became victims of their own control, most notably, the loss of Buddy Holly and the Big Bopper in a snow storm air crash.[2] Among the leaders of the teenagers today is a group called 'Kool and the Gang'. Need more be said?

Teenage motivation for causing winter is perhaps more difficult to ascertain. Perhaps they simply still like the fact that it annoys their parents, or they realise that Christmas and the concomitant gifts (a valuable economic incentive to this non-working class) require winter. It is known that as soon as they are allowed to conspire *en masse*, i.e. when school starts, winter is never far behind. It has even been noted that there is a declining intellectual climate in the schools.[3]

Much research remains. What is the effect of marijuana smoke or acne vapour on the ozone layer? Do the more efficient digestive systems of teenagers substantially reduce the amount of superheated gaseous effluent in the atmosphere? Can ice cream parlours and milk shakes be outlawed? What did Meg Trudeau do with the Rolling Stones?[4] Can teenagers and winter be eliminated?

Notes

1 Allen J.L. (1954 Chevrolet) 'Killer teens: the Lewis and Clark expedition' in Belmonts, Dion and the (eds) *Festschrift for Dobie Gillis* (Beach Blanket Press, Malibu CA), 212–490 + maps and apology
2 Allen J.L. (1985) 'The Holly–Bopper expedition' in Scott, Willard (ed.) *Flights of fancy* (Tomorrow's News Today Press, Burbank CA), available only on Video Disc
3 Willmott P.J. (1984) 'Climastrology: what's your sign and why do you treat me so cold?' *Journal of Adolescent Climatology* 17(2), 3–4
4 Steinbeck J. (1234) *The winter of our disco teens* (Clansfield State University Press, Clansfield)

FURTHER READING

There has been an explosion of interest in non-literary genre recently. Book length studies have appeared in 1987 (Ventola), 1990 (Swales) and 1993 (Bhatia; Suter). Ventola's *The Structure of Social Interaction* is a key work within the Hallidayan tradition which attempts to refine and develop some of the ideas that were taking shape earlier. She has a particularly interesting discussion of Hasan's concept of generic structure potential. Unfortunately, she concentrates her analysis on spoken service encounters and therefore some of her methods and conclusions do not transfer easily to the analysis of written genres. Hasan's views on genre are probably best represented in

Language, Context and Text (Halliday and Hasan, 1985/9), although she has written extensively on literary genres (see next chapter) and the interrelationship of language and culture. 'Ways of saying: ways of meaning' (1984b) can be particularly recommended for, although it is not centrally concerned with genre, it does suggest the ways in which the discursive practices of different societies invade and shape genres.

Halliday's writing on genre suggests that it is best situated within mode (e.g. Halliday, 1978, p. 145). This is a position which has been challenged by Martin (1985), and his detailed treatment of context in *English Text* (1992) is highly recommended. It should be obvious that I am more sympathetic to Martin's position. The relationship between genres and other social practices has been extensively explored by Kress (1989b) in *Linguistic Processes in Sociocultural Practices* working within a critical discourse analysis framework. A collection of papers in *Word* (1989; vol. 40) brings together the theoretical and practical difficulties of dealing with genre analysis from a largely systemic–functional perspective.

Different approaches are being developed within the US which relate genre study closely with the older traditions of rhetorical study, thus reviving interest in an area that was of considerable importance in education up until the nineteenth century. An interesting collection of papers occurs in Freedman and Medway (eds), *Genre and the New Rhetoric* (1994) and readers are particularly directed to the papers by Carolyn Miller. Another collection which touches on genre analysis is *Discourse Description* (1992) edited by Mann and Thompson. Although its focus is on the different ways in which a particular text can be analysed, the analyses themselves frequently comment (sometimes indirectly) on the relation of the particular text to its text-type.

Swales's *Genre Analysis* (1990) has been the inspiration for much of this chapter. His book is particularly good on the theoretical aspects of definition. The later chapters, however, concentrate on a particular subgenre (that of the academic research article) and relate it to the pedagogical concerns of the ESP class. Although he does have comments to make on more everyday genres, his work fails to deal with the kinds of texts that most people have to use as part of their 'ordinary' lives. Bhatia's *Analysing Genre* (1993) is slightly unfocused. Like Swales, he considers genre description largely in terms of *moves*, paying comparatively little attention to the ways these moves are realised linguistically. Given that he argues the psycholinguistic processes involved in recognising genres have been relatively neglected, this might be considered reasonable. He, too, has a number of pedagogical observations which are relevant to the ELT classroom, and he has some particularly interesting things to say about the growth, and adaptation, of genres in the 'new Englishes' of South East Asia. Suter's *The Wedding Report* (1993) is an interesting study of a particular genre which relates it very directly to its social situation. Although developed largely within the textlinguistic tradition of Germany, his work has considerable affinities with Swales. A collection of papers which approaches genre from a Swalesian position occurs in the *Revue Belge de Philologie et d'Histoire* (1993, vol. 71, 3) and includes my own paper where I develop in more detail some of my observations on advertising.

A useful starting point for relating parody to genre analysis occurs in Swales (1990). The literature on parody is extensive and a good general survey occurs in Rose (1993) *Parody: Ancient, Modern and Postmodern.* Unfortunately, most discussions of parody are concerned with literary parody and confuse what Ben-Porat (1985) calls 'genre parodies' with 'idiolectal parodies'. As will be clear from my discussion in this section, I am unconvinced that imitations of the particular authors should be considered as parodies (see discussion in Bex, forthcoming). Nevertheless, the various recent discussions contribute significantly to the literature on *intertextuality* in more general ways.

SOME QUESTIONS FOR CONSIDERATION

The following gem is an extract from a collection of parodies (Macdonald, 1960, p. 497). Commenting on a popular children's book *Strewelpeter*, Rudolph Friedmann produced the following psychoanalytic interpretation.

> The Inky Boys (to begin with quite white) breathe out racial hatred for the Black-a-moor symbolizing the exotic sinfulness of African and Asian potency. But the punishing father and still living German super-ego, Agrippa, lived close by 'so tall he almost touched the sky'; 'He had a mighty inkstand, too/In which a great goose-feather grew.'
>   (Cf. The long thin, almost imperceptible, black hair growing out of the palm of the left hand of masturbators.) Agrippa drops the three horrors into the inkstand so that they emerge blacker than Black-a-moor. The three are thrown back into the black well of the mother's womb to be reminded of their origin. 'Inter urinas et faeces nascimur.'

Friedmann assured Macdonald that this was not a parody, but gave him permission to reprint it anyway.

1 a How would you treat this?
   b If you consider it to be a parody, what genre is it parodying?
   c If you do not treat it as a parody, what genre do you feel it belongs to?
   d Is it possible to be a parody and instantiate a particular genre?

2 In my discussion of the problem page letters, I mentioned the ways in which the 'agony aunt' typically positioned her readers. Do you feel there is any justification for treating the letters and replies as two separate genres, or do you feel they are best treated as a single genre?

Chapter 8

The case of literature

INTRODUCTION

If my general argument is accurate it has particular consequences for literature. I have argued that texts enter into particular generic configurations precisely because writers and readers treat language as having social consequences. Writers therefore construct texts in conformity with perceived generic conventions because they intend their texts to have the particular 'meanings' associated with the genre and readers interpret such texts according to the same conventions because they are familiar with previous, similar texts and recognise the intentions. Genres are differentiated precisely to the extent that the social activities they symbolise can be differentiated. However, because individual social practices are embedded in a nexus of dominant practices (or discourses) which give them legitimacy, genres are likely to retain traces of such discourses. Thus, although genres may be realised as relatively distinct text types, individual texts may manifest features of other, overlapping genres.

Further, I have suggested that genres operate at the interface between linguistic and non-linguistic discursive practices. On this basis, the ultimate communicative success of any individual text must depend on the uses to which it is put. If we read a set of instructions, recognise them as instructions and then choose to ignore them, it is likely that the task they describe will be performed badly. Such texts, then, are intended to have immediate pragmatic consequences. To this extent, the texts we have been discussing seem to make direct reference to a phenomenal world.[1]

This raises a number of interesting problems in the case of a particular set of texts which do not seem to have the same kind of referential and pragmatic effects as those we have previously been discussing. Traditionally, such texts are referred to as literary texts and the fact that they are identified by a generic name suggests that they are recognised as performing some kind of function. However, the precise nature of this function is not immediately apparent. A further set of problems derives from the fact that a vast quantity of different text types are subsumed under the general heading of literature. I have already commented that the existence of a variety of text types may be subsumed within a specific genre, but the sheer diversity of literary texts suggests a number of problems that we have not met in our treatment of advertisements or letters. However, it may be that they will yield to the same kind of analysis, in which case we will have to posit a variety of discourse communities with rather looser connections than hold between the discourse communities that use other public genres.

With the notable exception of Hasan (1985), contemporary linguists have not been much concerned with the generic study of literature. They have made a number of interesting stylistic contributions to the study of literature, and some of them have been considerably exercised by the nature of 'literariness', but the ways in which literature functions as a genre and the relationships between the subgenres have been curiously under-investigated. This is somewhat surprising for, as Schaeffer argues:

> in these arts [by which he means music, painting, etc.] the need to distinguish between artistic and non-artistic practices does not arise . . . for the simple reason that they are intrinsically artistic activities. However, literature or poetry form local domains within a huge and integral semiotic domain, that of verbal practices, most of which are not artistic: the problem of defining and describing the field of literature (or of poetry) thus becomes vital.[2]
>
> (1989, pp. 8–9, my translation)

Of course, the genres within literature have been extensively explored by literary theorists and critics with varying degrees of success. Aristotle was one of the first to distinguish between kinds of literature and their different functions, and English critics have argued vehemently since the medieval period as to the proper 'forms' of language appropriate to particular kinds of literary production. More recently, Frye (1957) engaged in a detailed analysis of literary genres, and Alastair Fowler published his *Kinds of Literature: An Introduction to the Theory of Genres and Modes* in 1982. But the specific ways in which the existence of literary texts can be accommodated within a more general theory of language use has (at least recently) attracted relatively little attention.

THE GENRE OF LITERATURE

One way into this discussion would be to consider Fowler's (1982) distinction between 'types' and 'genres' within literature. My introduction started with a line from Sidney's sonnet-sequence *Astrophel and Stella*. The sonnet may be considered as a type which has developed independently of the functions to which it has been put. Thus a sonnet is recognised as a sonnet precisely because of a set of formal features: i.e. it has to contain fourteen lines, rhyme in certain ways and demonstrate a topical development from the octet to the sestet. In this sense, it can be considered as a text as described in Chapter 4. The uses to which particular sonnets may be put, though, are various. In Sidney's case, they were used both as an intimate form of address to his lover, and as a knowing reference to, and intervention in, the discursive practices associated with the 'courtly love' tradition. Milton and Shelley, on the other hand, used them for public exhortation and related them to quite different discursive practices within their society. For these reasons, Fowler considers the sonnet form as a 'type' which belongs to a formal taxonomy developed within literary studies. Genres, on the other hand:

> have to do with identifying and communicating rather than defining and classifying. We identify the genre to interpret the exemplar . . . In literary communication, genres are functional: they actively form the experience of each work of literature.
>
> (1982, p. 38)

This is a useful initial distinction, but if Fowler's argument is to be vindicated he needs to demonstrate precisely how the genres (or, in my terminology, subgenres) are functional. This must surely depend on a more general view of how literature is functional as a whole, and Fowler does not offer a clear answer to this problem.

Jakobson considered this issue from a slightly different perspective. He first identifies a set of functions that language typically performs, and then singles out the poetic function as 'the dominant, determining function' in verbal art (1960, p. 37). He argues that, 'The set toward the MESSAGE as such, focus on the message for its own sake, is the POETIC function of language.' And later he claims '*The poetic function projects the principle of equivalence from the axis of selection into the axis of combination*' (ibid., p. 39). These are interesting claims in the ways they assume direct and immediate relationships between the formal properties of language and the uses to which it is put. If we agree with Jakobson that particular syntagmatic arrangements signal the predominance of the poetic function of language, then we might conclude that unusual syntagms can be used as the identifying feature of literature. And indeed some scholars have investigated how (some works of) literature 'foregrounds' certain features of language through metaphoricity, the use of rhymes, etc. and used the notion of foregrounding as part of their definition of literature.[3] Although such investigations managed to capture some sense of the uniqueness of (certain kinds of) poetic texts, they tended to ignore the functional element that was intrinsic to Jakobson's characterisation.

Another way of dealing with Jakobson's characterisation was to recognise that all language use manifested a poetic function to some degree (cf. Werth, 1976) and that the classification of some texts as literature was undertaken for purely institutional reasons. Roger Fowler adopts this strategy in *Linguistic Criticism* (1986) where he argues that the use of language in literature is co-extensive with other uses of language and can therefore be analysed in the same ways. In so far as literature is considered to be unique (and therefore in some sense better) than other kinds of texts, it is because societies choose to classify them in this way for particular ideological reasons. Again, there is something uncomfortable about this claim. Although it seems to account for why some rhyming texts are treated as advertisements while others are treated as poems, it fails to capture the distinctive ways in which literature is used, and recognised, by individuals within a society. It is just not enough to say that text A is an advertisement and text B a poem simply because society has decreed this to be the case. The texts operate differently because they are perceived both by their writers and their readers as performing different functions.

Indeed, Fowler's argument takes us dangerously close to Fish's (1980) view that the identification of literary value is the function of an 'interpretative community'. Of course, the identification of aesthetic value is not quite the same thing as the identification of a text as literary *per se*, but the way in which Fish has constructed his argument certainly suggests a significant overlap between the two concepts. Fish refers to an experiment he conducted in which he invited his students to discuss a random list of names left on the board by a previous lecturer as though it were a poem. He comments that they were all prepared to engage in an analysis of the displayed text using the techniques appropriate to literary criticism, thus demonstrating that there is nothing intrinsic to any text which declares it to be a work of literature. This leads him to claim that:

> Skilled reading is usually thought to be a matter of discerning what is there, but if the experience of my students can be generalised, it is a matter of knowing how to *produce* what can thereafter be said to be there.
>
> (1980, p. 327)

It is doubtful that Fish would regard this brief test as being adequate proof of his thesis, but there are certain deeply flawed assumptions at play here. In the first place, we have to acknowledge that Fish was in a position of authority, and there is nothing unreasonable in a literature class assuming that the given text was literary if their teacher had asserted it was so. Perhaps, more importantly, acknowledging with Jakobson that the poetic function is present in all texts, it is not surprising that students, asked to find such features, should strive to identify them. However, this is not proof that literature is solely in the eye of the beholder, although it may be evidence to suggest that the analytic techniques appropriate to literary study are the possession of an interpretative community and can be applied by that community to other kinds of texts.

Nevertheless, the idea of an interpretative community is interesting since it obviously has resonances with Swales's references to a 'discourse community'. In the light of my previous arguments, there do seem good grounds for accepting the view that a literary reading of a particular text may be closely associated with a given 'discourse community', and I shall come back to this later. However, we still have to establish why a given range of texts are considered by a significantly large proportion of the reading public to be examples of literature while other texts are not. Simply appealing to some form of institutional authority, whether conceived in broad terms as with Fowler or in the narrower sense used by Fish, seems deeply unsatisfactory if only because readers, under normal circumstance, seem able to make such classifications on their first acquaintance with a given text.

This might seem to suggest that there is something intrinsic in the text which signals that it is to be read 'as literature' in which case we have come full circle to the original followers of Jakobson and which we earlier rejected. A recent attempt to square this circle has been made by Carter (1987a) who believes that there may be a cline of 'literariness', and that different texts will be more or less literary. This certainly has the merit of accounting for why it is that we view certain (non-literary) works as being more like literature rather than other works and it acknowledges that all texts demonstrate some degree of 'literariness'. But by tending to resituate the element of 'literariness' as to do with the choice of language rather than the use of the text as a communicative act, it leaves open the question as to how 'literary' a text has to be to count as literature.

LITERATURE AND RELEVANCE THEORY

What we need to consider is how readers read, and what it is in the work that they are reading *regardless of its form* that persuades them that they are reading literature. From there, we can construct a possible theory as to what functions literature performs within society. Consider a reader confronted with any one of the texts that I have considered earlier in the book. Following Sperber and Wilson's principle of relevance they would construct a context in which the utterance achieved maximum contextual effects. For example, when I read letters from my friends, I think about them, I am happy when they are, sad when they are. When I read a letter from the building society, I consider the effects it is likely to have on my bank account. When I read a recipe, I either choose to follow the instructions or decide that the dish is too difficult or inappropriate for the occasion. When I read an advertisement, I either seek out the goods and services on offer or forget them. All these acts of reading lead to quantifiable contextual effects and not merely to my cognitive environment. Suppose I were to read a recipe and find that the instructions were flawed in some way. I would still be likely to consider it as a recipe rather than as belonging to some other genre since I would assume that its function (although flawed) was to instruct me how to prepare a meal. If, on a careful re-reading, I notice some element that seems incommensurate with my experience of previous recipes, then I might be inclined to view it as a parody. But such re-classification also depends on my recognition that the use of texts as recipes has specific contextual effects which, in this case, are not taking place.

My claim, then, is that in most of our interactions with the written word we expect pragmatic consequences to follow on our interpretation. This is true even for those works which have an effect only on our cognitive environment. If I read a work of history, or a news report in the paper and am not convinced by the information offered, I have ways of confirming or denying what I believe to be the case. I can seek out another history book and search for an alternative interpretation of the event, or I can make contact with the people whose story has been reported and confirm its veracity. All these texts relate to the phenomenal world and the consequences of a particular interpretation can be tested empirically against this phenomenal world.

In the case of literary texts this is just not the case. When I open a novel, I cannot question the characters in it to discover whether they really did perform the actions that have been described. When I read a poem, I cannot directly question the accuracy of the feelings expressed in quite the same way as I can question whether the events in an autobiography actually occurred simply because the emotions are those of the writer and therefore unknowable except in the linguistic form offered. My central claim, then, is that literature is recognisable precisely because its propositions are not propositions about the phenomenal world and belief (or disbelief) in them has no necessary pragmatic consequences for the reader.

I can best illustrate this by considering a poem which, on the face of it, appears to be firmly rooted in the world that we typically experience. Auden's (1940, p. 47) 'Musée des Beaux Arts' seems to be a description of a set of paintings with special emphasis on Brueghel's *Icarus*. If we were to visit the gallery we would presume to see exactly the same paintings as Auden. The poem, then, could be considered to be a form of reportage or criticism and could therefore be treated in exactly the same way as any other art criticism. One might argue that the pragmatic consequences of reading the text in this way would be to enable a visitor to the museum to look at the paintings with new perceptions. Although such an outcome is likely to be the case, readers are left with certain puzzles. The first, and most obvious, is why Auden should have chosen to construct his art criticism using rhyme. This is not an insoluble problem, and can be treated as a textual feature which is of minimal significance in identifying this as a work of literature. However, it does hint that we are not reading a *catalogue raisonnée*. Related to the use of rhyme is the unusual typographical layout but this, again, is not in itself sufficient to assign it to literature (cf. the layout of certain advertisements). Another noticeable feature is the somewhat contorted syntax. The opening lines:

> About suffering they were never wrong,
> The Old Masters

are unusual in that the cataphoric use of the pronoun may well be more associated with speech than writing. A close reading is likely to identify a number of unusual collocations: e.g. 'the torturer's horse/Scratches its *innocent* behind on a tree'; while a still closer reading will pick out a higher than statistically likely number of rhymes and half-rhymes. However, if we use these features as a means of identifying the work as literary, we run the risk of assuming that literature can be distinguished by the use of a particular selection of 'literary' language.

But if we consider Auden's description of the pictures themselves, it slowly becomes apparent that we are being offered an interpretation rather than a description. This, of course, is signalled by the accumulation of adjectives, but again I want to discount the textual features of the poem to concentrate on what it seems to be saying. And it is quite clear that looking at the pictures themselves will not enable us to establish the truth of what Auden appears to be claiming. There is nothing directly present in Brueghel's *Icarus* to confirm his observation that:

> . . . everything turns away
> Quite leisurely from the disaster: the ploughman may
> Have heard the splash, the forsaken cry,
> But for him it was not an important failure . . .

because Auden is extrapolating from a visual experience to an entirely fictional textual world. While we can identify the ploughman, and may be inclined to agree with Auden's attribution of insouciance, we have no way of questioning the figure to find out whether it actually occurred. Further, of course, we may notice that the painting itself is not of a historical event and that at least one representation in the picture is of a mythical person. Thus, the world created in the poem is at two removes from the world we experience with our senses.[4]

If, then, we are able to recognise literature precisely because it does not refer (directly) to the phenomenal world, it follows that the classification contains a considerable number of disparate text types including jokes, riddles, conundrums, parodies as well as novels, drama and poetry. It also, of course, excludes a number of works that are highly valued because of their literary merit. The former claim obliges us to ascertain what such diverse texts have in common in the way of social function. The latter can be explained in terms of the former, because if it can be established that literary texts have certain valuable functions, then the reading strategies which are employed in reading literature will be transferred to those other texts which are perceived as making uses of similar linguistic resources.

THE SOCIAL FUNCTION OF LITERATURE

Although it is true that literature does not refer directly to the phenomenal world, this is not to say that it does not refer indirectly. The concepts and propositions which are evoked by reading a literary text may not have specific correlations with items and relationships in the non-fictional world, but they enable us to create relatively rich imaginary cognitive worlds which mimic the external world. However, given that these worlds are constructed of words rather than things, the choice of words takes on added significance. As Widdowson (1984, p. 158) explains, 'literature . . . represents realities other than those conventionally referred to by creating unique schemata which confer upon signs an additional dimension of meaning'. By this he seems to be referring to Jakobson's notion of the orientation towards the message itself. If language is not referring conventionally, then we as readers are likely to pay more attention to the materiality of language and recognise it for itself as well as for what it does. And this does, indeed, seem to occur in certain literary reading processes. With poetry, for example, we pay attention to the rhythms and rhymes and treat them as meaningful. In narrative, we pay attention to features such as the method of characterisation, the ways narrative has been constructed, and treat these as meaningful. Thus we engage in literary reading strategies (which is why we know how to apply them to non-literary texts should we so desire).

Cook (1994) has expanded on Widdowson's view by suggesting that literature tends to be 'schema-refreshing'. By this he means that conventional ways of perceiving the world are challenged by the ways created by literature. And this brings us to the social function of literature as a genre. It offers us an alternative world against which we can judge the phenomenal world. This possibility seems to be confirmed by the application of relevance theory. If readers initially approach written texts using the same cognitive interpretive processes, when they are faced with a text that clearly does not refer to the real world they will assign some relevance to the cognitive world they have created (Bex, 1992). Initially it is not entirely clear what kinds of contextual effects might be derived from the creation of a fictional world, and it is likely that these will vary from reader to reader. Some readers may well use the fictional world as a pleasant escape from the real world, but other readers are likely to assess its potentiality for existence and in that way use it as a means of criticising the external world.

However, given that my characterisation of literature allows in such a variety of different kinds of texts, it might be helpful to qualify this claim to some extent. Van Peer (1991, p. 134) has suggested that literary texts are essentially homiletic, i.e. that they are 'reflective, socially cohesive, and delight inducing'. Although he was almost certainly referring to those kinds of texts which have been traditionally classified as literature, this identification of a social function neatly fits most of the other texts which I have included. All of them, in some way or other, invite delight and some go beyond this and can be used as a means of reflection. Thus, they can all be classified as 'ludic' and therefore, following Widdowson and Jakobson, can be said to draw attention to themselves for what they are, as much as for what they do. However, only some of them are strictly socially cohesive since if one function (of some literary texts) is to offer an alternative world which calls into question the experienced world, this clearly has the potential for social conflict.

GENERIC DEVELOPMENT

Having gone some way to explaining how it is that literature can be treated as a separate genre because of the particular functions it serves, we need a further explanation both for the proliferation of subgenres within literature and for the development and changes that occur within any particular subgenre. It would be quite beyond the scope of this book to offer anything even remotely resembling a comprehensive explanation for either of these phenomena, although the general principles invoked to explain the existence of particular genres will obviously apply.

In fact, dividing this into two separate kinds of process is slightly misleading since it is fairly obvious that the evolution of one particular subgenre may well ultimately lead to the creation of something that is recognised as entirely new. Therefore, it is probably better to see this development more in terms of degrees of change. Put briefly, I shall be arguing that existing subgenres are likely to develop and change to the extent that the conventions which they habitually exploit have become so familiar that they are no longer deemed (either by writers or by readers) to be able to stimulate the imagination so as to create interesting or provocative alternative views of the world. For this to be the case, though, we need to posit a particular discourse community which has identified (for its own purposes) the social functions that the particular subgenre is performing (cf. Chapter 3).

On occasions, however, whole societies themselves may be undergoing such radical shifts of organisation and self-perception that existing subgenres are no longer adequate to express the interests of the discourse communities from which they arose. Alternatively, new discourse communities may develop with particular interests that are not represented within existing subgenres. In such cases, radically new subgenres are likely to develop. In fact, the dichotomy is never quite as extreme as this formulation suggests. On the one hand, subgenres are in a permanent state of evolution and development as are the societies which give them meaning; on the other, revolutions, both social and generic, always incorporate or absorb elements from the past against which they are reacting. Nevertheless, to the extent that they can be seen as involving slightly different members of the society as a whole, I shall treat them as methodologically separate. In the following sections, then, I shall briefly consider the evolution of the Pastoral Elegy and compare its development with the emergence of what appears to be a new subgenre, the novel.

THE PASTORAL ELEGY

Consider the following lines:

1   If, having come this far, somebody reads
        these verses, and he/she wants to understand,
        face this grave on Beeston Hill, your back to Leeds,
        and read the chiselled epitaph I've planned:

(Tony Harrison, 'v')

This is a very brief extract from a much longer poem in which Harrison describes himself visiting his parent's graveyard and finding it desecrated. He imagines the appearance of a skinhead whom he asks to justify such acts of vandalism. During the course of their discussion, Harrison makes some wide-ranging observations on British society with constant emphasis on the ways it is divided and tries to condemn the unemployed skinhead for behaving antisocially. At a critical moment in the poem, however, Harrison realises that he and the skinhead are inseparable as coming from the same society.

These lines are not difficult to understand, and most readers would be well able to interpret them. One of the interesting things about Harrison's poetry is that it is written in a particular dialect that is not typically associated with poetry (cf. another stanza of this poem which is quoted in Chapter 1). Thus we can assume that he is trying to appeal to a readership who themselves may not be avid readers of poetry, To this extent, he is attempting to enlarge the discourse community that reads and enjoys what appears to be a minority pursuit. We can assume that all readers of this poem would identify certain textual features as being particularly salient, and would therefore recognise it as a poem and engage in the reading strategies that they typically employ in reading poetry. Whether the poem will delight is an open question, but it is certainly likely to lead to reflection if only because the language of the poem is so often indecent. Thus, the generic expectations associated with literature as a communicative event (i.e. the creation of a fictional world which invites us to engage in enjoyment and reflection) will have been met.

However, Harrison as writer is situated in this discourse community in a very particular way. He is professionally engaged and could therefore be considered as an expert. One aspect of his expertise will be his knowledge of previous poems. This knowledge will be differently available to his actual readers, but some of them are also likely to be engaged professionally with literature either as writers, critics or teachers. Reverting to Lesley Milroy's description of sociolinguistic communities (see Chapter 3), those who are professionally engaged, or who otherwise have specialist knowledge can be considered as members of a close-knit discourse community and they will have reinforcing norms. One of these norms will be to anticipate that Harrison has actively chosen the poetic form he uses and that any intertextual references they identify will be present for a purpose. In this one respect, they will be like Fish's interpretive community (see above), but with the important difference that the interpretations they arrive at will have been signalled by the text as a communicative act within a sequence of previous communicative acts which have been designed to fulfil a similar function.

Given that Harrison's poem is self-evidently a meditation in a graveyard, it will hardly be surprising if this close-knit community remember previous poems which have chosen a similar theme and setting. In particular, they will recall Gray's lines:

2   For thee who, mindful of th'unhonoured dead,
       Dost in these lines their artless tale relate;
       If chance, by lonely Contemplation led,
       Some kindred spirit shall inquire thy fate,

       Haply some hoary-headed swain may say . . .
       'Approach and read (for thou canst read) the lay,
       Graved on the stone beneath yon aged thorn.'
                    (Thomas Gray, 'Elegy Written in A Country Churchyard')

Again, specialist readers will notice a similar set of themes. The poet is contemplating both the peasants who are buried in the churchyard, and contemplating his own grave and its epitaph. However, they will also be aware of subtle differences of approach. Gray's language is highly Latinate and difficult to disentangle, and therefore radically unlike Harrison's demotic. Again, the specialist member of the discourse community might call to mind Gray's view that 'the language of the age is never the language of poetry', and assume an implicit criticism in Harrison's choice of language. Such readers are also likely to be aware that, in the mid-eighteenth century, England was on the verge of the industrial revolution which led to social unrest and, ultimately, the kinds of townscapes that Harrison depicts. They are thus likely to assume that both writers are engaging in a similar kind of communicative act and that Harrison's poem takes some of its meaning from Gray's.

However, Gray also uses conscious archaisms (e.g. 'swain') which suggests that he too (as an expert member of the discourse community) is appealing to a set of anterior texts and that these are intended to be part of the meaning of his poem. The one that most obviously springs to mind is Milton's 'Lycidas':

3   So may some gentle Muse
       With lucky words favour my destined urn,
       And as he passes turn
       And bid fair peace be to my sable shroud.

                                          (Milton, 'Lycidas')

Milton's poem was written immediately prior to the civil war, and he too was contemplating a divided England and questioning the value of a poetic vocation. However, because of the considerable risks involved, he felt unable to speak directly, preferring instead to adapt the pastoral form. The pastoral was recognised at the time as one way of describing an ideal state and thereby indirectly criticising the actual state. However, Milton was also deeply concerned about his own vocation as a poet and needed to select a subgenre that was typically used for reflection. He chose the elegiac form and combined two subgenres to introduce a new subgenre to England: the pastoral elegy.[5]

What we can observe here then is a very complex development which will have different significance to different sets of readers. And these different sets of readers will be different precisely because of the ways they are situated towards the discourse community of poetry writers and readers. The non-specialist (i.e. those who are members of the loose-knit community) will approach the individual poems as representative of the genre of literature as a whole, although they are likely to have developed certain views as to how the subgenre of poetry typically communicates. The specialist readers (i.e. those who are professionally or otherwise engaged in literature, who communicate regularly with each other in various ways, and who are members of the close-knit community) will read the poems recognising them as representatives of a specific subgenre of poetry which has developed to fulfil specific communicative functions. They will also be aware of how this subgenre has developed over the centuries to accommodate the changes that have occurred within the societies they are describing. Put loosely one might claim that the subgenre of pastoral elegy has developed as a way of contemplating the divisions that exist within society and the relationships that the (mortal) poet has with that society. In their different ways, Milton, Gray and Harrison all engage in this kind of communicative act, but Harrison can incorporate (and change) some of the features present in Gray, as can Gray with Milton. Nevertheless, the 'meanings' developed by Harrison depend in part on the poem being an instantiation of the pastoral elegy, and these meanings are accessible to the discourse community of which he is an expert member.

THE NOVEL

As the name implies, the novel is a relatively recent appearance on the literary scene, although it evidently has literary forebears. In its early form, it typically related the adventures of a single protagonist and therefore bears some relationship to the epic (which is why Fielding could introduce epic elements into *Tom Jones*). What was new about the novel was that the protagonist possessed a number of 'realistic' characteristics with which people could identify. In the words of Watt the novel's primary convention is that:

> [it] is a full and authentic report of human experience, and is therefore under an obligation to satisfy its reader with such details of the story as the individuality of the actors concerned, the particulars of the times and places of their actions, details which are presented through a more largely referential use of language than is common in other literary forms.

> (1957, p. 32)

It would be interesting to compare the emergence of the novel with the development of the epic. If we wish to claim that the epic exists as a distinct subgenre with a particular communicative function then we need to account for such disparate examples as *Beowulf*, *The Faerie Queene*, *Paradise Lost*, *The Rape of the Lock*, *The Prelude* and *The Waste Land*.[6] One way of dealing with these heterodox examples would be to consider the hero. If we consider him (and it is usually a male), then he is conceived as containing all the virtues necessary for the preservation of the health of the nation or tribe, and he demonstrates these virtues through heroic actions. However, the characterisation of these virtues undergoes subtle shifts as the society (or discourse community) to which these heroes are appealing changes. Beowulf is the warrior prince making the tribe safe from the unknown terrors that lurk on its margins; the various knights in Spencer's epic embody the appropriate moral virtues necessary for the maintenance of social order in late feudal England; in *Paradise Lost* the intended hero is a God[7] who has a peculiarly ambivalent relationship to the world he has created, being both immanent (like Satan) and absent (unlike Satan). The hero of *The Rape* is less easily identifiable with a particular person. As a comic epic concerned with manners, the presiding virtue seems to be politeness as manifested through forgiveness and can therefore most easily be identified with Belinda. In *The Prelude*, the hero is unmistakeably the poet himself but his heroism depends not so much on military, moral, religious or sociable virtues as on the right education and use of the imagination. Finally, the hero of *The Waste Land* would seem to be the learned 'shorer-up' of fragments desperate to preserve a set of (historical) values that he perceives to be crumbling. Therefore it might be possible to maintain that as communicative acts, the epics have the function of educating their readers as to how to behave but that with the increasing fragmentation of the society such a function becomes difficult to maintain. But if the discourse community that epics appealed to largely consisted of the highly educated and privileged members of the larger society, then these shifts in the characterisation become easier to understand.

One of the more interesting shifts occurs between Milton and Pope. Whereas earlier heroes had typically possessed 'supernatural' powers, after Pope they became more terrestrial and localised (cf. Pope's facetious use of fairies in *The Rape of the Lock*). This development seems to be occurring in parallel with the early development of the novel and it suggests a significant shift in the ways literary genres interacted with society. Exactly why this should have happened is highly complex and Watt (1957) and McKeon (1987) have offered detailed analyses of the philosophical and cultural changes which contributed to such a development. However, as we have seen in Chapter 2, there was also the growth of a significantly new reading public who were relatively unfamiliar with the classical tradition. Langford reports how James Beattie

> deplored the collapse, as he saw it, of the classical culture on which he had been reared. Its cause he identified in the growing purchasing power of the new, barely literate, who had never been exposed to the civilizing influence of the ancients.
>
> (1989, p. 95)

The new heroes and, even more, heroines appealed to this new readership quite directly and, in the case of Richardson particularly, contributed to their moral education. If we reinvoke the notion of a discourse community, we can observe a new discourse community developing with increasing economic power that had not previously been significant consumers of literature. This community would be unfamiliar with (and in some cases inimical to) the values that attached to the classical models and references and were such a significant feature of the epic. They would therefore fail to recognise their generic significance. However, one of the social functions of the epic was preserved, though in significantly altered form. Given that the epic offered models of behaviour which ideally could be emulated in everyday life, this function was supplied by the new hero(ines) acting in an imaginary world which better represented the concerns of the new discourse community. In this way, a new subgenre slowly emerged through the selective grafting together of features from existing subgenres (and here one would include the romance) which were better able to represent the discursive practices of this new discourse community. Of course, as we have seen, the subgenre 'epic' did not disappear, but its appeal was to a progressively smaller and more marginalised discourse community. Indeed, it is at least possible that the marginalisation of this old discourse community contributes to the despair of *The Waste Land*.

It might appear that I am citing economic change as the primary mover in generic change. In fact, that is not my intention. Certainly, the growth of a new reading public is likely to lead to the development of new forms of reading matter to satisfy the demand. And this evidently happened in the eighteenth century. Equally clearly, Pope's *Rape of the Lock*, which represented a significant development of the epic form, was not written with this new reading public as its intended audience. But the fact that its protagonist was a woman, and that a significant proportion of the new readership that developed was also female, suggests that there were complex interrelationships between the ways in which the epic was undergoing shifts in its communicative functions and the development of a new genre. I have suggested, in my discussion of the changes that affected the pastoral elegy, that these evolutions were a necessary consequence of the changing historical circumstances in which they were written. It seems that similar reasons may be invoked to explain the shifts in the epic. For various philosophical reasons it may just not have been possible to invest the tragic hero with supernatural powers (although it is interesting to see how the supernatural reappeared in the Gothic novel later in the century). If this speculation is accurate, then it follows that the communicative act which was previously performed by the epic had also changed. The epic itself need not die because it would continue to appeal to a discourse community (of expert readers) who would recognise its earlier functions and be variously entertained at the rewritings that occurred. We have seen how this happened with the pastoral elegy, and it no doubt happened with the epic. The communicative act then in itself would continue and would be acknowledged by the discourse community for which it had meaning, but the specific meanings would have undergone changes in parallel with social changes.

CONCLUSION

Although this chapter has been highly speculative, its central claim has been that literature is capable of being characterised as a genre in the same ways as other genres are characterised. That is to say that it performs recognisable functions within society. These functions are essentially 'ludic' in that they do not directly refer to the phenomenal world. One consequence of this is that the interpretation of a literary text has no pragmatic consequences. This, however, does not lead to 'meaningless' since the interpretation of literary texts depends on the same cognitive processes as the interpretation of any other text. However, two important consequences follow from this lack of reference. The first is that the imagined worlds which they create lead to contextual effects on the range of assumptions that readers currently hold. Given that these assumptions are likely to be about the world they experience, then the imagined world will be seen as holding some sort of relation to the experienced world. This relation may of course be treated as trivial, in which case the literary work will be treated as a form of escapism. On the other hand, it may be treated as significant, in which case the imagined world will be used as a measure against which the experienced world can be judged. The second consequence of non-referentiality is that readers are likely to pay closer attention to the material substance of the text precisely because it is the sole means by which the imagined world is being created. Of course, in my characterisation of literature I allowed in a range of texts which are not usually included, but this is precisely because such texts are seen as performing the same social function as all other literary texts. A joke, except when it is in the telling of a true story, clearly manifests the ludic nature of literature. That it only utilises a narrow range of the full potential of a literary work does not make it any less literary because it manages to fulfil part of the same function as these other works.

One further consequence of my characterisation is that the genre of literature *in itself* gives us no obvious clue as to why specific subgenres have developed. I have suggested that they may perform quite specific functions, in the same ways as a joke fulfils a specific function. However, appreciation of these various functions and of the meanings they create depends on the ways in which the reader is situated in relation to the discourse community. Some people might be described as experts in that they write poetry, read about it, teach it or otherwise consider it to be an important part of their communicative existence. These people will treat the existence of subgenres as having a specific set of meanings which have developed historically and which are in a continuing state of evolution. To some extent, they are like Fish's interpretive community, in that their practices are passed down through education. However, this is not quite the same as claiming that the meanings they develop from particular subgenres are simply a construction of the readers. To the extent that the discourse community is 'close-knit', the meanings are certainly verified by the community, but since this community also includes producers of literary texts, it is reasonable to assume that such producers choose generic forms precisely because they can anticipate the kinds of meanings such forms will evoke. In other words, the genre which a particular work instantiates is part of the meaning of that work and is recognised as such by other members of the close-knit community.

Other readers may be less familiar with the subgenres that coexist within the body of work that is literary, although they will surely be familiar with the broad distinctions that exist between drama, prose fiction and poetry. They will therefore be less inclined to derive the specific interpretations that are signalled by a subgenre, being members of the 'loose-knit' discourse community. However, they will still be capable of recognising the general communicative functions of literary texts and offering interpretations that can be challenged and refined in the act of discussion.

Of course, I realise that my cursory discussions of the pastoral elegy and the novel were insufficient to substantiate these claims, but the need to situate the genre of literature within a rich linguistic theory of genre seems to me paramount and these comments are offered in the hope that somebody will be stimulated to investigate the area considerably more thoroughly.

FURTHER READING

As must be obvious, this chapter covers a lot of ground and the potential range of recommended reading is vast. At best, I can only give some indications as to where to search for useful bibliographies. Alastair Fowler's (1982) *Kinds of Literature* is a very useful introduction to the literary study of genre, and his list of references will repay exploration. A very useful compendium of literary theorists is Lodge's *Modern Criticism and Theory* (1988). This contains papers by Jakobson, but also other theorists whom I have not mentioned but who are germane to my discussion. Todorov's paper 'The origin of genres' (1976) is particularly illuminating, as is anything by Bakhtin but especially the collection of his late writings that appeared in 1986. Watt's (1957) *The Rise of the Novel* is still unrivalled as a study of the development of a particular genre, although McKeon's (1989) *The Origins of the English Novel* has developed some of Watts' ideas in interesting ways.

An excellent collection of papers on stylistics is Short's *Reading, Analyzing and Teaching Literature* (1989) as is Carter and Simpson's *Language, Discourse and Literature* (1989). Cook's (1994) *Discourse and Literature* can be recommended as an interesting discussion of schema theory and its literary applications. Widdowson is always interesting. His *Explorations in Applied Linguistics 2* (1984) has some very useful papers on literary analysis, and his more recent *Practical Stylistics* (1992) is an indication of the ways in which his ideas have developed.

Within the systemic–functional tradition, Hasan's *Linguistics, Language and Verbal Art* (1985) is a very useful discussion of the ways literary texts can be analysed. A paper which has a very direct bearing on some of my observations in this chapter is Threadgold's 'What did Milton say Belial said and Why don't the Critics believe him?' (1988).

SOME QUESTIONS FOR CONSIDERATION

A popular form of romantic fiction is referred to as Mills and Boon fiction. This suggests that it has acquired a generic title.

1 a What social functions do you think that this subgenre has?
  b Are you able to characterise its discourse community?
  c Has it undergone any changes is recent years and, if so, what are these changes?
  d What do such changes suggest about the changing nature of society in which it performs a communicative act?

Comics might be considered a subgenre of literature.

2 a What kinds of comics are you familiar with?
  b Do you feel that they share a common readership?
  c What social functions do the different types of comic perform?
  d How do you feel their development has been affected by the graphic element?

Conclusion

It remains to gather together the arguments I have been advancing in this book. The central claim is that the variety of written texts that we encounter in our daily life is far greater than is typically acknowledged by populist writers and speakers on language. To the extent that these populist views prevail, our children's education is impoverished. In Chapter 1, I argued that the dominant view suggested that there was a single 'correct' way of writing and that this model appealed to an extremely limited range of socially situated written texts. One author who is frequently cited as a master of written English is, of course, Shakespeare. While not denying Shakespeare's supreme ability to shape the written language for specific dramatic purposes, I suggested that people who held him up as an exemplar to be followed by contemporary writers ignore the various different functions for which we typically compose written messages. However, it would be dangerous to dismiss the promulgators of such a view as simply naive. Their appeal to Shakespeare has resonance largely because it is an appeal to an ideologically driven view as to what it means to be 'English' (and, in this case, 'English' is not equivalent to 'British' however much the proponents of such a view might wish it to be).

Others adopt a slightly different tactic, arguing that there is a 'correct' form of written English that needs to be taught in schools simply in order to preserve comprehensibility. Again, it would be foolish to dismiss this as naive. There are undoubtedly occasions when particular 'wordings' are, or seem to be, required in the construction of a written message for the message to be deemed acceptable. There are also occasions when inappropriate 'wordings' may lead to ambiguity. However, in recognising this, we are not obliged to extend the argument, as so many do, and claim that there is therefore one model of written English which will be appropriate for all occasions. On the contrary, we need to recognise the extent to which different communicative purposes require different forms of writing. For example, the kind of linguistic organisation that may be appropriate for a legal document or scientific report would read very oddly in a postcard or a recipe. Nevertheless, the search for a single model has led to the belief that there is (or should be) a linguistically describable variety of English that is often referred to as 'Standard' English.

My discussion of these overlapping views and their historical development may seem tangential to the main purposes of the book, but I am firmly convinced that we cannot talk meaningfully about a language without some sense of its history and the things people have said about how it should be used. This theme is developed in Chapter 3 where I argue that any particular language – in this case English – is the possession of a particular society and that the meanings that are assumed to reside in the language are, in fact, not immanent but are created by that society. Societies, however, are rarely homogeneous. Rather, they consist of groups of people (i.e. smaller social groupings) who ally themselves together because they identify common, shared goals and histories, and are governed by similar discursive practices. Such larger groups are inherently unstable, though, simply because the smaller groupings of which they consist have their own particular interests which may, at times, conflict with the interests of the dominant group. Another way of putting this might be to claim that any particular society is always historically transient. The language used within that larger society will therefore always manifest variety. In the case of written English, I suggested that these varieties are best seen as the possession of 'discourse communities'. Each discourse community is situated slightly differently in relation to the larger society of which it is part, and each discourse community will have its own specific history. However, the differences between such communities may not be vast simply because people – the users of language – are necessarily members of a wide range of discourse communities. This overlapping membership contributes to the stability of a particular language but at the same time encourages variety within a language since any particular discourse community will develop its own meanings and its characteristic ways of expressing them. Indeed, I argued that one of the signs of a healthy society was precisely the extent to which it tolerated such variation since a society which suppressed linguistic variation (through prescribing some usages and proscribing others) was indirectly suppressing social diversity.

My primary aim, of course, has been to show how and why written texts were so various. To show *how* they are various is a relatively simple matter: one need only point to differences in lexis and syntax. But this kind of analysis remains on the surface of the text without telling us anything very obvious about how these differences lead to changes in meaning. To do this, we need a coherent theory which links linguistic choice clearly to linguistic function. Paradoxically, such a theory may be logically impossible simply because in the act of describing a text *as though* it were performing a particular function we are using the text to perform a different function. I therefore proposed a threefold model of description which distinguished between 'language-in-observation' (i.e. discussion about texts as objects), 'language-in-action' (i.e. what a given text may be said to be doing at any particular time), and 'users of language' (i.e. the people who are intending that language should be performing a specific function at a particular time). Although I acknowledge this to be rather clumsy and capable of refinement, I adopted it in order to avoid the danger of assuming that a given linguistic construction necessarily indicated a circumscribed social function.

This enabled me to consider the kinds of choices that were typically available to writers in order to make their contributions cohesive and coherent. Although they cannot guarantee that they will be read in the ways they intend, writers can make reasonable assumptions that given choices are likely to lead to given interpretations within specific contexts. Of course, this confidence depends on their knowledge of how previous writers have constructed similar messages (cf. my mention of history). Writers may therefore be said to create texts according to a particular register, i.e. a configuration of what the text is about, to whom it is addressed and the circumstances under which it will be read.

Although register theory is a powerful means of describing how writers make their linguistic choices, it fails to show how individual readers interpret written texts. There seems little doubt that different readers can and do produce quite different readings of the same text. This is most obviously evident in the discussion of literary texts, but it also occurs with other texts. So, for example, lawyers can argue quite vociferously as to how a piece of (written) legislation should be interpreted. One way of explaining this kind of variability has been developed within relevance theory, which claims that readers establish that interpretation which is most salient to their knowledge and interests.

In Chapter 7 I draw the various threads of my argument together. While recognising that each written message is unique, I argue that writers construct their messages with the intention of being read according to the norms of particular discourse communities. Given that these discourse communities have different interests and different histories, it follows that writers have to shape their writings according to the norms of such communities. These differences therefore lead to different text types, or genres. Variation in written English therefore reflects the different interests of sections of our society. Readers identify certain salient features of a given text and use these to assign the text to a genre. Indeed, the existence of genres is attested to by the fact that people label texts as being advertisements, letters, reports, etc., and in the act of naming imply that such texts have been designed to perform particular functions. They then interpret the text as a communicative intervention in the social discourses that are mediated through the genre and their interpretations are subsequently validated by being treated as meaningful by other members of the discourse community. The choice of genre is thus considered to be both relevant and part of the meaning of the text.

However, discourse communities are fluid entities in two important respects. On the one hand, they contain expert members, neophytes and 'tourists'; on the other, they consist of people who necessarily also belong to other discourse communities. For these reasons, the boundaries between genres are also fluid since they will admit, to varying degrees, the 'meanings' of other discourse communities at least to the extent that such meanings overlap with their own meanings, and will tolerate (again, to varying degrees) inexpert interventions. And I should stress here that an intervention can be either in the form of a written text or in the form of an interpretation of a text. The genre's meanings are therefore also fluid since they are constantly in the process of being revalidated and subtly changed by the discourse community. Necessarily, the kinds of shifts that I am referring to typically take place over longer periods of time. If they did not, there would be an insufficient body of texts that had been used to perform specific social functions to allow us to identify a (sub)genre.

Chapter 8 is frankly speculative. I believe that any theory which attempts to explain the existence of genres should also be able to encompass the great variety of literary texts that we encounter. The first task then must be to establish the general social functions of those works we identify as literary. To some extent we are faced with a circular argument at this point since the identification of function is a necessary condition for the given work to be classified as literary, and it may be that some readers will consider writings to be literary which do not obviously perform such functions. While recognising this to be the case, I would argue that such apparent anomalies can be explained in three ways. First, there will be some historical texts that were originally produced to perform quite other functions but which, by virtue of possessing certain qualities which we value in prototypical examples of literature, have come to be regarded as literary. Second, that the historically shifting boundaries between genres have moved in such a way that these works are no longer considered to be performing their original function. And third, that generic assignment is the role of interpreters of texts rather than of texts themselves. Of course, this last assertion does not mean that writers do not attempt to indicate the genre to which they intend their writings to belong, but they cannot guarantee that readers will necessarily interpret the (linguistic) signals in quite the ways they originally intended. This, of course, is because readers themselves may be expert or inexpert members of the discourse community which consumes and creates such texts.

I chose to identify the social function of literature as essentially ludic. However, I also contended that some works of literature have a homiletic function in that they invite us to compare the fictional worlds they create with the phenomenal world that we experience in our everyday life. I further contended that literature does not refer directly to this phenomenal world and therefore does not have the same pragmatic consequences as other written texts. I did not mean by this that literature has no effects. Clearly, it is capable of affecting us profoundly. But the truths it offers are of a different order to those offered by other writings since they are not empirically verifiable. Having established the general functions of literature, I proceeded to consider some literary subgenres. I argued that these served specific functions although, again, these specific functions would be recognisable to different degrees according to whether their readers were 'expert' members of the literary discourse community or were relatively inexpert. For the experts, generic choice can be regarded as part of the specific meanings of the work under investigation. For others, the more general social function that attaches to literature as a whole is salient. I attempted to demonstrate this by looking both at a specific subgenre, the novel, which developed from earlier subgenres but which took on particular characteristics because of the historical circumstances in which it was formed; and at another subgenre, the pastoral elegy, which has survived as a recognisable and identifiable form of communication even though it has undergone various mutations historically.

I have little doubt that better linguists than I will find flaws and inconsistencies in my arguments, and my hope is that they will develop better theories to explain the phenomena under investigation here. About one thing, though, I remain adamant. A proper understanding of the various ways people use language to achieve different ends will lead to a richer understanding of society as a whole. For this reason, I believe that the study of language variety should be at the centre of language education. I find it anomalous that our children should so often be taught to value the huge variety of literary texts that exist, but be encouraged to despise, or ignore, the kinds of variety that are such a feature of non-literary written texts in our society.

Notes

INTRODUCTION

1 I am not, of course, suggesting that children will not be aware of and use a tremendous variety of written language in their lifetime, simply that their perception of this variety will be deeply flawed to the extent that they believe it to be 'wrong' in some way.

1 VARIETY AND 'STANDARD ENGLISH'

1 My choice of the word 'English' here is quite deliberate. Scotland retained a separate king and legislature; Ireland was the subject of frequent invasions to suppress independence movements; and Wales still contained a significantly high proportion of Welsh speakers.
2 In my discussion of these two surveys I shall concentrate on those findings which relate to the written language. Both surveys also considered the spoken language with equally predictable results.
3 It is interesting to observe that many people consult dictionaries as though they had the authority of 'divine right'. Few people acknowledge that the great reference dictionaries are the works of individuals writ large, preferring to regard them as authoritative statements as to what the language is like.
4 In all fairness, Lamb (1992) produced some examples where wrong choices led to considerable ambiguity so that serious misunderstandings could have arisen. However, these were certainly a minority.
5 Although I have endeavoured to reproduce these texts as accurately as possible, some of their graphic features have inevitably been lost. They come from:

    1 A life assurance policy
    2 'v' by Tony Harrison
    3 A solicitor's letter
    4 A private letter (originally in handwriting)
    5 A record club brochure
    6 A local paper

6 A piece by Robert Fisk in the magazine section of the *Independent*, 2 August 1995.
7 From a travel agent's computer printout.
8 G. Kress, 'History and language: towards a social account of linguistic change', *Journal of Pragmatics* 13 (1989), p. 449.
9 A Christmas card, picked up for use as a shopping list.

10 Part of a legal notice that appeared in the newspaper.
11 From a packet of tea.

2 A (VERY BRIEF) HISTORY OF ENGLISH

1 It is important to remember that reference to Anglo-Saxon in this period is imprecise. Although there are sufficient structural similarities between the different dialects to suggest significant features in common, the term Anglo-Saxon is often used as a blanket term to refer to quite distinct geographical features in grammar and lexis.
2 The first is from an advertisement in a Nottingham newspaper of 1717; the second from a newspaper report from 1751; the third from a letter written in 1761; and the fourth from an anonymous letter of complaint (which is partly akin to a political pamphlet) directed against a local magistrate in 1762. The first, second and fourth are all from Porter (1982, pp. 280, 32, 118) and the third from Beresford (ed., 1925, p. 233).

3 TEXTS IN SOCIETIES: SOCIETIES IN TEXTS

1 For various reasons, this is unlikely to occur, precisely because such signs are often supported by other semiotic devices, e.g. pictorial representations of cartoon characters crossed by a red line. These features will be discussed later under register, but the point still holds in principle.
2 Cf. Hodge and Kress's (1988, pp. 37–8) interesting discussion of the 'meaning' of traffic lights. They illustrate that even fixed semiotic codes are liable to different pragmatic interpretations according to the drivers.
3 Although in 1920s slang the term could refer to a clever, witty fellow.
4 The first text is taken from the back of a Bank of Scotland MasterCard statement, the second from the back of an Access statement.
5 I should make it clear that discursive practices may be carried on by other symbolic means than language, although they often have linguistic concomitants. Commercial transactions may be made electronically, for example, but customers are still required to sign the invoice.
6 Some theorists prefer to use the term 'ideology' to refer to such systems of belief (e.g. Haynes, 1989). However, I prefer to reserve the term 'ideology' to describe organised and largely coherent sets of ideas which can be clearly articulated. Eagleton (1991, p. 194) suggests that ideology is 'less . . . a particular *set* of discourses, than . . . a particular set of effects *within* discourses'. Discursive practices are more unconscious than ideologies and they can often be ambiguous and contradictory (cf. Pennycook, 1994).
7 I fully recognise that membership of groups and the exercise of power within them are frequently realised in other ways, but it is rare for other symbolic actions not to be preceded, or followed, by some form of words.
8 Halliday (1978, Chapter 9) has suggested that antilanguages are relatively untainted forms of discourse. To the extent that they exist in conscious opposition to the forms used by the dominant society, they represent alternative ways of constructing social reality. However, to the extent that they draw on forms that are already established in the dominant society (whether through inversion or some other means), they can be seen as one among many varieties of the language. What is interesting is that they seem to be consciously developed (although they may presumably develop into creoles – Halliday is not entirely clear on this). In this respect, they are not significantly different

from other genres which have been developed and refined to express a particular representation of the world.

4 SOME DEFINITIONAL PROBLEMS

1 For a fascinating account of this phenomenon in the reporting of parliamentary speech, see Slembrouck (1992).
2 For a fuller discussion of this point, see Rose (1993).
3 Halliday and Hasan (1976, 1985/9) describe the development of the term *context* from its uses by Malinowski and subsequently by Firth. They distinguish between 'context of situation' and 'context of culture'. Certainly, if we wish to engage in delicate analyses of the ways in which texts may be interpreted, this distinction is a valuable one. However, as I shall be arguing below, culture is largely inseparable from situation. The distinctions between the two will therefore be an idealisation that may obscure important information about how texts are used and interpreted.
4 A fuller discussion of the cognitive processes involved in establishing appropriate contexts occurs in Chapter 6.
5 Barristers, for example, are not barristers simply because they use barristers' language, but also because they have passed certain kinds of exams (which is certainly a linguistic activity, but also involves sitting in exam halls, watching the clock, etc.), wearing funny clothes on occasion, eating so many meals in chambers, etc.
6 This seems to be a fundamental problem in Biber's research (1989). Large-scale cluster analysis certainly shows us how certain linguistic elements recur in different texts, but it does not explain their functional uses within such texts. These have to be assumed with the result that '[functional] categories are assigned *a priori* to language forms, thereby entrapping the analyst in the circular exercise of proving what one has already decided to be the case from the very beginning' (McCarthy and Carter, 1994, p. 12). A further problem is that Biber relates his findings to genres without showing exactly how he has defined genre with the same result as indicated by McCarthy and Carter.

5 COHESION, COHERENCE AND REGISTER

1 In Halliday and Hasan (1985/9, p. 85) Hasan suggests that the presence of overlapping similarity chains within different texts indicates genre-specificity, while identity chains are text (or in my use) register-specific. In fact, as we shall see, the first of these claims seems unfounded because genres as communicative acts can be about very different topics.
2 Although I do not have the space to discuss this in any detail, the communicative approach to language teaching has been heavily involved in discovering the 'functions' of language, and one of the best introductions to language functions remains Widdowson's (1977) *Teaching Language as Communication*. The fullest exploration of the relationships that may hold between clauses is that undertaken by Winter. Two recent publications which give useful summaries of his approach are Winter (1992) and Winter (1994). The former has some interesting observations on lexis in texts also.
3 Halliday suggests that there were only about a hundred coded sentences available for use during the wartime restrictions. In this sense, it does seem more satisfactory to invoke Firth's term of a 'restricted language' to describe

such a situation. However, although the range of options was limited, an ingenious soldier could in principle produce 10,000 different messages by constantly recombining the available options since different clause sequences would indicate different clause relations.

Halliday continues by referring to the language of air traffic control and the language of bridge as further examples of restricted registers. I would take issue with this on the grounds that there are, presumably, a number of different combinations of call signs, speed, height, wind direction, provenance and destination that might be reported, and that the reporting might take place in a variety of different intonations and accents. I have no knowledge of bridge but, again, I doubt whether a player's call is predictable either in terms of content or manner. (How many times is an identical sequence of play repeated?)

Since all these features contribute to the identification of register, it would seem that the notion of a closed register is highly questionable.

4 I have chosen these two texts as examples precisely because they are the sorts of texts which are regularly encountered by most adults.

5 For critics who suggest that I might be reading too much into this form of address, I would argue that forms of address are significant and interesting ways in which societies maintain social hierarchies and structures. I am not suggesting that Seeboard (and you will notice that I am unable to single out any particular individual within the company) have adopted this mode of address consciously, or with the intentions that I have referred to. However, it is clearly in their interests to assume a stable ordered society which meets its obligations since prompt payment of bills depends precisely on such a society (cf. Hunston, 1993).

6 The advent of recorded speech has made this true to a greater extent also of spoken interaction. Pre-war newsreels are frequently used for purposes that could not possibly have been foreseen when they were originally produced. I have seen Neville Chamberlain's famous return from Munich when he declared 'Peace in our time' used for poignant effect, for historical reporting and for hilarious purposes in a *Monty Python* sketch. The form of words was originally tied to a particular context of situation. The subsequent uses of the newsreel have not altered that particular context although they have resituated it in such a way that the co-text significantly influences our interpretation. In a very important way, the words no longer quite mean what they originally meant.

This is even more true of written texts. In *Labyrinths* (1970), Jorge-Luis Borges tells the (fictional) story of Pierre Menard, a twentieth-century writer who sets out to write *Don Quixote*. After a lifetime of study and struggle, he manages to produce some fragments which are identical, in wording, to the original. But, as Borges makes clear, Menard's text cannot be interpreted in the same way as Cervantes's text. If this is true, then it is questionable whether written texts can, through their registerial selections, signal their intent quite as directly as Halliday suggests. I shall be considering this in more detail when I discuss parodic texts.

Elsewhere Halliday and Hasan consider issues of intertextuality and 'context of culture', and I shall consider these in due course. My point here is to establish that, however carefully writers attempt to construct ideal readers in ideal situations, they will always be challenged by actual readers situated in particular relations to the texts they are reading.

7 I have adapted Halliday's detailed analysis of grammatical functions and also some of his terminology for the sake of simplicity.

8 I consider 'drop me a line' to be an idiom on the grounds that it behaves as a lexical unit, i.e. its parts can not be reordered, nor can other elements be substituted for them. It is therefore quite unlike such set phrases as 'We are pleased to advise . . .'. The latter may be genre-specific whereas the former can probably be used in a variety of different genres.

9 Some of the more important contributions include Martin (1992) and the collections of papers edited by Ghadessy (1988, 1993).

6 INTERPRETING THE LANGUAGE

1 Were this to happen, it could be argued that the maxims were being violated, although it would be difficult to decide which of the four was in abeyance. Clearly, the response is informative (but not strictly as informative as required); it is true; it is brief; but it is not obviously relevant (though it may be). The principle of defeasibility is interesting, and seems to be at the root of the 'good news/bad news' jokes, e.g. 'First, the good news – I've cooked you the most delicious salmon souffle. Now, the bad news, I dropped it on the floor.'

2 For further discussion of this issue, see Sarangi and Slembrouck (1992).

3 In fact, this may not always be the case. In my workplace, the fire alarm is tested regularly every Tuesday morning, thus my interpretation when it rings varies depending on when I hear it. On Tuesday morning, it signals a test; at all other times, it signals potential danger. This raises problems for me should it be rung on Tuesday morning as a result of a fire. Nevertheless, the general principle is fairly clear.

4 This is a difficult area to explore adequately. It is always open to Sperber and Wilson to argue that the slightest contextual effect is an indication of the relevance of, say, graffiti. Thus if I feel disgust on reading the graffiti, some kind of communicative effect has been achieved, i.e. it has proved to be relevant to me. However, if this is the case, it would seem that anything that I observe and which has some effect on my cognitive environment may be deemed to be an example of ostensive–inferential communication. Clearly this seems to stretch the concept of relevance beyond that intended by Sperber and Wilson.

5 Even the choice of the modal 'may' does not give direct access to a particular interpretation. Consider the difference in interpretation between the following two utterances:

She may have carried it in her hand . . . (but she didn't).
She may have carried it in her hand . . . (but I don't know).

6 If we consider my example: 'Get some bread from the bank', it will be clear that the assumptions that might have been held by the writer are significantly under-represented in the message. Imagine a situation in which somebody has £50, but has suddenly realised that she needs £65 in order to buy a particular item of which the addressee might be unaware. Further, she needs it tomorrow because the item is only available at a sale price, etc. All of these assumptions might have contributed to the construction of the message, but they are essentially unrecoverable by the reader, although what might be recoverable, through a series of implicatures, is something along the lines of:

1 I have been asked to get some money from the bank.
2 I know that x has (or had) £50.

Implicated conclusion:

    a) The £50 has been spent *or*
    b) *x* needs more than £50

and

    c) No explanation has been given for this request.

Implicated conclusion:

    d) There is some urgency behind it *or*
    e) *x* does not want me to know why the extra money is needed.

This process of internal argument could continue *ad infinitum*, but all the time I, as reader, am computing these extra implicatures, I am denying that the message is intended to be optimally relevant.

7 Cf. my discussion of cohesion in the previous chapter.

8 Of course, this does raise interesting questions as to the accuracy of formal linguistic descriptions of language. It is possible to assume, with Sperber and Wilson, that there are formal properties which have (as yet) not been fully described, and which are part of the input system. On the other hand, it is possible to adopt a different position based on fuzzy logic, and argue that the kinds of relationships expressed through lexicogrammars are far more conventionally based than was previously assumed (cf. Bex, 1993b; Lakoff, 1987; Taylor, 1989). If we adopt the latter view, then it would suggest that my example sentence does not so much violate the semantics of 'bachelor' as extend the range of its possible meanings.

9 This, of course, is remarkably similar to the characterisation of I-language offered by Chomsky (e.g. Chomsky, 1986).

10 A have used the phrase 'word shape' because I am referring quite specifically to written language. It is possible that some readers engage in subvocalisation in which case their mental dictionary may be represented in a phonological form.

11 I should stress here that I am referring quite particularly to written forms. Whether spoken language follows the same rhetorical patterns as written language is an open question, and one that I do not intend to discuss. However, it is important to recognise that Sperber and Wilson's theory seems to be built largely on the analysis of conversational exchanges, and that therefore some of what they say may not apply to the construction and interpretation of written texts.

12 I should stress that I am recalling this from memory. My memory may be wrong, but that is not the point. False memory may often play an extremely important role in the development of those assumptions which are used in interpretation.

13 Cf. my reference to Bakhtin in Chapter 3, and the notion of discourse communities.

14 Although this text may be slightly esoteric in its choice of subject matter, it is remarkably similar to other announcements that we find on billboards, in shop windows, etc.

15 Unfortunately, there is insufficient space to discuss frame/schema theory here, although some linguists (e.g. Cook, 1994) believe it is a powerful way of explaining how we interpret texts. Good general treatments occur in Brown and Yule (1983) and Sperber and Wilson (1986).

16 These were notes to myself while I was writing this book. In fact, I have not used them, but they may be of some interest in their own right as glosses on this and an earlier chapter.

7 GENRE

1 In this case, the joke is signalled by its context. *Viz* is known to be a slightly scurrilous and satirical magazine. Readers would therefore expect its contents to be comic. However, as we shall see later, context is not always a reliable guide to content.

2 Cf. my discussion at the end of Chapter 4.

3 Of course, there are some diaries which are deliberately written for publication (usually by politicians, cf. Benn), or which are subsequently published (cf. Pepys). In the former case, they can best be regarded as a hybrid genre mid-way between the private diary and the public history. The latter are a classic example of social reclassification. They become public not through any desire of their author, but in entering the public sphere they are read in a different way than originally intended although they retain all the linguistic features of a private genre. The private examples which I quote in this book (all of them with permission!) might also be considered to be similar hybrids. See also note 5.

4 It is interesting here to note that this is a particular feature mentioned by Catherine Snow in her discussion of Child Directed Speech (Fletcher and Garman, 1986). Given that genres are examples of contextualised language, it is not surprising that recurrent contexts are likely to produce similar linguistic choices. I am not, of course, suggesting that the language of intimacy between adults is necessarily identical to that between adults and children (although the display of Valentine messages in the press on 14 February might suggest otherwise), merely that genres are, typically, learnt (cf. Hicks, 1990).

5 As we shall see later, however, there is a new mode of instant communication being developed (email) which can be highly interactive, but which does not necessarily use such markers. It will be argued that the discussions about appropriate conventions for email communication suggest we are witnessing the development of a new genre.

6 There is an intrinsic problem in discussing the nature of private communications. Once they have been made public, as in this instance, they are recontextualised and tend to lose the force they originally had. More particularly, the shared assumptions that might exist between the sender and the receiver cannot easily be recovered by outsiders, and therefore meaningful analysis is likely to be skewed towards the possibly unjustified assumptions of the analyst. This will be true even of private communications that are stored on a database. Although I have tried to overcome this problem by selecting private communications addressed to me, I cannot be fully confident that any generalisations I want to make genuinely hold for other examples.

7 It is interesting to compare this letter with a postcard that was delivered to my address in error. (The address was mine, but I was clearly not the intended recipient.) Unfortunately, for technical reasons, it is impossible to reproduce exactly. However, I would assume that most of my readers will recognise it as a postcard rather than a letter. The message reads:

Natasha,
Having a splendid holiday out here in Tenerife!! Food's lovely men are even nicer but most of them are *GERMAN!!* One very nice Spanish waiter called Juan or John in english. You know I'm a dreadful flirt, anyway on the 3rd day he asked me out to a disko! And I'll fill you in when I see you at school. I'm missing Mark. Hmm . . . weather's lovely,
Corgii

The message has been partly overprinted by a smudged postmark, and the ink is so pale as to be almost unreadable. The sender has identified herself (although I realise this is a gender-specific assumption that may not be justified) with a set of icons following the name, including that for infinity.

Many of the features present identify it as a private communication. There is a degree of intimacy indicated by such features as verbal contractions, markers more frequently associated with speech ('Hmm'), reference to a joint acquaintance, etc. However, the absence of specific deictic markers of time and place are more commonly associated with cards than with letters. The assumption is that the separation between sender and recipient is of a brief duration and that the exact place from which the card has been sent is of relatively little importance. Also, of course, the physical constraints of size limit what can be included in the message.

8 In this way, they may be akin to Swales's characterisation of an ideal discourse community.

9 I have quite deliberately chosen to describe the features in this way to demonstrate how the language associated with one type of communication is often quite inappropriate when used in other forms of communication. Although there has been some research into the interaction between non-linguistic visual symbols and linguistic symbols and the effect this has on the interpretation of 'mixed' texts, this has tended to concentrate on specific areas (e.g. Bernhardt, 1985; Bex, 1994b; van Peer, 1993).

10 Readers who are interested in the development of this new genre might also be interested in the effects it has on the compilation of bibliographies by looking at the entry under Kehoe, 1992.

11 And it is by considering these as typical features and functions of the subgenre 'Letters to the Editor' that we recognise the letter quoted at the beginning of the chapter as a parody. Essentially, it works by telling a story so preposterous that it cannot be taken as true. It therefore subverts the conventions of the traditional letters by indirectly calling into question their own veracity.

12 There are, of course, letters which are intentionally anonymous although I have not been able to lay hold of any. Whether they give any indication of their sender or their intended recipient I cannot, therefore, judge. Letters which appear in the press with the legend 'name and address withheld' can be considered as similar to those which are sent to the problem page.

13 To be fair, there is also a visual representation of the product being advertised in the bottom right hand corner of the page. But this is not particularly prominent and, because of its position, can easily be overlooked by the reader.

14 It is interesting to observe that although we refer to such advertisements as 'small ads' in English, other languages use different terms to distinguish them from those advertisements which direct readers to business retailers. This gives further support to the view that genres are the creation of specific social activities as viewed from a particular perspective. In Britain, we might assume that being a 'nation of shopkeepers', to use Napoleon's phrase, economic activity involving buying and selling is seen as an undifferentiated whole.

15 I have chosen this advertisement partly because I have no idea what 'four-six' actually means in this context. My interpretation here is pure guesswork, but had I belonged to that section of the population who buy Booster bikes, I would no doubt understand the reference (cf. Toolan's [1988, p. 63] comments on the Silk Cut advertisements).

16 In this case, the presumed common interests will be the selling and buying of

the particular goods on offer and the assumption that the goods will be cheaper than those on offer in more public venues.

17 This compares interestingly with a garage in Canterbury which calls itself Man On Wheels. The notion that 'real driving' is mainly done by men is something that evidently dies hard!

18 Clearly, there are some such interactions. If I dash into a strange shop to buy something in a hurry, I may pay little or no attention to the person serving me as other than occupying a given role in the transaction. However, such occasions are comparatively rare and, in the case of written texts, may only occur in the construction of public notices which are addressed to all readers regardless of their status.

8 THE CASE OF LITERATURE

1 This is not, of course, the same as saying such texts *must* be interpreted as relevant in this way. Readers are always free to construct alternative interpretations (e.g. that a menu is 'really' a poem). It is just that such interpretations are unlikely to be validated by other readers.

2 The French text is as follows:

dans ces arts la nécessité de distinguer entre pratique artistique et pratique non artistique n'existe pas, . . . pour la toute simple raison qu'il s'agit d'activités intrinsèquement artistiques. A l'inverse, la littérature ou la poésie constituent des domaines régionaux à l'intérieur d'un domaine sémiotique unifié plus vaste, qui est celui des pratiques verbales, celles-ci *n'étant pas* toutes artistiques: le problème de la délimitation extensionnelle et définitionnelle du champ de la littérature (ou de la poésie) peut donc paraitre crucial.

3 For a fuller discussion of this and, indeed, of formalist and structuralist approaches to literature see Cook (1994), Chapter 5.

4 I have chosen this example precisely because it seems so amenable to empirical investigation. I believe that similar observations would obtain if we were to consider a poem which was ostensibly about a poet's feelings. Although such a poem could be regarded as 'reporting' emotions in the same ways as a personal letter might report emotions, in the act of telling these emotions are being restructured (or re-presented) in a way that renders them fictional (i.e. empirically unverifiable). Even if this analysis were to be proved wrong, however, it would still leave open the question as to what relevance (in the Sperber and Wilson sense) the report of a stranger's feelings could have for the reader's cognitive environment.

5 Of course, this had existed in classical literature, as Milton would have been aware.

6 Although not a random list, this is highly selective. Blake's 'Prophetic Books' might be considered as in the same tradition and Byron's *Don Juan* could also have been included. However, my selection serves to illustrate some of the significant changes that overtook the epic during the eighteenth century.

7 Although some, and most notably Blake, have argued that the real hero of *Paradise Lost* is Satan, this is an essentially romantic view which depends on the assumption that it is individualistic action rather than submission to God that is most heroic.

Bibliography

Aarsleff, H. (1983) *The Study of Language in England: 1780–1860*, London: Athlone Press.

Adamson, S. (1989) 'With double tongue: diglossia, stylistics and the teaching of English', in M. Short (ed.) *Reading, Analyzing and Teaching Literature*, London: Longman, 204–40.

Aitchison, J. (1989) *The Articulate Mammal*, (3rd ed.), London: Routledge.

Anderson, R.C. and Pearson, P.D. (1988) 'A schema-theoretic view of basic processes in reading comprehension', in P.L. Carrell, J. Devine and D. Eskey (eds) *Interactive Approaches to Second Language Pedagogy*, Cambridge: Cambridge University Press, 37–55.

Auden, W.H. (1940) *Another Time*, London: Faber and Faber.

Augst, G. (1992) 'Aspects of writing development in argumentative texts', in D. Stein (ed.) *Cooperating with Written Texts*, Berlin: Mouton de Gruyter, 67–82.

Austin, J.L. (1976) *How to Do Things with Words*, (2nd ed.), Oxford: Oxford University Press.

Bach, U. (1992) 'From private writing to public oration', in D. Stein (ed.) *Cooperating with Written Texts*, Berlin: Mouton de Gruyter, 417–36.

Bacon, F. [1605] *The Advancement of Learning*, (ed. with an introduction, G.W. Kitchin, 1915), London: Dent.

Bailey, R.W. (1991) *Images of English: A Cultural History of the Language*, Cambridge: Cambridge University Press.

Bakhtin, M. (1981) *The Dialogic Imagination*, (trans. C. Emerson and M. Holquist, ed. M. Holquist), Austin: University of Texas Press.

Bakhtin, M. (1986) *Speech Genres and Other Late Essays*, (trans. V.W. McGee, ed. C. Emerson and M. Holquist), Austin: University of Texas Press.

Barber, C. (1976) *Early Modern English*, London: Andre Deutsch.

Barber, C. (1993) *The English Language: A Historical Introduction*, Cambridge: Cambridge University Press.

Barthes, R. [1977] 'The death of the author', in D. Lodge (ed.) *Modern Criticism and Theory*, London: Longman, 167–72.

Barton, D. (1994) *Literacy: An Introduction to the Ecology of Written language*, Oxford: Blackwell.

de Beaugrande, R. (1993) ' "Register" in discourse: a concept in search of a theory', in M. Ghadessy (ed.) *Register Analysis: Theory and Practice*, London: Pinter Publishers, 7–25.

de Beaugrande, R. and Dressler, W. (1981) *Introduction to Text Linguistics*, London: Longman.

Ben-Porat, Z. (1985) 'Ideology, genre and serious parody', in C. Guillen and P.

Escher (eds) *Proceedings of the Xth Congress of the Comparative Literature Association: Vol. II Comparative Poetics*, New York: Garland Publishing Inc., 180–7.

Bennett, H.S. (1952) *English Books and Readers: 1475–1557*, Cambridge: Cambridge University Press.

Benson, J.D. and Greaves, W.S. (eds) (1985) *Systemic Perspectives on Discourse*, New Jersey: Ablex.

Benson, J.D., Cummings, M.J. and Greaves, W.S. (eds) (1988) *Linguistics in a Systemic Perspective*, Amsterdam: John Benjamins.

Beresford, J. (ed.) (1925) *The Letters of Thomas Gray*, Oxford: Oxford University Press.

Bernhardt, S.A. (1985) 'Text structure and graphic design: the visible design', in J.D. Benson and W.S. Greaves (eds) *Systemic Perspectives on Discourse: Vol. 2*, New Jersey: Ablex, 18–38.

Bex, A.R. (1992) 'Genre as context', *Journal of Literary Semantics*, XXI/1: 1–16.

Bex, A.R. (1993a) 'The genre of advertising', *Revue Belge de Philologie et d'Histoire*, 71, 3: 719–32.

Bex, A.R. (1993b) 'Language and the linguists', *Social Semiotics*, 3, 2: 161–81.

Bex, A.R. (1993c) 'Standards of English in Europe', *Multilingua*, 12, 3: 249–64.

Bex, A.R. (1994a) 'The problem of culture and language teaching in Europe', *IRAL*, XXXII/1: 57–67.

Bex, A.R. (1994b) 'The relevance of genre', in Roger D. Sell and P. Verdonk (eds) *Literature and the New Interdisciplinarity: Poetics, Linguistics, History*, Amsterdam: Rodopi, 107–29.

Bex, A.R. (forthcoming) 'Parody, genre and literary meaning', *Journal of Literary Semantics*.

Bhatia, V.K. (1993) *Analysing Genre: Language Use in Professional Settings*, London: Longman.

Biber, D. (1989) *Variation Across Speech and Writing*, Cambridge: Cambridge University Press.

Blake, N.F. (1969) *Caxton and His World*, London: Andre Deutsch.

Blake, N.F. (1981) *Non-Standard English in English Literature*, London: Andre Deutsch.

Blake, N.F. (ed.) (1992) *The Cambridge History of the English Language: Vol.2: 1066–1476*, Cambridge: Cambridge University Press.

Blakemore, D. (1987) *Semantic Constraints on Relevance*, Oxford: Blackwell.

Blakemore, D. (1988) ' "So" as a constraint on relevance', in R.M. Kempson (ed.) *Mental Representations*, Cambridge: Cambridge University Press, 183–95.

Blakemore, D. (1989) 'Denial and contrast: a relevance theoretic analysis of *but*', *Linguistics and Philosophy*, 12, 1: 15–37.

Blakemore, D. (1992) *Understanding Utterances*, Oxford: Blackwell.

Blakemore, D. (1993) 'The relevance of reformulations', *Language and Literature*, 2, 2: 101–20.

Bolton, W.F. (ed.) (1966) *The English Language: Essays by English and American Men of Letters: 1490–1839*, Cambridge: Cambridge University Press.

Borges, J.L. (1970) 'Pierre Menard, author of the *Quixote*', in D.A. Yates and J.E. Irby (eds) *Labyrinths*, Harmondsworth: Penguin.

Bourdieu, P. (1991) *Language and Symbolic Power*, Oxford: Polity Press.

Briggs, A. (1994) *A Social History of England*, (2nd ed.), London: Weidenfeld and Nicolson.

Bright, W. (ed.) (1992) *International Encyclopedia of Linguistics*, (4 vols), Oxford: Oxford University Press.

Brown, G. and Yule, G. (1983) *Discourse Analysis*, Cambridge: Cambridge University Press.

Bullokar, W. [1586] *Pamphlet for Grammar*, (ed. and introduction, J. Turner, 1980), Leeds: University of Leeds School of English.

Burnley, D. (1992) *The History of the English Language: A Sourcebook*, London: Longman.

Burrow, J.A. and T. Turville-Petre (1994) *A Book of Middle English*, Oxford: Blackwell.

Burton, R. [1621] *The Anatomy of Melancholy*, (ed. and introduction, A.H. Bullen, 1923), London: Bell.

Butler, C.S. (1985) *Systemic Linguistics: Theories and Applications*, London: Batsford.

Cable, T. (1984) 'The rise of written Standard English', in A. Scaglione (ed.) *The Emergence of National Languages*, Ravenna: Longo, 75–94.

Cameron, D. (1995) *Verbal Hygiene*, London: Routledge.

Carrell, P.L. and Eisterhold, J.C. (1988) 'Schema theory and ESL reading pedagogy', in P.L. Carrell, J. Devine and D. Eskey (eds) *Interactive Approaches to Second Language Pedagogy*, Cambridge: Cambridge University Press, 73–92.

Carrell, P.L., Devine, J. and Eskey, D. (eds) (1988) *Interactive Approaches to Second Language Reading*, Cambridge: Cambridge University Press.

Carter, R.A. (1987a) 'Is there a "literary" language', in R. Steele and T. Threadgold (eds) *Language Topics: Essays in Honour of Michael Halliday, Vol. 2*, Amsterdam: John Benjamins, 431–50.

Carter, R.A. (1987b) *Vocabulary*, London: Unwin Hyman.

Carter, R.A. (1993) 'Language and literature in the British National Curriculum', Keynote lecture delivered at the PALA Conference, Abo.

Carter, R.A. (1995) *Keywords in Language and Literacy*, Routledge: London.

Carter, R.A. and Nash,W. (1990) *Seeing Through Language*, Oxford: Blackwell.

Carter, R.A. and Simpson, P. (eds) (1989) *Language, Discourse and Literature*, London: Unwin Hyman.

Chametsky, R. (1992) 'Pragmatics, prediction and *relevance*', *Journal of Pragmatics*, 17, 1: 63–72.

Chomsky, N. (1959) 'A review of Skinner's *Verbal Behaviour*', in J.P.B. Allen and P. van Buren (eds) (1971) *Chomsky: Selected Readings*, Oxford: Oxford University Press, 136–9.

Chomsky, N. (1965) *Aspects of the Theory of Syntax*, Cambridge, Mass.: M.I.T. Press.

Chomsky, N. (1980) *Rules and Representations*, Oxford: Blackwell.

Chomsky, N. (1986) *Knowledge of Language*, New York: Praeger.

Chomsky, N. (1988) *Language and Problems of Knowledge*, Cambridge, Mass.: M.I.T. Press.

Clanchy, M.T. (1993) *From Memory to Written Record: England 1066–1307*, (2nd ed.), Oxford: Blackwell.

Cobbett, W. [1819] *A Grammar of the English Language*, (ed. and introduction, R. Burchfield, 1984), Oxford: Oxford University Press.

Colley, L. (1992) *Britons: Forging the Nation 1707–1837*, Yale: Yale University Press.

Conte, M.-E., Petöfi, J.S. and Sözer, E (eds) (1989) *Text and Discourse Connectedness*, Amsterdam: John Benjamins.

Cook, G. (1990) 'Goals and plans in advertising and literary discourse', *Parlance*, 2, 2: 48–71.

Cook, G. (1994) *Discourse and Literature*, Oxford: Oxford University Press.

Coulthard, M. (1977) *An Introduction to Discourse Analysis*, London: Longman.
Coulthard, M. (ed.) (1994) *Advances in Written Text Analysis*, London: Routledge.
Cox, B. (1991) *Cox on Cox: An English Curriculum for the 1990's*, London: Hodder and Stoughton.
Crowley, T. (1989) *The Politics of Discourse*, London: Macmillan.
Crowley, T. (1990) 'That obscure object of desire: a science of language', in J.E. Joseph and T.J. Taylor (eds) *Ideologies of Language*, London: Routledge, 27–50.
Crowley, T. (1991) *Proper English: Readings in Language, History and Cultural Identity*, London: Routledge.
Crystal, D. (1988) *The English Language*, Harmondsworth: Penguin.
Davis, S. (ed.) (1991) *Pragmatics: A Reader*, Oxford: Oxford University Press.
Downes, W. (1984) *Language and Society*, London: Fontana.
Dryden, J. (1958) *Poems and Fables*, (ed. J. Kinsley), Oxford: Oxford University Press
Eagleton, T. (1991) *Ideology*, London: Verso.
English for Ages 5–16 (1989) London: Department of Education and Science and the Welsh Office, H.M.S.O.
English for Ages 5–16 (1993) London: Department of Education and Central Office of Information, H.M.S.O.
Enkvist, N.E. (1990) 'Discourse comprehension, text strategies and style', *AUMLA*, 73: 166–80.
Enkvist, N.E. (1991) 'On the interpretability of texts in general and of literary text in particular', in R.D. Sell (ed.) *Literary Pragmatics*, London: Routledge, 1–25.
Enkvist, N.E. (1994) 'Context', in R.D. Sell and P. Verdonk (eds) *Literature and the New Interdisciplinarity: Poetics, Linguistics, History*, Amsterdam: Rodopi, 45–60.
Evans, M. (ed.) (1977) *Elizabethan Sonnets*, London: Dent.
Fairclough, N. (1989) *Language and Power*, London: Longman.
Fairclough, N. (1995) *Critical Discourse Analysis*, London: Longman.
Fawcett, R.P., Halliday, M.A.K., Lamb, S.M. and Makkai, A. (eds) (1984) *The Semiotics of Language and Culture: Vol. 1 Language as Social Semiotic*, London: Pinter.
Fish, S. (1980) *Is There a Text in This Class?*, Harvard: Harvard University Press.
Fisher, J.H. (1984) 'Caxton and Chancery English', in R.F. Yeager (ed.) *Fifteenth Century Studies*, Connecticut: Archon, 161–85.
Fletcher, P. and M. Garman (eds) (1986) *Language Acquisition*, (2nd ed.), Cambridge: Cambridge University Press.
Fodor, J.A. (1983) *The Modularity of Mind*, Cambridge, Mass.: M.I.T. Press.
Foucault, M. (1972) *The Archaeology of Knowledge*, (trans. A.M. Sheridan Smith), London: Routledge.
Fowler, A. (1982) *Kinds of Literature: An Introduction to the Theory of Genres and Modes*, Oxford: Clarendon Press.
Fowler, R. (1986) *Linguistic Criticism*, Oxford: Oxford University Press.
Freedman, A. and Medway, P. (eds) (1994) *Genre and the New Rhetoric*, London: Taylor and Francis.
Frye, N. (1957) *Anatomy of Criticism*, Princeton: Princeton University Press.
Gaile, G.L. and Hanink, D.M. (1985) 'Agents of ice', *Area*, 17, 2: 165–7.
Ghadessy, M. (ed.) (1988) *Registers of Written English*, London: Pinter.
Ghadessy, M. (ed.) (1993) *Register Analysis: Theory and Practice*, London: Pinter.
Goodman, A. (1992) *John of Gaunt*, London: Longman.
Goody, J. (1977) *The Domestication of the Savage Mind*, Cambridge: Cambridge University Press.

Goody, J. (1986) *The Logic of Writing and the Organization of Society*, Cambridge: Cambridge University Press.

Gray, T. (1984) 'Elegy written in a country churchyard', in R. Lonsdale (ed.) *The New Oxford Book of Eighteenth Century Verse*, Oxford: Oxford University Press.

Grice, P. [1968] 'Logic and conversation', reprinted in S. Davis (ed.) (1991) *Pragmatics: A Reader*, Oxford: Oxford University Press, 305–15.

Guillen, C. and Escher, P. (eds) (1985) *Proceedings of the Xth Congress of the Comparative Literature Association: Vol. II Comparative Poetics*, New York: Garland Publishing Inc.

Halliday, M.A.K. (1975) *Learning How to Mean*, London: Edward Arnold.

Halliday, M.A.K. (1978) *Language as Social Semiotic*, London: Edward Arnold.

Halliday, M.A.K. (1985) *Spoken and Written Language*, Victoria: Deakin University Press.

Halliday, M.A.K. (1988) 'On the ineffability of grammatical categories', in J.D. Benson, M.J. Cummings and W.S. Greaves (eds) *Linguistics in a Systemic Perspective*, Amsterdam: John Benjamins, 27–51.

Halliday, M.A.K. (1994) *An Introduction to Functional Grammar*, (2nd ed.), London: Edward Arnold.

Halliday, M.A.K. and Hasan, R. (1976) *Cohesion in English*, London: Longman.

Halliday, M.A.K. and Hasan, R. (1985/9) *Language, Context and Text: Aspects of Language in a Social-Semiotic Perspective*, Victoria: Deakin University Press.

Harrison, T. (1987) *Selected Poems*, (2nd ed.), Harmondsworth: Penguin.

Hasan, R. (1984a) 'Coherence and cohesive harmony', in J. Flood (ed.) *Understanding Reading Comprehension*, Delaware: International Reading Association, 181–219.

Hasan, R. (1984b) 'Ways of saying: ways of meaning', in R.P. Fawcett, M.A.K. Halliday, S.M. Lamb and A. Makkai (eds) *The Semiotics of Language and Culture: Vol. 1 Language as Social Semiotic*, London: Pinter, 105–62.

Hasan, R. (1985) *Linguistics, Language and Verbal Art*, Victoria: Deakin University Press.

Haugen, E. (1966) 'Dialect, language, nation', in J.B. Pride and J. Holmes (eds) (1972) *Sociolinguistics*, Harmondsworth: Penguin, 97–111.

Haynes, J. (1989) *Introducing Stylistics*, London: Unwin Hyman.

Herford, C.H. and P. and E. Simpson (eds) (1947) *Ben Jonson: Vol. VIII*, Oxford: Clarendon Press.

Hickey, L. (1992) 'Notice is hereby given to hide ulterior motives', in D. Stein (ed.) *Cooperating with Written Texts*, Berlin: Mouton de Gruyter, 459–66.

Hicks, D. (1990) 'Narrative skills and genre knowledge: ways of telling in the primary school grades', *Applied Psycholinguistics*, 11, 1: 83–104.

Hill, C. (1993) *The English Bible and the Seventeenth Century Revolution*, London, Allen Lane.

Hodge, R. and Kress, G. (1988) *Social Semiotics*, Oxford: Polity Press.

Hoey, M. (1991a) 'Another perspective on coherence and cohesive harmony', in E. Ventola (ed.) *Functional and Systemic Linguistics: Approaches and Uses*, Berlin: Mouton de Gruyter, 385–414.

Hoey, M. (1991b) *Patterns of Lexis in Text*, Oxford: Oxford University Press.

Holmes, G. (1993) *The Making of a Great Power: Late Stuart and Early Georgian England*, London: Longman.

Holmes, G. and Szechi, D. (1993) *The Age of Oligarchy: Pre-industrial Britain*, London: Longman.

Holmes, J. (1992) *An Introduction to Sociolinguistics*, London: Longman.

Hudson, R.A. (1980) *Sociolinguistics*, Cambridge: Cambridge University Press.

Hunston, S. (1993) 'Evaluation and ideology in scientific writing', in M. Ghadessy (ed.) *Register Analysis: Theory and Practice*, London: Pinter, 57–73.

Hurford, J.R. and Heasley, B. (1983) *Semantics: A Coursebook*, Cambridge: Cambridge University Press.

Jakobson, R. [1960] 'Linguistics and poetics', in D. Lodge (ed.) (1988) *Modern Criticism and Theory*, London: Longman, 32–57.

Jones, R.F. (1953) *The Triumph of the English Language*, Stanford: Stanford University Press.

Joseph, J.E. (1987) *Eloquence and Power: The Rise of Language Standards and Standard Languages*, London: Pinter.

Joseph, J.E. and Taylor, T.J. (eds) (1990) *Ideologies of Language*, London: Routledge.

Kachru, B.J. (1985) 'Standards, codification and sociolinguistic realism', in R. Quirk and H.G. Widdowson (eds) *English in the World*, Cambridge: Cambridge University Press.

Kehoe, B.P. (1992, February) *Zen and the Art of the Internet: A Beginners Guide to the Internet* [Online]. Available telnet:bubl.bath.ac.uk. Directory:BC-Information Networking: Networks: Internet File: Zen and the Art of the Internet.

Keynes, G. (ed.) (1968) *Sir Thomas Browne: Selected Writings*, London: Faber.

Kingman, J. (1988) *Report of the Committee of Enquiry into the Teaching of the English Language*, London: H.M.S.O.

Kress, G. (1989a) 'History and language: towards a social account of linguistic change', *Journal of Pragmatics*, 13: 445–66.

Kress, G. (1989b) *Linguistic Processes in Sociocultural Practices*, Oxford: Oxford University Press.

Kress, G. (1993) 'Against arbitrariness: the social production of the sign as a foundational issue in critical discourse analysis', *Discourse and Society*, 4, 2: 169–91.

Kress, G. (1994) *Learning to Write*, (rev. ed.), London: Routledge.

Lakoff, G. (1987) *Women, Fire and Dangerous Things*, Chicago: University of Chicago Press.

Lamb, B.C. (ed.) (1992) *A National Survey of UK Undergraduates' Standards of English*, London: The Queen's English Society.

Lamb, B.C. (ed.) (1994) *A National Survey of Communication Skills of Young Entrants to Industry and Commerce*, London: The Queen's English Society.

Langford, P. (1989) *A Polite and Commercial People: England 1727–1783*. Oxford: Oxford University Press.

Lask, R. (1987) *The Shape of English*, London: Dent.

Lecercle, J.-J. (1990) *The Violence of Language*, London: Routledge.

Lee, D. (1992) *Competing Discourses: Perspective and Ideology in Language*, London: Longman.

Leith, D. (1983) *A Social History of English*, London: Routledge.

Lemke, J.L. (1988) 'Text structure and text semantics', in E. Steiner and R. Veltman (eds) *Pragmatics, Discourse and Text*, London: Pinter, 158–70.

Leonard, S.A. (1929) *The Doctrine of Correctness in English Usage: 1700–1800*, (reprinted 1962), New York: Russell and Russell.

Levinson, S.C. (1983) *Pragmatics*, Cambridge: Cambridge University Press.

Lodge, D. (ed.) (1988) *Modern Criticism and Theory: A Reader*, London: Longman.

Lyons, J. (1977) *Semantics*, Cambridge: Cambridge University Press.

Lyons, J. (1981) *Language and Linguistics: An Introduction*, Cambridge: Cambridge University Press.

McCarthy, M. (1993) 'Spoken discourse markers in written text', in J.M. Sinclair, M. Hoey and G. Fox (eds) *Techniques of Description: Spoken and Written Discourse*, London: Routledge, 170–82.

McCarthy, M. and Carter, R. (1994) *Language as Discourse: Perspectives for Language Teaching*, London: Longman.

Macdonald, D. (ed.) (1960) *Parodies: An Anthology from Chaucer to Beerbohm*, London: Faber.

McKeon, M. (1987) *The Origins of the English Novel: 1600–1740*, Baltimore: Johns Hopkins University Press.

Mann, W.C. and Thompson, S.A. (eds) (1992) *Discourse Description: Diverse Linguistic Analyses of a Fund-Raising Text*, Amsterdam: John Benjamins.

Martin, J.R. (1985) 'Process and text: two aspects of human semiosis', in J.D. Benson and W.S. Greaves (eds) *Systemic Perspectives on Discourse*, (vol. 1), New Jersey: Ablex, 248–74.

Martin, J.R. (1992) *English Text: System and Structure*, Amsterdam: John Benjamins.

Matthiessen, C. (1993) 'Register in the round', in M. Ghadessy (ed.) *Register Analysis: Theory and Practice*, London: Pinter, 221–92.

Mey, J.L. (1991) 'Text, context, and social control', *Journal of Pragmatics*, 16: 399–410.

Mey, J.L. (1993) *Pragmatics: An Introduction*, Oxford: Blackwell.

Michael, I. (1987) *The Teaching of English: From the Sixteenth Century to 1870*, Cambridge: Cambridge University Press.

Miller, C.R. (1994) 'Rhetorical community: the cultural basis of genre', in A. Freedman and P. Medway (eds) *Genre and the New Rhetoric*, London: Taylor and Francis, 67–78.

Milroy, J. (1992) *Linguistic Variation and Change*, Oxford: Blackwell.

Milroy, J. and Milroy, L. (1991) *Authority in Language*, (2nd ed.), London: Routledge.

Milroy, L. (1987) *Language and Social Networks,* (2nd ed.), Oxford: Blackwell.

Milton, J. (1940) 'Lycidas', in H.C. Beeching (ed.) *The English Poems of John Milton*, Oxford: Oxford World Classics.

Mueller, J.M. (1984) *The Native Tongue and the Word*, Chicago: Chicago University Press.

Mühlhäusler, P. (1987) 'The politics of small languages', *Language and Communication*, 7, 1: 1–24.

Mühlhäusler, P. (1990) ' "Reducing" Pacific languages to writings', in J.E. Joseph and T.J. Talbot (eds) *Ideologies of Language*, London: Routledge, 189–205.

O'Donnell, W.R. and Todd, L. (1980) *Variety in Contemporary English*, London: Allen and Unwin.

Ong, W.J. (1982) *Orality and Literacy: The Technologizing of the Word*, London: Methuen.

Ormrod, W.M. (1990) *The Reign of Edward III*, Yale: Yale University Press.

Patten, M. (1980) *5000 Recipe Cookbook: Meals Without Meat*, Optimum Books: London.

Patterson, F.A. (ed.) (1933) *The Student's Milton*, New York: Appleton-Century-Crofts.

van Peer, W. (1989) 'The concept of cohesion: its empirical status in a definition and typology of texts', in M.-E. Conte, J.S. Petöfi and E. Sözer (eds) *Text and Discourse Connectedness*, Amsterdam: John Benjamins, 291–308.

van Peer, W. (1991) 'But what *is* literature', in R.D. Sell (ed.) *Literary Pragmatics*, London: Routledge, 127–41.

van Peer, W. (1993) 'Typographic foregrounding', *Language and Literature*, 2, 1: 49–61.

Pennycook, A. (1994) 'Incommensurable discourses?', *Applied Linguistics*, 15, 2: 115–38.

Perera, K. (1984) *Children's Writing and Reading*, Oxford: Blackwell.

Phillips, M.K. (1988) 'Texts, terms and meanings: some principles of analysis', in J.D. Benson, M.J. Cummings and W.S. Greaves (eds) *Linguistics in a Systemic Perspective*, Amsterdam: John Benjamins, 99–118.

Pilkington, A. (1994) 'Against literary reading conventions', in R.D. Sell and P. Verdonk (eds) *Literature and the New Interdisciplinarity: Poetics, Linguistics, History*, Amsterdam: Rodopi, 93–106.

Plumb, J.H. (1956) *Sir Robert Walpole: The Making of a Statesman*, London: Cresset Press.

Poole, A.L. (1955) *Domesday Book to Magna Carta: 1087–1216*, Oxford: Clarendon Press.

Porter, R. (1982) *English Society in the Eighteenth Century*, Harmondsworth: Penguin.

Pride, J.B. and Holmes, J. (eds) (1972) *Sociolinguistics*, Harmondsworth: Penguin.

Quirk, R and Widdowson, H.G. (eds) (1985) *English in the World*, Cambridge: Cambridge University Press.

Rabinow, P. (ed.) (1986) *The Foucault Reader*, Harmondsworth: Penguin.

Reid, W. (1991) *Verb and Noun Number in English*, London: Longman.

Roden, C. (1985) *A New Book of Middle Eastern Food*, Harmondsworth: Penguin.

Rose, M. (1993) *Parody: Ancient, Modern and Postmodern*, Cambridge: Cambridge University Press.

Samraj, B.J.T.R. (1989) 'Exploring current issues in genre theory', *Word*, 40: 189–200.

Sarangi, S.K. and Slembrouck, S. (1992) 'Noncooperation in communication: a reassessment of Gricean pragmatics', *Journal of Pragmatics*, 17, 2: 117–54.

Scaglione, A. (ed.) (1984) *The Rise of Written Standard English*, Ravenna: Longo.

Schaeffer, J.-M. (1989) *Qu'est-ce qu'un genre litteraire?*, Paris: Editions de Seuil.

de Selincourt, E. (ed.) (1936) *The Poetical Works of Wordsworth*, (2nd ed.), Oxford: Oxford University Press.

Sell, R.D. (ed.) (1991) *Literary Pragmatics*, London: Routledge.

Sharrock, R. (ed.) (1966) *Bunyan:* Grace Abounding *and* The Pilgrim's Progress, Oxford: Oxford University Press.

Short, M. (ed.) (1989) *Reading, Analyzing and Teaching Literature*, London: Longman.

Simpson, P. (1993) *Language, Ideology and Point of View*, London: Routledge.

Sinclair, J.M. (1991) *Corpus, Concordance, Collocation*, Oxford: Oxford University Press.

Sinclair, J.M. (1993) 'Written discourse structure', in J.M. Sinclair, M. Hoey and G. Fox (eds) *Techniques of Description: Spoken and Written Discourse*, London: Routledge, 6–31.

Sinclair, J.M., Hoey, M. and Fox, G. (eds) (1993) *Techniques of Description: Spoken and Written Discourse*, London: Routledge.

Slembrouck, S. (1992) 'The Parliamentary Hansard "verbatim" report: the written construction of spoken discourse', *Language and Literature*, 1, 2: 101–19.

Smith, O. (1984) *The Politics of Language*, Oxford: Clarendon Press.

Sperber, D. and Wilson, D. (1986) *Relevance: Communication and Cognition*, Oxford: Blackwell.

Stein, D. (ed.) (1992) *Cooperating with Written Texts*, Berlin: Mouton de Gruyter.

Steiner, E. and Veltman, R. (eds) (1988) *Pragmatics, Discourse and Text*, London: Pinter.

Strang, B. (1970) *A History of English*, Methuen: London.

Stubbs, M. (1986) *Educational Linguistics*, Oxford: Blackwell.

Sundby, B., Bjørge, A.K. and Haugland, K.E. (1991) *A Dictionary of English Normative Grammar: 1700–1800*, Amsterdam: John Benjamins.

Suter, H.-J. (1993) *The Wedding Report: A Prototypical Approach to the Study of Traditional Text Types*, Amsterdam: John Benjamins.

Swales, J. (1987) 'Utilizing the literatures in teaching the research paper', *TESOL Quarterly*, 21, 1: 41–68.

Swales, J. (1988) 'Discourse communities, genres and English as an international language', *World Englishes*, 7, 2: 211–20.

Swales, J. (1990) *Genre Analysis*, Cambridge: Cambridge University Press.

Swales, J. (1993) 'Genre and engagement', *Revue Belge de Philologie et d'Histoire*, 71, 3: 687–98.

Taylor, J.R. (1989) *Linguistic Categorization: Prototypes in Linguistic Theory*, Oxford: Oxford University Press.

Thibault, P.J. (1991) *Social Semiotics as Praxis*, Minneapolis: University of Minnesota Press.

Thomas, K. (1986) 'Literacy in early modern English', in G. Baumann (ed.) *The Written Word: Literacy in Transition*, Oxford: Clarendon Press, 97–131.

Threadgold, T. (1988) 'What did Milton say Belial said and Why don't the Critics believe him?', in J.D. Benson, M.J. Cummings and W.S. Greaves (eds) *Linguistics in a Systemic Perspective*, Amsterdam: John Benjamins, 331–92.

Todorov, T. (1976) 'The origin of genres', *New Literary History*, 8, 1: 159–70.

Toolan, M. (1988) 'The language of press advertising', in M. Ghadessy (ed.) *Registers of Written English*, London: Pinter, 52–64.

Trudgill, P. (1983a) *On Dialect*, Oxford: Blackwell.

Trudgill, P. (1983b) *Sociolinguistics*, (rev. ed.), Harmondsworth: Penguin.

Turner, E.H. and Cullingford, R.E. (1989) 'Using conversation MOPs in natural language interfaces', *Discourse Processes*, 12, 1: 63–90.

Ventola, E. (1987) *The Structure of Social Interaction*, London: Pinter.

Ventola, E. (1989) 'Problems of modelling and applied issues within the framework of genre', *Word*, 40: 129–61.

Ventola, E. (ed.) (1991) *Functional and Systemic Linguistics: Approaches and Uses*, Berlin: Mouton de Gruyter.

Vygotsky, L. (1986) *Thought and Language*, (rev. ed.), Cambridge, Mass.: M.I.T.

Wakelin, M. (1988) *The Archeology of English*, London: Batsford.

Wales, K. (1989) *Dictionary of Stylistics*, London: Longman.

Watt, I. (1957) *The Rise of the Novel*, London: Chatto and Windus.

Werth, P. (1976) 'Roman Jakobson's verbal analysis of poetry', *Journal of Linguistics*, 12, 1: 21–73.

Widdowson, H.G. (1977) *Teaching Language as Communication*, Oxford: Oxford University Press.

Widdowson, H.G. (1984) *Explorations in Applied Linguistics 2*, Oxford: Oxford University Press.

Widdowson, H.G. (1992) *Practical Stylistics*, Oxford: Oxford University Press.

Widdowson, H.G. (1995) 'Discourse analysis: a critical view', *Language and Literature*, 4, 3, 157–72.

Winter, E. (1992) 'The notion of unspecific versus specific as one way of analysing the information of a fund-raising letter', in W.C. Mann and S.A. Thompson (eds) *Discourse Description: Diverse Linguistic Analyses of a Fund-Raising Text*, Amsterdam: John Benjamins, 131–70.

Winter, E. (1994) 'Clause relations as information structure', in M. Coulthard (ed.) *Advances in Written Text Analysis*, London: Routledge, 46–82.

Yeager, R.F. (1984) *Fifteenth Century Studies*, Connecticut: Archon.

Zimmerman, E.N. (1994) 'Definition and rhetorical genre', in A. Freedman and P. Medway (eds) *Genre and the New Rhetoric*, London: Taylor and Francis, 125–32.

Ziv, Y. (1988) 'On the rationality of "relevance" and the relevance of rationality', *Journal of Pragmatics*, 12, 5/6: 535–45.

Index

Academic writing as performance